The Battle for Sabarimala

The Battle for Sabarimala

Religion, Law, and Gender in Contemporary India

DEEPA DAS ACEVEDO

OXFORD
UNIVERSITY PRESS

Oxford University Press is a department of the University of Oxford.
It furthers the University's objective of excellence in research, scholarship,
and education by publishing worldwide. Oxford is a registered trade mark of
Oxford University Press in the UK and in certain other countries

Published in India by
Oxford University Press
22 Workspace, 2nd Floor, 1/22 Asaf Ali Road, New Delhi 110 002, India

© Oxford University Press India 2023

The moral rights of the author have been asserted

First Edition published in 2023

All rights reserved. No part of this publication may be reproduced, stored in
a retrieval system, or transmitted, in any form or by any means, without the
prior permission in writing of Oxford University Press, or as expressly permitted
by law, by licence or under terms agreed with the appropriate reprographics
rights organization. Enquiries concerning reproduction outside the scope of the
above should be sent to the Rights Department, Oxford University Press, at the
address above

You must not circulate this work in any other form
and you must impose this same condition on any acquirer

ISBN-13 (hardback): 978-9-39-105013-9
ISBN-10 (hardback): 9-39-105013-1

ISBN-13 (eBook): 978-9-39-105014-6
ISBN-10 (eBook): 9-39-105014-X

ISBN-13 (oso): 978-9-39-105018-4
ISBN-10 (oso): 9-39-105018-2

DOI: 10.1093/oso/9789391050139.001.0001

Typeset in Minion Pro 10.5/14
by Newgen KnowledgeWorks Pvt. Ltd., Chennai, India
Printed and bound in India by Replika Press Pvt. Ltd.

For amma and John, who make everything worthwhile.

Contents

Preface	ix
Note on Non-English Terms	xiii
Acronyms	xv
Chronology	xvii
Copyright Permissions	xxv
Supreme Court Benches	xxvii

Introduction	1
I.1 From Temples to Secularism, and Back Again	4
I.2 The Curious Case of Women's Entry	11
1. The Setting	17
1.1 Kerala Mahatmyam?	18
1.2 God's Own Country	26
1.3 Keralite Temples, Indian Secularism	32
2. The Counterprotests	41
2.1 *Aachaaram* Meets the Women's Wall	42
2.2 A Gandhi in Wayanad	50
2.3 A Diminishingly Supreme Court	56
3. The Case	67
3.1 Anatomy of a Case	68
3.2 *IYLA* Redux	73
3.3 Sovereign Citizens | Sovereign State	86
4. The Scandal	93
4.1 Separate but Equal	98
4.2 'Doing a Jayamala'	106
5. The Rule	113
5.1 Babies, Bundles, and Books	117
5.2 Invisibility, Then and Now	128
6. The Protests	131
6.1 #HappyToBleed	134
6.2 Chingari	138

    6.3 Whose Temples? Whose Entry?   144
    6.4 Temple Entry, Then and Now   146

Conclusion   149

Acknowledgements   161
Appendix A: A Note on Interdisciplinary Interventions   165
Appendix B: Legal Materials   175
Notes   183
Bibliography   215
Index   239

Preface

The prince smiled to himself, but said nothing. Manikantan knew that his mother, the queen, was not really unwell, that the illness she complained of had nothing to do with her health and everything to do with her frustration. Just yesterday morning, the king had announced that Manikantan would be named crown prince. The palace had been ringing with the queen's complaints ever since.

Why would the king choose Manikantan, she had demanded, who was after all only an adopted son, a baby they had found in a basket on the river Pamba, lying abandoned and naked save for the golden bell around his neck after which they had named him? Why would he have overlooked Manikantan's younger brother, their own—and only—biological child? The queen was beside herself. She loved Manikantan, as the king ought to well know. They had been desperate for a child when he had come, like a gift from the gods, into their lives. But unlike the king, her love did not blind her to their younger son's superior claims to the throne of Pandalam.

Manikantan could see the queen struggling with herself as she lay on her sickbed, not wanting to send him off on what they both knew was a fool's errand, and a dangerous one at that, yet not wanting to let him stay. Tiger's milk would not cure her—only his departure would do that. He knew he would have to go. He would have to leave this kingdom that had been his only home for the twelve short years of his life, and he would have to wander deep into the surrounding forests that were full of dangerous animals and poisonous plants in search of the tiger's milk that the queen said was her only hope. Manikantan knew this with complete certainty, not because of the queen's obstinacy or the king's sorrow, but because it was foreordained. He *was* a gift from the gods. And so, he left.

From the heavens above came a great sigh of relief. This child of theirs, this miraculous son of two male gods, the product of Vishnu's womb when he assumed the form of Mohini the enchantress and Shiva forgot himself in lust—this progeny of Ayyan and Appan, this *Ayyappan* would save them from themselves. Only Vishnu and Shiva's son could do so, the curse had stipulated... and now he would.

Eventually, tales of Manikantan's exploits in the forest began making their way back to the palace: how he had defeated fierce wild animals in singlehanded combat; how he had won many victories against warlords and brigands, like the muslim Vavar, who had afterwards become Manikantan's devoted friend; and, most of all, how he had slayed the terrifying demoness Mahishi.

When Mahishi died, the heavens rained down flowers and songs of gratitude, and Manikantan knew that he had fulfilled his earthly purpose. He refused the entreaties of the beautiful woman who had been cursed to assume the demoness' awful form, the woman he had liberated when he slayed Mahishi. He would only marry her, he said, when no new supplicants came to the forests seeking his help. Until that day, he would remain a celibate youth, a *brahmachari*, devoted to his followers. The love-struck woman declared her willingness to wait for him and him alone just as a jasmine flower waits until night before blooming. 'Malikapurathamma!' came the refrain from the forests—the lady jasmine who waits outside.

Soon afterwards, the king of Pandalam awoke to see Manikantan descending the hills in front of the palace, surrounded by Vavar and others, astride an enormous tigress. He was magnificent. The king ran out to meet his son, crying with joy. Whoever this glorious being was, from wherever he had really come, he was still his son. The queen waited nervously. Manikantan greeted them both with a smile and a shake of his head. He would not be staying in Pandalam, and he would not be accepting the throne. He was going home, to the forest.

When the king pleaded with him to not leave his father, his family, Manikantan took pity on the old man. He shot an arrow into the forests surrounding the palace, the same forests from which he had just descended and said that wherever the arrow landed, that place would be his new home. There, he would practice the austerities to which he now wished to devote himself, always remaining a youth and retaining his celibacy, guarded by his friend Vavar and awaited by Malikapurathamma, ready to receive and protect those who loved him. The hill on which the arrow landed, Sabarimala, would become the most famous temple dedicated to him—to *Ayyappan* as he would now be known in recognition of his divine fathers: a god who was also an ascetic, a warrior, and a prince.¹

* * *

This is the story of a dispute over an unusual god, his unusual temple, in an unusual state, in India, where nothing is ever unusual. The dispute likely began, as Indian jurists enjoy saying, some time 'since time immemorial'. It began ending in 2018, and it has been ending ever since.

In September of that year, the Indian Supreme Court told the Hindu temple at Sabarimala, in the Communist-led state of Kerala, that it could no longer exclude women aged ten to fifty from its premises on the grounds that their presence offended the temple's presiding deity, a bachelor god named Ayyappan. Observers on both sides of the dispute, who had until then been expressing themselves via passionate letters-to-the-editor and duelling hashtag campaigns, poured onto the streets and up the hillsides surrounding Sabarimala in corporeal shows of solidarity or dismay. In the months that followed, Sabarimala was on the tip of every politician's tongue and many lawyers' pens as they relitigated the Court's decision.² Several dozen petitioners demanded that the Court confess itself mistaken as to its own law.

How did a long-simmering dispute come to such a sudden and violent climax? Why has there been no lasting resolution despite decades of jurisprudence and a decision from the country's generally well-respected Supreme Court? Can it really be that Ayyappan's preferences are actionable under Indian law? What circumstances make this dispute possible, ordinary, and extraordinary in India?

I have been asking myself these questions with respect to Sabarimala for around a dozen years. For much of that time, neither Sabarimala nor its dispute over women's entry were particularly well known north of the Vindhya mountains; today, the temple figures regularly in national newspapers and Delhi conversations, and it not infrequently surfaces outside India as well. This book chronicles the dispute, which I have found to be at once teleological, circular, legally constrained and legally generative, historically situated, and charmingly ahistorical. And it does so by taking seriously both the lawyer's imperative to consider what the law *is* and the anthropologist's mandate to explore what law (*sans* definite article) tells us about society.

Note on Non-English Terms

This book occasionally makes use of terms from Indian languages, most especially Malayalam and Sanskrit (as well as a Malayalam-ized Sanskrit). In transcribing these terms, I have not used diacritics because, as others also note, diacritics tend to provide information for those who don't need it while alienating those who do.* Instead, I usually italicize and define non-English terms in the main text, although on rare occasion and in the interests of readable prose I have relegated some definitions to the notes. Where I have relied on a particular source to provide a translation, I indicate as much in the notes. Where I have not indicated a source, the translation is my own.

---

* This is a rough paraphrasing of Geraldine Heng's position with regard to diacritics, which in turn relies on David Nirenberg's views (Heng 2018, 6).

Acronyms

The following acronyms, listed in alphabetical order, appear with varying regularity throughout the book.

BJP   Bharatiya Janata Party
CPI(M)   Communist Party of India (Marxist)
IYLA   Indian Young Lawyers Association

Readers should note that I use the un-italicized version (IYLA) to refer to the organization, and the italicized version (*IYLA*) to refer to the litigation and judicial opinion.

KHC   Kerala High Court
PIL   public interest litigation
NSS   Nair Service Society
TDB   Travancore Devaswom Board

Chronology

The following timeline is a rough approximation of events relevant to the dispute over women's entry. Like all timelines, it is partial. Like many timelines, it is only partially reliable: many of these events took place over thirty years ago and were heavily contested even as they unfolded.

In instances where the specific date on which an event occurred might be of interest, I have indicated this in parentheses. In instances where a date is particularly unclear, contested, or open to interpretation, I have indicated this with an asterisk. **Bolded** entries are particularly significant.

1924–25	February–November	Vaikom *satyagraha*[†] led by T. K. Madhavan seeks access to roads surrounding Vaikom temple in erstwhile Kingdom of Travancore*
1929–30	October–January	Pune *satyagraha* led by S. J. Kamble and P. N. Rajbhoj seeks access into Parvati temple in erstwhile Bombay Presidency
1930–35	March–	Nashik *satyagraha* led by B. R. Ambedkar seeks access into Kalaram temple in erstwhile Bombay Presidency*
1931–32	November–October	Guruvayur *satyagraha* led by K. Kelappan seeks entry into Guruvayur temple in Malabar District of erstwhile Madras Presidency

[†] The term *satyagraha* is commonly translated as "truth force" or "insistence on truth" and is mostly associated with M. K. Gandhi's non-violent approach to civil resistance. When *satyagraha* is accompanied by a place or other specific noun (e.g., "Guruvayur" or "flag"), it refers to a specific campaign conducted along Gandhian principles of non-violence. A *satyagrahi* is one who participates in *satyagraha*.

1950		A fire at Sabarimala prompts major reconstruction and, it is later asserted, changes to temple customs
1986	March	Sudha Chandran allegedly visits Sabarimala
1987	April	Girija Lokesh allegedly visits Sabarimala
		Jayamala allegedly visits Sabarimala*‡
1990	August	Newspaper report surfaces of S. Chandrika and other women conducting rice-feeding ceremonies for infants at Sabarimala
	October	First hearings in *S. Mahendran v. TDB*
1991	April	Opinion issued in *S. Mahendran v. TDB*
2002	December	KHC directs TDB to conduct probe after news reports of young women seeking *darshan* of Ayyappan during *arat* procession
2006	June	*Devaprasnam* ceremony is conducted at Sabarimala by Unnikrishnan Panicker (16th–19th)
		Jayamala faxes her confession (17th)
		Meera Jasmine allegedly visits Rajarajeshwara temple at Taliparamba
	July	TDB delegation questions Jayamala at her home in Bangalore

‡ In her faxed confession, Jayamala stated that she visited Sabarimala during one of the five-day *maasa puja* periods that occur every month; however, at least one news report, *Times of India* (2011), suggests that she visited in April, which is the month of Vishu (New Year) festivities and has a roughly week-long opening rather than a traditional *maasa puja* period.

		Tantri Kandararu Mohanaru orders purification ritual allegedly unrelated to Jayamala's entry
		Indian Young Lawyers Association files Supreme Court writ petition challenging Sabarimala's admission practices
	August	First Supreme Court hearing in *IYLA v. State of Kerala*
2007	June	NSS demands publication of state investigation into Jayamala episode
		Kerala Police files First Information Report in connection with Jayamala episode but does not name the actress as an accused
	July–December	Multiple Supreme Court hearings in *IYLA*
2008	March	Two-judge Supreme Court bench refers *IYLA* writ petition to three-judge bench
2010	September	Kerala Police amends FIR to include Jayamala
	December	Kerala Police files final report regarding Jayamala episode
2011	April	KHC clears Jayamala of charges on procedural grounds
	June	Magistrate judge allows Kerala Police investigation to continue despite procedural flaws
	October	Dipak Misra is elevated to the Supreme Court
2012	April	Ranjan Gogoi is elevated to the Supreme Court

	July	KHC clears Jayamala on substantive grounds (no intent to harm religious sentiments)
2013	April	S. A. Bobde is elevated to the Supreme Court
2015	November	Prayar Gopalakrishnan gives a speech in which he suggests women may enter Sabarimala when a machine to determine their menstrual status has been invented (13th)
		Nikita Azad posts her open letter on *Youth ki Awaaz* (20th)
		Nikita Azad posts her second open letter (23rd)
		#HappyToBleed campaign begins
	December	**Trupti Desai and the Bhumata Brigade conduct their first temple entry agitation at the Shani Shingnapur temple in Maharashtra**
2016	January	**After eight-year gap, Supreme Court resumes hearings in *IYLA***
	January–July	Multiple Supreme Court hearings in *IYLA*
	April	Trupti Desai and the Bhumata Brigade conduct temple entry agitations at two more temples in Maharashtra
	June	**Bombay High Court issues opinion in *Niaz v. State of Maharashtra*, ordering Haji Ali *dargah* to allow women access on par with men**
	August	Trupti Desai announces her intention to visit Sabarimala during the annual pilgrimage season in light of *Niaz*

CHRONOLOGY xxi

	September	#ReadyToWait campaign begins*
2017	February	Various applications to intervene in *IYLA* are allowed
	August	Dipak Misra becomes Chief Justice of India
	October	Three-judge Supreme Court bench refers *IYLA* to five-judge bench
2018	January	Justices Kurian Joseph, Jasti Chelameswar, Ranjan Gogoi, and Madan Lokur conduct a press conference critiquing CJ Misra and current practices at the Supreme Court (12th)
		CJ Misra appoints a five-judge bench, including himself, to hear *IYLA*; the bench does not include any judge who participated in the press conference (15th)
	July	A new five-judge bench is appointed to hear *IYLA*
		The five-judge Supreme Court bench conducts hearings in *IYLA*
	July–September	One of the original *IYLA* petitioners, Prerna Kumari, asks to be removed from the case after experiencing a change of heart; she is told it is too late
	September	**Supreme Court issues 4:1 opinion in *IYLA v. State of Kerala* declaring Sabarimala's admission practices to be unconstitutional**
	October	Dipak Misra retires from Supreme Court
		Ranjan Gogoi becomes Chief Justice of India

		Dozens of review petitions are filed in *IYLA*
	October–December	Multiple attempts by women aged ten to fifty to visit Sabarimala; Trupti Desai reaches Kerala but leaves without exiting Kochi International Airport; Bindu Ammini and Kanakadurga make their first attempt at visiting Sabarimala
	November	The same five-judge bench that heard *IYLA* (with Gogoi replacing Misra) begins hearing review petitions; Congress MP Shashi Tharoor writes op-ed critiquing *IYLA*
2019	January	An over 600 kilometre long *vanitha mathil* ('women's wall') is formed to support gender equality and the Supreme Court decision in *IYLA* (1st)
		Bindu Ammini and Kanakadurga become the first women aged ten to fifty to enter Sabarimala after *IYLA*; *tantri* Kandararu Rajeevaru orders purification ritual allegedly unrelated to their entry; Congress Party MPs attempt 'black armband' protest in the Lok Sabha but Sonia Gandhi prevents it (2nd)
		Kerala is overwhelmed by riots, strikes, and protests (3rd)
		Kanakadurga is taken to hospital after her mother-in-law physically assaults her
	February	Bindu Ammini petitions the Supreme Court over the continued lack of access to Sabarimala and the purification ritual conducted after her January visit

		Supreme Court continues review petition hearings
	April	Congress Party announces its president, Rahul Gandhi, will contest from northern Kerala seat of Wayanad in addition to Gandhi family stronghold of Amethi in Uttar Pradesh
	May	Congress Party wins landslide in Kerala during national elections despite dismal performance overall; Rahul Gandhi wins Wayanad but loses Amethi; the CPI(M) is reduced to one MP from Kerala
	June	First private member's bill in new Lok Sabha is a bill to overturn *IYLA* proposed by an MP from Kerala
	July	Rahul Gandhi resigns as president of Congress Party following its poor electoral performance
	October	CPI(M) performs well during Kerala by-elections
	November	**Supreme Court issues 3:2 opinion in *Kantaru Rajeevaru v. IYLA*; it favours keeping the review petitions pending and refers broader questions of religion and law to five-judge bench**
		Ranjan Gogoi retires from Supreme Court
		S. A. Bobde becomes Chief Justice of India
2020	January	Nine-judge bench assembles for hearings on referral questions associated with *Kantaru Rajeevaru*

January–February	Multiple Supreme Court hearings in *Kantaru Rajeevaru*
February	**Supreme Court issues unanimous order holding it has authority to proceed with referral questions (10th)**
	Final hearings in *Kantaru Rajeevaru* (17th)
March	TDB urges devotees to avoid visiting Sabarimala in light of COVID-19
April	TDB closes Sabarimala to pilgrims through 14 April (Vishu)
May	**Supreme Court issues unanimous order explaining February 2020 order**
June	TDB announces Sabarimala will open in June using a virtual queue but with limited capacity, safety precautions, and no accommodations for pilgrims
	TDB reverses course, says Sabarimala will not open to pilgrims in June
October	Sabarimala opens to pilgrims for first time in seven months with max daily capacity of 250; TDB announces pilgrims under 10 and over 60 prohibited until COVID-19 situation improves
	Gov't of Kerala announces max capacity of 1,000–2,000 per day during 2020 pilgrimage season and makes negative COVID-19 tests mandatory
November	Preliminary TDB figures suggest 97% fewer pilgrims visiting Sabarimala than usual

Copyright Permissions

Portions of the following works have been reprinted with permission:

"From Mythic Saviors to #MeToo at the Indian Supreme Court," *Asian Journal Of Law And Society* 8(2): 226–254 (2021) (Cambridge University Press)

"Just Hindus," *Law & Social Inquiry* 45(4): 965–994 (2020) (Cambridge University Press)

"Gods' Homes, Men's Courts, Women's Rights," *International Journal Of Constitutional Law* 16(2): 552–73 (2018) (Oxford University Press)

"Temples, Courts, and Dynamic Equilibrium in the Indian Constitution," *American Journal Of Comparative Law* 64(3): 555–82 (2016) (Oxford University Press)

"Celibate Gods and 'Essential Practices' Jurisprudence at Sabarimala, 1991-2011," in *Filing Religion: State, Hinduism, And Courts Of Law* 101–123 (Daniela Berti et al, eds.) (2016) (Oxford University Press)

"Divine Sovereignty, Indian Property Law, and the Dispute Over the Padmanabhaswamy Temple," *Modern Asian Studies* 50(3): 841–865 (2016) (Cambridge University Press)

"Secularism in the Indian Context," *Law & Social Inquiry* 38(1): 138–67 (2013) (Cambridge University Press)

Supreme Court Benches

Over fifteen years, many justices of the Indian Supreme Court have heard portions of the Sabarimala dispute; the timeline below indicates when each bench took over the litigation.§

2006	August	Y. K. Sabharwal (CJ), S. H. Kapadia, C. K. Thakker
2007	July	S. B. Sinha, H. S. Bedi
	November	S. B. Sinha, J. M. Panchal
	December	S. B. Sinha, H. S. Bedi
2008	March	S. B. Sinha, V. S. Sirpurkar
2016	January	Dipak Misra, P. C. Ghose, N. V. Ramana
	April	Dipak Misra, Gopala V. Gowda, Kurian Joseph
	July	Dipak Misra, C. Nagappan, R. Banumathi
2017	February	Dipak Misra, R. Banumathi, Ashok Bhushan
2018	January	Dipak Misra (CJ), A. K. Sikri, A. M. Khanwilkar, D. Y. Chandrachud, Ashok Bhushan
2018	July–September	Dipak Misra (CJ), A. M. Khanwilkar, D. Y. Chandrachud, R. F. Nariman, Indu Malhotra

§ This list may overlook some benches, but at minimum it demonstrates that many members of India's most powerful court have been involved in this dispute. Much of this information is sourced from Rajagopal (8 July 2016), *Economic Times* (15 January 2018), and *The New Indian Express* (7 July 2018).

2018–19	October–November	Ranjan Gogoi (CJ), A.M. Khanwilkar, D.Y. Chandrachud, R.F. Nariman, Indu Malhotra
2020	January–May	S. A. Bobde (CJ), R. Banumathi, Ashok Bhushan, L. Nageswara Rao, Mohan M. Shantanagoudar, S. Abdul Nazeer, R. Subhash Reddy, B. R. Gavai, Surya Kant

Introduction

To everyone's surprise, the actress Jayamala confessed that she had done it.

It was the summer of 2006, and all was not well at the Sabarimala temple. A hired astrologer had just announced that the deity was displeased: rituals were being inadequately observed, development projects were causing no end of trouble, and contrary to the temple's long-standing rules, a woman had entered its premises. Things would have to change. For a split second after Jayamala's confession came in, via fax to the temple administrator's office, it seemed as if matters were coming to a head.

Within days, however, it had all fallen apart. Jayamala's confession was universally disbelieved. How could any beautiful, young actress—no megastar, she, but in 1987 still a charming twenty-seven-year-old—have gone unnoticed in a crowd of male worshippers? How could *any* woman have accidentally tripped across 15 feet of well-guarded space and up the final steps into the inner sanctum? Sabarimala's chief priest was confident in his dismissal of the story, but he oversaw a purification ritual nonetheless.[1]

Soon, hints of a darker offence began to emerge, of conspiracy and deception and a determination to achieve fame by any means. The astrologer and the actress were in cahoots, the media concluded, and turned to other matters. The courts, on the other hand, were just getting started.

Over the next six years, the Jayamala scandal would ricochet among multiple tribunals, the government of the State of Kerala, the Crime Branch of the Kerala Police, and various members of Sabarimala's religious and administrative hierarchies. Every so often, a new official would rediscover the episode, and the media, which never tired of stories involving one of Kerala's most powerful temples, would obligingly follow suit. Jayamala herself was eventually charged with the crime of 'hurting religious sentiments' under India's labyrinthine nineteenth-century penal code. The charges were carefully constructed: although it was by now assumed that she could not have actually visited Sabarimala, and although her visit—had it happened—would not have broken any laws, Jayamala's *claim* to have violated the temple's proscription against fertile women was itself said to offend believing Hindus. At long last, in 2012, a judge of the Kerala High Court dismissed all the charges against her.

The Jayamala scandal was not the first time Sabarimala's 'ban on women' had inspired legal action, and it would not be the last or even the most important. In fact, throughout the six-year saga that followed her faxed confession, the ban itself played second fiddle to the woman who had supposedly violated it. In 2006, nobody argued that Sabarimala should not be allowed to exclude women from its premises, and nobody questioned the temple's rationale for doing so. But the Jayamala scandal opened the door for a broader debate over Sabarimala's admission practices, and for one of the most hotly litigated cases in contemporary India.

The lawsuit that eventually emerged from Jayamala's confession, *Indian Young Lawyers Association v. State of Kerala*,[2] inspired protests across India and influenced the national elections of 2019. It was filed in 2006 by a group of lawyers in New Delhi, some 2,600 kilometres and a universe away from Sabarimala, who had read about the purification rituals conducted in the aftermath of Jayamala's improbable visit. It did not matter, the lawyers argued, that only women between the ages of ten and fifty were forbidden from entering the temple. It also did not matter that some temple authorities believed the ban to be religiously necessary. No temple in modern India ought to exclude devotees on the basis of their sex, said the lawyers—certainly no temple associated with Hinduism, which they argued was a uniquely inclusive religion, and most definitely no temple that was managed by public officials and associated with a democratically accountable government. When the Supreme Court declared, in 2018, that the lawyers were right and that Sabarimala could no longer enforce its ban, all of India erupted in simultaneous shows of celebration and dismay.

The *IYLA* litigation is itself a fascinating window into the complicated and always-evolving way that secular governance is understood in the world's largest democracy. Like many landmark cases, it has inspired a small flurry of scholarship and a rather more sizeable volume of media coverage. And yet, as the Jayamala scandal suggests, *IYLA* is just one moment in a broader dispute that is far more intricate, porous, and non-linear than any single lawsuit.

This book is about the dispute over women's entry into Sabarimala. It chronicles the various stages of the dispute as well as its eclectic cast of characters: a hereditary priest of impeccable orthodoxy, his media-savvy grandson, an astrologer, a minor actress, various religious associations and their feminist others, a housewife-turned-activist, a college student, polished New Delhi lawyers, phlegmatic communist state officials, a bachelor god, and a couple of chief justices eager to rehabilitate their reputations. It argues that despite this colourful roster and the unusual nature of the religious practice in question—exclusion on the basis of gender, rather than caste—the dispute over women's entry replicates typical tensions between individual and group rights, as well as tensions among different types of individuals (and among different types of groups). Lastly, the book demonstrates how the dispute over Sabarimala has been heavily judicialized and, in the end, has itself become something of a turning point for the Indian judiciary.

Above all else, this book explains why the dispute over women's entry has proven both dynamic *and* intractable. The battle over Sabarimala mirrors the constant push-pull between two very distinct visions of India: one in which the state has the authority to reform and regulate society, and the other in which the state respects its limited role as the agent of a sovereign people. Both of these impulses are encoded into the country's famously lengthy constitution, meaning that whether we view constitutions as chronicles or blueprints or wish lists, India has *two*—and they are often, if not always, at odds with one another. When Indians go to court to litigate disputes over religious freedom, as they have done over and over again regarding Sabarimala, they do so against the backdrop of these twin impulses and with the effect of redefining the perpetual, unresolvable, and dynamic equilibrium in which they exist.[3]

The battle for Sabarimala may, in other words, be a battle for India, but it is also the kind of battle that is essential to India. There are serious criticisms to be made about how this particular struggle has been fought, and I make many of those criticisms in the pages that follow. None of these take away from the fundamental and frequently inconvenient truth that battles like Sabarimala are best fought well and often rather than never at all.

I.1 From Temples to Secularism, and Back Again

Although anthropology is no more driven by personal interests than, say, economics, the anthropologist is a more visible character in the story she tells and consequently merits some introduction. I grew up the only child of two professors, my time largely divided among Canadian schools, Bharatanatyam dance lessons in Chennai, and Penguin editions of the English canon. During our months-long trips to India, I would sometimes break up my days with visits to an Ayyappan temple in Anna Nagar, the once-backwater, now-bustling Chennai neighbourhood where my grandfather and aunt both lived, and which my parents and I considered home. Although known around our neighbourhood as 'the Ayyappan *koyil*', a common pronunciation of the Tamil word for temple (*kovil*, literally, 'god's home'), the Anna Nagar Ayyappan temple is built in the distinct low-slung, high-pitched, white-plastered style of Keralite *ambalam*s and *kshethram*s.[4] I loved its rhythms and sounds, the smells of flowers and camphor, and—despite coming from several generations of unimpeachably atheistic stock—I did my best to pray as I made my way around it.

As a sophomore in an American college, I applied for a quirky internal grant whose only requirement was that recipients design a summer project of personal significance that involved no classrooms or structured programmes. Since I was a Bharatanatyam dancer by training and predilection, if not entirely by aptitude, I wrote in my application that, after a decade of studying India's most famous classical dance form, I wanted to see the even more legendary temples where it is said to have originated. I visited over sixty temples in Tamil Nadu that summer, travelling alone in India for the first time and marvelling at the way these centuries-old, physically gorgeous institutions fit seamlessly into the mundane routines of twenty-first-century India. Two years later, as a college senior studying abroad in Delhi, I again hopped on buses and trains to visit some of north India's most famous religious sites, bathing in the Ganga beside the Kashi Vishwanath temple in Benares (and then in disinfectant in my hostel bathroom), and trying very hard to not cry as I toured the scarred remains of the Babri Masjid in Ayodhya.

When it came time to formalize a dissertation project for graduate school, I scanned databases of Indian newspapers from my apartment in Chicago, looking for a puzzle to solve. What I kept seeing were stories noting how this or that person had been refused entry to a temple, or that priests had performed purification rituals after discovering some individual's impermissible presence. The stories were usually short, rarely more than snippets, but they were persistent. Sometimes the unwanted visitors were women, at other times, they were low caste or Christian. A few were decidedly elite: a star playback singer from Kerala's film industry and the child of a national cabinet minister. More often than not, the parties disagreed as to whether the state should—or could—step in.

How could it be, I wondered, that in 2009 debates were still raging over whether the state could control access to Hindu temples? In the first few decades of the twentieth century, before independence, some soon-to-be-Indians had led a series of social movements demanding that other soon-to-be-Indians (and, very often, their colonial allies) open temples to persons of all castes. These caste-based temple entry agitations were inextricable from governmental action. If the movements did not directly involve or appeal to a state authority—if, for instance, the temple was governed by powerful private actors—state authorities were nonetheless drawn into them and impacted by them. Soon after the agitations concluded, royal proclamations, colonial statutes, the new Indian Constitution, and several landmark judicial opinions by the country's Supreme Court all worked to address the fundamental problem of caste-based discrimination in temple access. Collectively, these developments make temple entry seem like one of the precious few aspects of religion-state relations in independent India that has been jurisprudentially resolved if not practically realized.

But if temple entry was what drew me to the study of religion-state relations in contemporary India, the dissertation that I eventually wrote and for which I conducted ethnographic fieldwork between 2009 and 2011 set out to explore something much broader than the issue of access to temples. I conducted interviews, observation, and archival research that used temple governance in Kerala as a way to understand the everyday workings of secular governance in India. Temple entry was a part of that story, to be sure, but it was far from the whole—or even the main—event.

I spent a majority of my doctoral fieldwork period in Ernakulam, the central business district of Kerala's commercial capital, Kochi. Twice a week, I attended hearings of the 'temple bench' at the Kerala High Court under the aegis of Krishnakumar Mangot, to whom I was introduced by a fortuitously rediscovered cousin. Mangot, who has since passed away, was a semi-retired lawyer who had been appointed to the pro bono position of counsel to the *devaswom* ('god's own') ombudsman.[5] The ombudsman himself was an advisor of sorts to the rotating two-judge temple bench of the High Court; he provided information and opinions on temple operations as needed by the bench and dispensed with small matters that did not require judicial attention. Although this arrangement placed Mangot into the rather attenuated position of being an advisor's advisor, his seniority, his commitment to the role, and the generally high esteem in which he was held made him an excellent guide into the world of temple governance at the High Court. He was not, like many key interlocutors, an 'insider-outsider' so much as an insider now technically on the outside.[6]

On our court days, I would go to Mangot's house in the morning to discuss the matters scheduled for hearing that day and to review the case files that he had received in advance. At first we would have tea and biscuits as we talked, but as the months passed and we fell into greater familiarity with one another, these niceties disappeared and we got quite unceremoniously down to business. We quarrelled once or twice, exactly and embarrassingly like the disagreements I used to have with my grandfather, but we reconciled in much the same way too. I miss him.

After these morning conversations, Mangot and I would take an autorickshaw to court and observe proceedings until lunchtime—sometimes eating lunch together in the courthouse canteen—before going our separate ways in the afternoon. We spent much of the day sitting far away from one another, with him always self-effacingly choosing the second of two front tables that had been reserved for government lawyers, and me at the very back of the courtroom in a row of benches occupied by members of the public or, more often, by disconcertingly youthful law students whose awkward and unpopular classmate I undoubtedly appeared to be. In between matters, Mangot frequently called me over to him for a quick introduction or to clarify a point of law.

On non-court days, I alternated between more interviews or observations and a species of archival research. I met with lawyers who had argued before the temple bench, either on behalf of the government or for private litigants, many of whom I knew courtesy of Mangot, and with sitting and retired judges associated with the temple bench. I spent some time at two local law schools, partly out of a general curiosity regarding

Indian legal education and partly to meet law professors who might be well informed regarding court operations. For a couple of months, I passed a day or two each week collecting stories pertaining to any aspect of temple governance in the local offices of *The Hindu*, south India's most influential broadsheet and one of India's few truly national newspapers. I sat alone in a small reading room to which someone would bring elephant folios of the paper's old editions, sometimes scribbling in my notebook, sometimes scanning articles with one of the exciting gizmos that anthropologists now regularly carry into the field, and either because of the solitude or the scanner I was rather indiscriminate in my selection.

During the summer of 2011, I decamped to the state capital, Trivandrum. At the Kerala State Archives and the Kerala Council for Historical Research, I read government memos, extracts from legislative debates, edicts related to temple governance, and other primary sources that provided content, as well as a great deal of colour, to the landscape I was trying to map. In Trivandrum, I was also able to speak with the Minister for Devaswom Affairs as well as the grandson of Sabarimala's chief priest, who served, for several years, as something of a self-appointed public relations officer for his family.

Beyond this, there were interviews that I conducted in both locales (for instance, with representatives of various Ayyappan devotee associations), over the phone (most relevantly, with Jayamala's husband), and on occasional day trips outside either Kochi-Ernakulam or Trivandrum. Into this last category fall my conversations with Kandararu Maheshwararu, who was then the eldest of Sabarimala's chief priests, along with his wife, Devaki Antharjanam; with the heads of two erstwhile royal families who still serve as titular guardians of prominent temples (including Sabarimala); with the superintendent of police responsible for overseeing Sabarimala's district; and with a few academics and priests who had long interested themselves in temple governance. Towards the end of my fieldwork, I also spent some time in the Chennai offices of *The Hindu* and a few days in New Delhi, where I was able to speak with the lead plaintiff in the *IYLA* case.

None of this was done with a view to studying temple entry in particular, much less the question of women's entry at Sabarimala. I was after a set of questions regarding secular governance and citizen-state relations that extended far beyond any one issue or institution, and so I studied administrative hierarchies for temple governance and bureaucratic reform proposals, changes in statutory and judicial authority over temples, case law and legislation governing the regulation of religious institutions both within Kerala and across India, as well as too many discrete cases or investigations unconnected to either Sabarimala or women's entry for me to name here. Truthfully, while I was still in Kerala and for several years afterwards, my attentions were mostly given over to a judicial enquiry regarding the climax of Sabarimala's annual pilgrimage season and its production, in 2010–11, of a stampede that caused over one hundred casualties. I have always felt that public and governmental responses to this incident better exemplify the dual understandings of sovereignty that I describe in this book, but neither the stampede nor the investigation it triggered is the stuff of national drama in the way that women's entry has been.

Unsurprisingly, then, no matter how far afield I explored, Sabarimala's ban on women stayed close at hand. The Jayamala scandal continued to evolve while I was in the field and I wrote a dissertation chapter on the dispute as I knew it then. Not long after I thought I had packed my dissertation away for good, the question of women's entry began to resurface in the media, from which arena it has never truly departed. Ultimately, and as it happens all too often with both anthropologists and lawyers, I have found myself writing and speaking more frequently about a topic that I thought was largely settled when I began studying it than I have about any other aspect of my research.

This durability of the battle for Sabarimala is only partly owing to its particulars. To be sure, the juxtaposition of progressive politics and conservative norms that characterize Kerala, and the prominence of Sabarimala itself, go part of the way towards explaining why so many people have become invested in the ostensible preferences of a celibate deity or in the admission practices of a moderately inaccessible temple that is open for around one hundred days each year. But Sabarimala's quirks only enhance the ways in which contestations over it are emblematic of other, broader developments in Indian politics, or foundational features of Indian jurisprudence.

After much of the mid-to-late twentieth century, during which political belonging was more frequently negotiated in terms of access to wells or slums or universities, religious spaces have once again become the kind of public spaces that Indians fight over. Kalighat, Padmanabhaswamy, Raghunath, Ayodhya, and Haji Ali: the list is not short (nor is this one exhaustive), and the conflicts themselves are varied in both substance and longevity.[7] What they share in common with the dispute over women's entry is the view, held by all participants to firm and frequently contrasting effect, that one's degree of belonging within a religious space is both a measure and an element of one's belonging within the polity.

Similarly, for many of us observers—including for one of the authors of *IYLA*—the spectacle of women battling for 'temple entry' in the early twenty-first century provokes, willy-nilly, recollections of those earlier efforts that took place in other places and in connection with other kinds of marginalized bodies. Admittedly, those early twentieth-century caste-based agitations were often part of a project to consolidate Hindu identity in ways that their contemporary counterparts are not. And yet, the simple act of having to specify *which* set of 'temple entry movements' one is discussing makes it inescapably apparent that gender facilitates a kind of violence and a set of practices regarding ritual pollution that were once overwhelmingly, if not exclusively, associated with caste.

Even this is only half the story. The longevity of the battle for Sabarimala as well as the remarkable ways in which it blends the peculiar with the familiar are, in the end, *legal* stories as much as they are social or political ones. Understanding the one requires grappling with the other, not always on its own terms, but not to their total exclusion either. The stark reversals, internal contradictions, and curious twists that fill the pages of this book are reversals, contradictions, and twists that are also reflected in the substance of Indian law and, particularly, in the words of the Indian Constitution. This idea—that the *content* of law is at least but only an equal partner in the analysis of social phenomena—is likely to displease both anthropologists (for whom it is crassly functionalist) and lawyers (for whom it is contemptibly timid). It is, nonetheless, an idea that becomes difficult to resist when one's frame of analysis is neither a court document nor a community, but something in between and, consequently, it is an idea that informs both the content and structure of this book.

At this point, it is perhaps no very great admission to say that this book stands apart from many recent ethnographies that bear more than a passing connection to law. Its true focus is not a place, a practice, or a set of people—no forms of legal expertise are studied here, no courthouses or law firms, no particular variety of litigants.[8] This is the ethnography of a single dispute, the most recent phase of which has lasted some sixteen years, but that has had a great many earlier iterations that are, equally, part of its story. It is also the ethnography of a concept underlying that dispute, secularism, and of that concept's articulation and adventures through a written constitution as well as the courts that interpret it. As such, there is precious little direct observation to be had or ordinary life to participate in. For better and for worse, this is often in the nature of a scholarly genre that, as I explain in an appendix, is best thought of as 'constitutional ethnography'.[9]

Finally, a note on nomenclature for places as well as for persons. Beginning in the mid-1990s, there was a concerted push to accelerate a process of renaming Indian cities and states that had been proceeding, in typically ad hoc fashion, since independence. A slew of revised names appeared during this period, all of which reflected either the non-anglicized versions of names that had vernacular counterparts or vernacular names that had been displaced in favour of English ones. In this way, Madras became Chennai, Bombay became Mumbai, and Orissa and Pondicherry became Odisha and Puducherry, respectively. Changes within Kerala were plentiful but perhaps milder, since many traditional names had been anglicized rather than ousted, and they remained, even when unofficial, in active circulation; for some people, and in some contexts, Trivandrum has always been Thiruvananthapuram, Cochin always Kochi, and Quilon—for the vast majority of us, I suspect—always Kollam. (By the same token, Travancore has largely remained Travancore, and Malabar, Malabar.) Throughout this book, I have tended to use place-names as I most often encountered them in fieldwork conversations rather than as they appear by official designation. Thus: Trivandrum and Delhi, but Chennai and Kochi.[10]

Additionally, and in deviation from an anthropological practice that is now virtually obligatory, almost none of the individuals I spoke with have been given pseudonyms. This is not, despite recent argumentation emanating from the legal academy, because I believe ethnography should be or even can be 'fact-checked', as if facts are pebbles on the road waiting to be picked up by any stray comer and capable of being passed unchanged from pocket to pocket.[11] I do not use pseudonyms because, in the context of one of twenty-first-century India's most widely reported and analysed disputes, it would be silly to do so. Much of what my interlocutors said was said in public spaces like the courthouse, and much of what they told me was also told to journalists and lawyers. Indeed, many of the statements directly quoted throughout this study have been sourced from the news media.[12] By weaving them together or by juxtaposing them against one another, and by adding in generous handfuls of legal and historical analysis—in short, by telling a more multifaceted story of the Sabarimala dispute and teasing out its implications—I do not make these comments more secret or more sensitive or less significant than they already were. Attentive analysis is not dependent on privileged statements.[13]

I.2 The Curious Case of Women's Entry

Chapter 1 establishes three contexts, successively broader yet overlapping, for the dispute over women's entry. First, in observance of anthropological norms, it introduces an immediate geographic setting for the dispute over women's entry: Kerala, the south-western Indian state that has become famous for progressive politics, unusual demographics, and striking cultural practices. Second, the chapter sketches the history of temple-state relations in Kerala, which is both unique in its particulars and representative of general patterns among southern Indian states. Finally, the chapter goes on to outline the Indian constitutional prose and jurisprudence that is most relevant to the Sabarimala dispute. I focus, in particular, on Article 25 (religious freedom, emphasizing individuals), Article 26 (religious freedom, emphasizing groups), and the 'essential practices doctrine'. There is more relevant law, of course—far more than can be satisfyingly discussed in a chapter or a book, much less in part of one chapter of one book—but this chapter aims to round out a vocabulary, not write a sonnet.

The rest of the book recounts major episodes in the dispute over women's entry, but not quite in their chronological order. No stage of the Sabarimala dispute had to happen as it did, no moment is self-evidently earlier or later in this assemblage of events. I have stopped announcing, to myself and to others, that the dispute over women's entry is finished because, in the decade or so since I began exploring it, it has ended multiple times, usually in ways that are fascinatingly and obligingly unpredictable. To tell this story as a sequence of temporally ordered occurrences would be to irreparably naturalize the ordering.

Consequently, this book begins more or less at the end—or what has sometimes passed for an end—and proceeds, in fits and starts, towards various possible beginnings. Chapter 2 opens on 29 September 2018, one day after the Supreme Court issued its opinion in *IYLA*. By that point, the Shiv Sena, a Hindu nationalist organization with roots in Maharashtra, had already called for a protest *hartal* (strike) across Kerala, while domestic and international English-language media were already celebrating another win in the 'long-running conflict between India's modern, liberal court system and deeply conservative elements of its ancient culture.'[14] The headlines were suitably heady. 'Exclusionary practices violate right to worship' announced *Scroll*.[15] 'Opening the gates' trumpeted *The Indian Express*.[16] *The News Minute* was even less restrained, declaring that the judgement represented a moment '[w]hen reason triumphed over prejudice.'[17] Admittedly, the outcome in *IYLA* had been widely expected—a day before the opinion was released, the *New York Times* published a sketch of the Indian Supreme Court that was equal parts effusive praise and 'juicy' exotica (the *Times*' own term for the type of debates preferred by the Court)—but it triggered widespread jubilation nonetheless.[18]

Just three weeks after *IYLA* was released, the *Times*' coverage of Sabarimala was markedly less triumphant. Two of its journalists, including one woman, had been forcibly turned back by crowds guarding the hills and pathways leading to the temple. Dozens of other aspiring visitors had fared similarly, and soon supporters and detractors of the *IYLA* opinion were busily exchanging marches, protests, editorials, and social media offensives, while Kerala's government tried and failed to implement the Court's order. Chapter 2 explores these reactions to the Supreme Court opinion as well as the way in which *IYLA* was mobilized during India's 2019 national elections to the detriment of Kerala's ruling Communist Party of India (Marxist) and the unexpected benefit of the Indian National Congress. The chapter also discusses recent developments at the Indian Supreme Court that were roughly contemporaneous with the Sabarimala litigation and that, I think, cannot be omitted from any discussion of it.

Chapter 3 conducts an in-depth tour of the source of all this commotion, the *IYLA* opinion, which at some 170 pages is almost succinct for a major Indian Supreme Court decision. Judicial opinions do not often figure in anthropological monographs except as plot twists or supporting cast; they are largely treated as products of highly formalized and overdetermined systems, and as artefacts that are less interesting for their own sake than for the wider social forces at which they gesture. *This* judicial opinion, however, with its four component parts and five authors, figures centrally and fascinatingly in the story of the women's entry dispute. Accordingly, the decision itself, along with details of the hearings, speculations, and interpretations that it has generated, takes up the entirety of this chapter.

Chapter 4 turns from the *IYLA* opinion to the event that directly precipitated it: the Jayamala scandal. Despite the universal disbelief that greeted her original claim, and despite the fact that she was not even the only actress to have issued a confession in 2006 about a visit to Sabarimala in 1987, Jayamala's declaration generated six years of legal wrangling and public debate. And yet, because it did not result in a pronouncement regarding the legal validity of the ban on women, the Jayamala scandal is now rarely featured in the canonical sequence of legal events that comprise the Sabarimala dispute. This chapter corrects that exclusion and demonstrates why an episode in which the ban itself was never seriously contested is nonetheless central to understanding both its contours and those of the Essential Practices Doctrine that has been suddenly, but profoundly, rendered vulnerable by the dispute over women's entry.

In Chapter 5, I head further back in time, to the Kerala High Court's 1991 opinion in *S. Mahendran v. Travancore Devaswom Board*.[19] Like *IYLA*, *Mahendran* grew out of a writ petition filed in response to newspaper coverage of one particular woman's interactions with Sabarimala—but there end the similarities. *IYLA* was filed by a distant petitioner in order to protest the exclusion of women aged ten through fifty; *Mahendran* was filed by a petitioner some 60 kilometres away from Sabarimala to protest the presence of women in the prohibited age range. *IYLA* sought to rationalize Ayyappan worship by bringing it into conformity with certain constitutional values like equality and nondiscrimination; *Mahendran*'s rationalization of religion lay in its imposition of uniformity and hierarchy where these were perceived to be missing or inadequate in Sabarimala's administration. *Mahendran* has not aged gracefully—since the commencement of the *IYLA* hearings, it has been either critiqued or ignored, and it is now effectively overruled—but its analytic framework hangs persistently over the Sabarimala dispute, even if only as a foil.

The final chapter advances to the recent past. Beginning in 2015, two social movements brought Sabarimala to national attention in a way that the *IYLA* writ petition had not, until that point, managed to achieve. First, much like some latter-day *satyagrahi*—albeit with smaller crowds and moderately violent tactics—the community organizer Trupti Desai started campaigning against Hindu temples that restricted or excluded women from their premises. By late 2016, Desai had set her sights on Sabarimala, which she repeatedly (though never successfully) pressured to let women in. Around the same time that Desai was making her initial foray into temple entry, a college student named Nikita Azad posted an open letter on a youth discussion forum critiquing a Keralite temple administrator who had defended Sabarimala's ban and, more generally, who had promoted conservative Hindu views on menstruation and ritual cleanliness. Azad's letter went viral and inspired duelling social media campaigns; she eventually went on to join the *IYLA* litigation as an intervenor in support of the suit for entry. Like the Jayamala scandal that occurred a decade earlier, these social movements are part of the dispute over women's entry without, in much meaningful sense, being part of the legal case.

If many academic monographs are akin to suspense stories, the story of Sabarimala's dispute, and especially of its finale, is far more like a mystery. Even in the aftermath of the aftermath, Sabarimala refused to recede from the national spotlight: the 2019 elections concluded, the angry rallies reduced in frequency, and India, like the rest of the world, was brought to a standstill by the coronavirus pandemic. Still, the litigation lived on in the Supreme Court—first via the medium of the review petitions, and later via the Court's determination to consider, inter alia, 'the scope and ambit of [the] right to freedom of religion.'[20] When this introduction was first written, there simply *was* no conclusion to describe. There was not even, it seemed, any sense in which the dispute over women's entry was any longer just a dispute over women's entry. Instead, it had subtly but definitely been transformed into a reassessment of India's approach to religion-state relations. The relationship between the particular and the general, always lurking in the background of anthropological analyses as well as Common Law adjudication, had become suddenly and unabashedly visible.

Lastly, for readers wondering how a book primarily standing on the shoulders of anthropology and law can have so little to say about anthropology or law, I include some observations on interdisciplinary interventions by way of an appendix. Despite its back-of-the-bus location, this reflection defines the story of the Sabarimala dispute more than any of the chapters that precede it; it is an account, or perhaps a manifesto, of storytelling itself, told in a peculiarly legal-anthropological key. Without precisely saying that anthropologists should become lawyers or lawyers should become anthropologists, I want to suggest that each of them could do with being a little less like themselves and more like the other in the interest of constructing stories that are better told and more widely heard.

The dispute over women's entry appears in its provisional entirety between the end of this introduction and the beginning of the conclusion. As I recount it here, that story is both ethnographic and archival, theoretical and doctrinal, peculiar and emphatically routine. It is also the sum—and, hopefully, the enhancement—of over a decade's writings on the issue of women's entry at Sabarimala.[21] Those earlier publications have never been gathered together, and I do not reproduce them here. Nevertheless, the story of this dispute is one that I have told often, and those earlier tellings inescapably inform the pages that follow.

1
The Setting

Despite being one of India's smallest states—around one-tenth the size of India's geographically largest state—Kerala commands considerable attention in international circles for its religious diversity, political progressiveness, and high achievement along various human development indices. It is, at first glance, an odd setting for this story. Indeed, to audiences elsewhere who have only ever heard of the 'Kerala model' for development on the cheap, or (notwithstanding the prior claims of tiny San Marino) of the 1957 installation of the world's 'first' democratically elected communist government, the women's entry dispute, with its focus on menstruation and ritual impurity, might appear perplexingly out of place. Not least among Kerala's successes, nor among the ironies of the Sabarimala dispute, are that the state boasts fertility and female literacy rates that are, respectively, low enough and high enough to rival most of the global north. Religious confrontation also sits poorly with the image projected outwards and held internally by many Keralites, who regularly bemoan the importation of Hindu nationalist politics from other parts of India. The kind of frothing rage and showy saffronization that now marks politics across large swaths of the country is not, so the story goes, native to *our* natives.

There are truths behind these caricatures, although it is not academically fashionable to say so, and yet caricatures they also and undoubtedly are. Kerala both is and is not the paragon of progressive, ecumenical, gender-equal politics it is often made out to be. It is and is not inexplicable that a controversy over whether Hindu women have the right to enter a Hindu temple should have exploded there. And, while there is certainly a sense in which Kerala's idiosyncrasies, whether these be of the heartwarming or -rending variety, define and permeate and make possible the events described in this book, the Sabarimala dispute is no more an exclusively Keralite phenomenon than either communism or coconuts.

From the local idiosyncrasies of Nair matriliny to the regionally familiar infrastructures of temple governance and the national mandates of constitutional law, the dispute over women's entry exists in a series of nested realities that simultaneously reach deep within the state's boundaries and extend far beyond them. It is not possible to understand how the battle for Sabarimala is Indian without also understanding how it is south Indian and Keralite—and vice versa.

1.1 Kerala Mahatmyam?

Even in a country marked and often riven by religious diversity, Kerala stands apart.[1] India's three largest faith communities—Hindus, Muslims, and Christians—are more equally distributed here, in a ratio of roughly 3:1.5:1, than anywhere else in the country.[2] There are more Christians in Kerala than in any other state, and India's oldest Jewish and Christian communities are also Keralite, with roots, it is said, dating to the destruction of the Second Temple in 70 CE and the arrival of St. Thomas in Muziris, a central Keralite port city that is now lost to history.[3] Conventionally and not altogether untruthfully, these groups are said to have lived in greater amity in Kerala than elsewhere in the subcontinent.

To be sure, the state has not lacked for inter-religious conflict. Twenty-first-century Kerala produced several of the most widely publicized accusations of 'love jihad', in which malevolent and conversion-minded Muslim men are said to pursue impressionable Hindu women as part of a zero-sum game for human souls and reproductive potential.[4] Kerala was also recently upset by the Marad Massacres of 2002–2003, in which Hindus and Muslims killed one another, and then Muslims revisited the issue by dispatching more Hindus. Somewhat less recently, during the Moplah Rebellion of 1921, Muslim agricultural workers in the Malabar region of northern Kerala slaughtered British-backed Hindu landlords until both Hindus and British returned the favour. The Rebellion threatened to become a distracting thorn in the side of India's burgeoning nationalist movement, which was increasingly committed to the ideal of Hindu-Muslim unity, until Gandhian critique and British military might put it forcefully to rest. Nevertheless, it was more than minimally thorny for the 2,000-odd Moplahs (Malabar Muslims) who were killed as, indeed, it was for my great-grandfather, who spent almost fourteen years in jail for having engaged in the seditious act of helping them.[5]

And yet, even if Hindus, Muslims, and Christians do not exist in a kind of ahistorical harmony set against the backdrop of Kerala's suitably exotic landscape, it is also true that religious strife in this small, south-western state is of a particular and generally less spectacular order.[6] Say what you will, the bloody drama that carved out India and two Pakistans from British India, displacing 10–12 million and killing as many as 2 million, did not find an equal expression in Kerala.[7] The bombs that periodically punctuate life in Delhi and Mumbai have not, thus far, been replicated here. The anti-cow slaughter campaigns of the BJP and RSS have gained unsurprisingly little traction among Keralites, roughly 45% of whom comprise beef-eating non-Hindus and the rest including many who, Hinduism notwithstanding, would be loath to give up their coconut-flecked beef fry. Indeed, when a band of youth activists attached to the local branch of the Congress Party publicly killed and consumed a cow in 2017, as a way of protesting the national government's ban on cattle sales for slaughter, the Congress' regional opponents, usually scathing in their criticism, merely remarked that it was 'a thoughtless act' that would 'only help Sangh Parivar [Hindu nationalist] outfits'.[8]

The image of harmonious cohabitation that anchors Keralite conceptions of self also draws on a belief in a specifically Keralite aptitude for religious syncretism. Besides the *avarna* ('without caste') reformer Narayana Guru and his famous slogan *oru jathi, oru matham, oru deivam, manushyanu* ('one caste, one faith, one god, for all'), Kerala boasts a plethora of Hindu deities and Christian saints' functioning as sibling pairs, as well as more than one Christian celebrity with a well-known propensity for visiting Hindu temples.[9] The state also has long-standing conventions of cross-community participation in religious festivals. Thrissur Pooram, a wildly popular Hindu festival centred on the Vadakkunnathan temple in central Kerala, features materials crafted or donated by Muslims and Christians, and representatives of all three communities engage in the prestigious task of feeding coconut buds to the temple's resident elephants.[10] Sabarimala itself not only welcomes men of all faiths (and ages) onto its premises, but it also houses a shrine dedicated to Ayyappan's Muslim friend and follower, Vavar. In a daily reminder of its religious eclecticism, the temple closes its doors every night to the sounds of the Hindu devotional lullaby *Harivarasanam* as recorded by the Christian singer and frequent visitor to Sabarimala, K. J. Yesudas.

If Kerala's religious plurality has always occasioned more or less positive commentary—the sixteenth-century Italian traveller Ludovico di Varthema marvelled at the 'very large number of merchants' he beheld in the northern city of Calicut, hailing from over twenty 'different countries and nations'[11]—the state's most celebrated gender practice has had a more uneven reception. Kerala is home to the largest matrilineal caste in India, the Nairs, who are, by virtue of their unique kinship practices and flexible conceptions of marital relationships, one of the most anthropologically well-studied communities in the world, as well as the one to which my own family belongs. Nineteenth-century anthropologists and the colonial officials who read them largely looked upon matriliny as the province of licentious savages for whom paternity was more hypothesis than fact.[12] Nairs were doubly suspect according to this world view, since they were not only matrilineal and matrilocal, but, especially in large parts of northern and central Kerala, their relationships were polyandrous and easily dissoluble, rather than monogamous (or at least polygamous) and permanent.[13] Male partners visited at night, left in the morning, and spent the rest of their days in their own joint family compounds among people who could—unlike their wives and children—be properly considered family.

But what was once odd and scandalous has become striking and even a touch progressive, so that Nair matriliny and its attendant conjugal practices are never totally absent from descriptions of Kerala's many successes in advancing women along human development matrices: as early as 1875, a Census Commissioner in what is now southern Kerala observed that 'there are 101 females to every 100 males' before coyly adding that 'it is a fact that among the "marumakkathayam" [matrilineal] people a female child is prized more highly than a male one'.[14] Kerala is the only Indian state to have had more women than men in every census taken since 1901,[15] these women live seven years longer than their counterparts elsewhere in India,[16] they die around three times less frequently in childbirth,[17] their state has population replacement metrics closer to the United States and United Kingdom than to India,[18] and over 94% of them were considered literate as of 2012, which was almost 12% more than the global average.[19] Even those of us professionally conditioned to know better often struggle to disassociate the feminist appeal of 'strong grandmothers'[20] and 'sexual freedoms'[21] from compelling but prosaic statistics; who is to say, after all, whether the kinship practices of a dominant caste community and the demographic indicators of its surroundings are related in a way that is correlative, causative, or merely coincidental?

If matriliny is part of Kerala's success story, it is sifted into a mix of political developments that is, I think it is not hyperbolic to say, extraordinary. Kerala's peaceful election of a communist government in 1957, just ten years after India's independence, was simply the first of these remarkable firsts. Although communism had been a prominent force at the all-India level through much of the nationalist movement, and although West Bengal would later replicate Kerala's achievement by electing its own communist government in 1977, Kerala demonstrated for India and the world that communist politics could be blended with electoral, postcolonial democracy. Since 1957, the state has more or less alternated between communist and Congress governments.[22]

Once elected, Kerala's first communist administration immediately set to work by passing India's most famous land reform legislation. The *Kerala Stay of Eviction Ordinance*, passed the very year the communists came to power, kept tenants on their lands pending the arrival of the *Kerala Agrarian Relations Bill*, passed two years later.[23] Together, these laws and their subsequent iterations established some of the guiding principles for land reform politics in Kerala over the next twenty years, with the most scandalous among them including the redistribution of land to a maximum of 25 acres per family and the empowerment of tenants vis-à-vis their landlords.[24] Indeed, Kerala's land reforms proved to be so significant that, before they could be implemented, Prime Minister Jawaharlal Nehru dismissed the state government and, we are told, either his party or his daughter Indira accepted American money to help combat the nascent communist threat.[25] The real work of land reform in Kerala would only be achieved twenty years later (by another communist administration), but the project that had been started back in 1957 burnished Kerala's progressive credentials on the global stage.

Twenty or so years after Kerala's land reforms finally went through, India decided to open itself up to the world and the world responded with foreign direct investment and mutton cheeseburgers. The move towards neoliberal globalization was followed, in 1992 and 1993, by constitutional amendments affirming and expanding the importance of local government institutions within the country's political architecture. Kerala took to the mandate for political devolution with orderly zeal. It launched the People's Planning Campaign (PPC) in 1996 as a many-millions-strong vote of confidence in the idea that political decentralization promotes engaged citizenship.[26] The agenda of the PPC was, moreover, famously shaped from the ground up through a series of assemblies held in Kerala's village schools on Sunday afternoons (to ensure widespread participation), and through locally led data gathering, community self-reporting, and development seminars.[27] Out of this bureaucratic pageantry emerged the Ninth Plan, which put Keralite money behind the national mouth. The plan reserved around 40% of state development funds for direct use by local institutions and mandated that 10% of *those* funds be used exclusively on 'women's projects'. At the time it was created, Kerala's decentralization programme was considered to be the largest of its kind in the world. To this day, the state continues to receive widespread acclaim for one of the PPC's most well-known components, a poverty-eradication and women's empowerment programme whose name, *Kudumbashree*, can mean, appropriately enough, either 'family prosperity' or 'lady of the house'.

Religion, gender, and politics: these are not Kerala's only claims to progressive fame. Near-universal literacy, powerful labour unions, savvy ecotourism, vibrant literary and art film cultures, ample primary healthcare, dynamic caste-uplift movements—Kerala has received so much international acclaim on so many fronts that the state is, within certain cosmopolitan circles, more of a Phenomenon than a Model. Indeed, for the better part of three decades, scholars writing on virtually any aspect of Keralite life have operated in the shadow of Kerala's glowing reputation and have consequently felt themselves obliged to temper its seemingly unflagging appeal with sobering statistics and re-evaluations. Seen through their differently tinted glasses, Kerala is, if not quite the inevitable backdrop for a landmark dispute over religious freedom and gender equality, a very plausible contender and a place whose faults are no less evident than its virtues.

Casteism, India's endemic and besetting sin, reaches heights of exquisite cruelty in Kerala. Most of the country has been content to structure its practices of caste discrimination around the concept that bodily contact and bodily fluids can cause ritual pollution when they are exchanged between persons of unequal caste status. In Kerala, however, the mere sight of a sufficiently low-caste person can pollute. Consequently, *Nambudiri*s (Keralite brahmins), who have long held their orthopraxy especially dear, were famous for shouting as they walked so that they could proceed along public roads without fear of inadvertently seeing a Pulaya or Paraya—the latter of whom gave us the common English word for a person whose very presence cannot be tolerated in polite society, *pariah*.

Nairs, meanwhile, enacted their own ritual and material superiority with cutting flair. Because the conventionally fourfold *varna* system (according to which all castes are either priests, warriors, merchants, or servants) is, in Kerala, mostly reduced to its highest and lowest components, Nairs are themselves considered to be 'servants', ritually speaking, despite their overall prominence in Keralite society. They walked a respectable distance away from Nambudiris, and they required those beneath them to appear topless in their presence (as, indeed, Nairs themselves were obliged to do before Nambudiris).[28] They used Christians, who were largely considered to be casteless, as neutralizers or absorbers of the pollution inhering in items received from the hands of lower castes. And, were all this not enough, Nairs demanded obsequious forms of speech or greeting from caste inferiors that included covering one's mouth while speaking and referring to oneself in the third person.[29]

The more egregious among these practices may not often manifest themselves in Keralite society anymore, but the spirit of discrimination behind them is alive and well. In the 1990s, anthropologists studying social mobility in village Kerala noted that 'we still often see ... people born in the 1960s using gestures like mouth-covering in front of "superiors" '.[30] Around the same time, my parents and I visited land that used to belong to my paternal grandmother's family, and I watched as an *avarna* former servant (who, thanks to those famed land reforms and literacy campaigns, was also a retired school principal and current homeowner) refused to sit, while in his own house, because he was in the company of the 'young master' he once cared for. My father twitched uncomfortably and made repeated entreaties, but Mambi would not be seated.

Keralite orthopraxy also persists in less obviously dehumanizing and casteist ways—for instance, in the painstaking enforcement of dress codes when visiting Hindu temples, which are more exacting here than in many other parts of the country.[31] Correct ritual observance is, in other words, a matter of some pride: our politics may be more progressive than yours, but our temples are more discerning and our brahmins more brahminical. This predilection for scrupulous orthopraxy was enthusiastically mobilized during the women's entry dispute, as supporters of the ban emphasized the Vedic credentials of Sabarimala's chief priest and the significance of certain ritual practices in which female devotees could not participate. Indeed Kerala's cultural rigidity provided the impetus for many of the state's most powerful progressive achievements, including the first law anywhere in India that opened temples to Hindus of all castes (1936) and two landmark non-violent agitations (in 1924–25 and 1932) that sought universal access to temples, or, at least, to the roads surrounding them.[32]

Keralite womanhood, too, it turns out, is not quite what it seems. Starting in the 1980s, but especially in the 1990s and early 2000s, a buzz began to emanate from scholarly and activist circles to the effect that the Kerala Model had not done well for women—or, more specifically, that what it *had* done for women should not (as it too often was) be extrapolated to indicate anything beyond those impressive lifecycle and literacy metrics. Yes, went the argument, Keralite women were literate, educated, healthy, and largely sheltered from the endless production of children in the service of patriarchal norms; they were indisputably better off than their counterparts across most of India. But they were far from enjoying parity with Keralite men, and, in some respects, their circumstances had actually deteriorated since independence. Most visibly, formal political power has remained largely inaccessible to women in Kerala.[33] Those who managed to enter official positions have done so largely through the local governance bodies that grew out of the PPC and its associated programmes, especially *Kudumbashree*. Even in these more limited contexts, women remain stuck in middle- to low-ranking positions, are often asked to do dangerous or menial service work with little assistance and less pay, and enjoy authority only to the extent that they align themselves with elite notions of feminine 'selfless service'.[34] Women's participation in public life is here, as it often is elsewhere, less a privilege than a third shift.[35]

As with politics, so too with work, love, and life: Keralite women participate in the labour force at a lower rate and in fewer sectors than other

Indian women; they suffer considerable and decidedly undercounted domestic abuse, often at the hands of alcoholic spouses; they increasingly choose or are pressured into sex-selective abortions; and they no longer enjoy advantages in matters of inheritance thanks to the abolition, in 1975, of all legal recognition for matrilineal succession to joint property.[36] None of these sobering truths renders the women of Kerala worse off than the women of Bihar or Haryana—certainly not—but they do place them at a disadvantage relative to the educated, independent, liberated, and thoroughly idealized selves they are widely assumed to be. They also explain why, for every scholarly work on Kerala titled something like *Politics, Women and Well-Being: How Kerala Became a 'Model'*, there is often one that is more forbiddingly headlined—say, *The Enigma of the Kerala Woman: A Failed Promise of Literacy*.[37]

Because we are, after all, concerned with one of the few reliably communist-democratic jurisdictions in the world, it bears mentioning that there are also materialist flaws in Kerala's progressive armour. Development on the cheap has not produced professional or financial stability for most Keralites, who are plagued by disproportionately high unemployment as well as an overwhelming dependence on the kind of low-wage, low-security jobs that characterize the informal economy and are beyond the reach of India's notoriously rigid yet largely worker-protective labour laws.[38] The land reforms that transformed so much of Keralite society socially and politically seem to have done little for it economically, inasmuch as the hundreds of thousands of miniscule landholders created by land legislation have struggled to secure viable livelihoods from their newfound properties, and agriculture itself has experienced minimal to negative growth despite providing a sizable proportion of jobs overall (33% as of 2010).[39] The People's Republic may have settled on a 'socialist market economy', but, in Kerala, communism and capitalism have not learned to live in polite ignorance of one another.

Not solely because of these failures, but not in spite of them, either, Keralites have long sought their fortunes elsewhere. They have emigrated in large numbers to construction, nursing, and miscellaneous domestic service jobs around the world, often enduring a modern variant of bonded labour in parts of the Middle East while funding 'Gulf pockets' and a 'money order economy' back home.[40] Those who remain in Kerala endure, engage in, and sometimes die from a 'strike culture' where labour agitations and work cessations are ubiquitous enough to generate the kind of traffic jams that boast their own fatality counts—not from crashes, but from delays in accessing medical attention or relief from the sweltering heat.[41] Not for nothing, then, did Kerala suffer the highest suicide rate in the country in the 1990s and early 2000s; as of 2014–18, it dropped to sixth out of twenty-nine states.[42]

This, then, is Kerala: a land of fabulous literacy, education, and healthcare; shaped by striking matrilineal traditions and impressive female well-being; home of the first major democratically elected communist government in the world as well as some of the world's most widely admired efforts at political decentralization and land reform; a place riven by biting caste oppression and bedevilled by patriarchy; where education begets joblessness, joblessness begets frustration, and frustration begets emigration or, too often, irreparable loss. To be sure, this is not all that Kerala is—there is plenty more, both good and bad, that lies unsaid here, and virtually everything that managed to be said was said too quickly. But this alone should establish two things: that Kerala is no progressive utopia unaccustomed to vehement protests or patriarchy or rigid religious norms, and that the state is stuffed every bit as full of contradictions as India itself.

1.2 God's Own Country

Amitabh Kant's late 1990s campaign to rebrand Kerala as 'God's Own Country' transformed the small south-western state into one of the hottest tourism spots in India.[43] Kant's vision was of a lush coastal land that was spiritual in its calm greenery and majestic in its exotic culture: image after image featured rustic houseboats, elephants, temples, and *kathakali* dancers in a kind of symbiotic nature-culture mélange that Kant would go on to use in his similarly successful 'Incredible India' campaign.[44] But the connection between religion and sovereignty in Kerala is of a much more long-standing and fundamental nature than Kant's slogan suggested: until quite recently, large parts of the state *were* in an important and entirely literal sense, God's own country.

On 17 January 1750, the middle-aged ruler of what is now south-central Kerala gave away his kingdom to his god.[45] Anizham Thirunal had acceded, when in his early twenties, to the throne of a minor chiefdom called Thiruvithamkoor. By the time the chiefdom was merged, two centuries later, with the newly created Republic of India—a merger overseen by a great-grandnephew many times removed and very likely no nephew at all (since the royals were both matrilineal and frequently lacking in female children)—Thiruvithamkoor had become 'Travancore' and a great deal had changed. Travancore, unlike Thiruvithamkoor, was a regional power and a national presence. It was a confirmed member of the second rung of Indian princely states within the British Empire: not so large or prestigious as Mysore and Baroda, but still one of less than a dozen to receive a nineteen-gun salute, a state respected for its prosperity and known for jealously guarding its reputation for enlightened governance.

However, back in the eighteenth century when Anizham Thirunal was just starting out, the throne of Thiruvithamkoor was not so very much to crow about. Anizham Thirunal set out to change that. Before his accession, the chiefdom had been one of many small principalities clustering around the southernmost tip of the subcontinent; to its immediate north lay the kingdom of Cochin (whose capital is the contemporary city of Kochi), while farther north still lay the kingdom of Calicut (soon to re-emerge as the British territory of Malabar). As Anizham Thirunal and his descendants added to their kingdom, Travancore become the largest and most powerful region in what is now the Indian state of Kerala. The cultural salience of this originally political designation, like that of Cochin and Malabar, remains considerable. Keralites are 'Keralites' to other Indians—that is, if they manage to be anything aside from fast-talking, coconut-loving communists—but amongst ourselves, the differences between Travancore, Cochin, and Malabar, to say nothing of the minute, village-level distinctions that exist within each one, can be articulated with a fervour that borders on the anthropological. As a geographic-cultural identity and an organizing principle for many governmental functions, *Travancore* is thus alive and well in twenty-first-century India despite not having had much political significance for over seventy years.

In the process of extending his borders outwards, Anizham Thirunal also deepened his reach within Travancore's borders. The title to which he had ascended barely made him first among equals within a circle of interrelated noble families who vied continuously for the crown; it left him decidedly inferior to a parallel line of authority emanating from the fabulously wealthy Padmanabhaswamy temple in Trivandrum. The temple owned, tax-free, so much of the land in Travancore that its governing body, the cheekily-named Assembly of Eight-and-one-half (where the king was the 'half') essentially functioned as a parallel state. Within four short years of assuming the throne, Anizham Thirunal successfully dispatched the Assembly and rebuilt the temple, thereby literally and figuratively transforming it into an expression of his sovereignty. Towards the end of his reign, he dedicated the same temple, along with all its considerable properties, the entire state of Travancore, and the familial properties of the royal household, to the temple's presiding deity, simultaneously inviting encomiums for supreme piety and a reputation as a wily statesman who knew a good public relations move when he saw one.[46]

Over the next 200 years, the rulers of Travancore would double and triple down on the connection between temples and state authority. At first, this was likely a matter of financial necessity more than anything else: a series of wars, domestic rebellions, and unrestrained spending had led Travancore to lease British battalions from the neighbouring Madras Presidency. With British debt came British agents and, soon enough, British legal reforms that were designed to improve Travancore's debt-servicing capacity. In 1811, for instance, with encouragement from its British Resident, Travancore nationalized many Hindu temples within its borders and brought their considerable earnings into state coffers. Sabarimala may have been swept up into Travancore's sphere of influence during this period. The Pandalam family, who recognize Ayyappan as their kin and Sabarimala as the object of their particular patronage, recall that the temple was first mortgaged to Travancore in 1794 to pay their share of the war effort against Tipu Sultan and then directly administered by Travancore beginning in 1820.[47]

But if money drove the integration of temple and government in the years immediately after Anizham Thirunal's reign, the two were soon entangled for reasons having far more to do with everyday life and changing royal perspective. A series of proclamations issued throughout the early to mid-1800s convey that the rulers of Travancore now felt themselves obliged to pronounce on the finer details of temple operations—on how devotee offerings should be collected, or on which non-Hindu communities might be excused from supplying the provisions used in temple rituals.⁴⁸ This was neither the purely arbitrative function ascribed to the Vijayanagara kings who ruled much of south India just before British arrival nor, at least initially, did it quite amount to the universalistic legislation of modern states.⁴⁹ Instead, many of these pronouncements 'were addressed to specific groups and individuals ... and were subject to alteration or repeal according to the pragmatic needs of kingship' but were also 'attributed to a constitutionally competent authority to pronounce rules having a general application'.⁵⁰

By beginning of the twentieth century, though, Travancore's governmental apparatus for temple management had expanded to include an entire department-level bureaucracy dedicated to *devaswom* ('god's own') issues.⁵¹ The rulers of Travancore had also seemingly come to view themselves as trustee-managers more than as proprietors. By 1922, Moolam Thirunal had embraced a rather striking reversal of the relationship between sovereigns and temples that had been established a century earlier. Henceforth, he declared, Travancore would hold itself obliged to meet the expenses of maintaining temple properties even if doing so required the state to draw on its own funds.⁵² This new policy would have managed to simultaneously alienate caste Hindus (who had long believed the state was usurping surplus temple revenues) as well as non-caste Hindus and non-Hindus (who suspected that temples, from which they were largely excluded, were absorbing general tax revenues).⁵³ But it was of a piece with the deep entanglement between sovereign and temple that had characterized Travancorean politics since at least 1750.

Finally, in 1936, the last reigning king of Travancore issued the subcontinent's first 'temple entry proclamation'.⁵⁴ Over the next few years—largely, but not exclusively after independence—some dozen similar proclamations would appear around India, opening Hindu temples to persons of all castes.⁵⁵ These would be superseded, in 1955, by national legislation that outlawed the exclusion of any person 'on the ground of "untouchability" ' from 'any place of public worship which is open to other persons professing the same religion or any sections thereof'.⁵⁶ Nevertheless, then as now, much was made of Travancore's (and thus Kerala's) successful sprint to the finish line. Within the kingdom, merchants proposed elaborate and predictably adulatory displays honouring Chithira Thirunal's proclamation, and the king's prime minister wrote angry letters to anyone who cast aspersions on royal motivations or legislative efficacy.[57] Outside the kingdom, however, even as nearby as Malabar and the rest of the Madras Presidency, Travancore's proclamation was sometimes critiqued as little more than upper caste condescension facilitated by arbitrary and autocratic royal action.[58]

The Travancore of Anizham Thirunal's imagination and his successors' efforts may have been unusual for its divine head of state and for its early adoption of temple entry reforms, but it was not, at its core, exceptional for the way in which it linked political power with Hindu temples. Temples and sovereign authority, particularly in south India, have long been viewed as inextricably caught up in one another. Precolonial south Indian kings gave generously to temple endowments and received copiously in the form of temple honours, they protected temples in times of conflict (but relied on them for war monies, too), and they intervened in disputes over temple management, which was otherwise the domain of local elites. Much of the scholarship exploring this connection has focused on the especially close link between temples and sovereigns in Tamil-speaking parts of south India—in a show of linguistic economy that is as typical as it is delightful, the Tamil word for temple (*kōvil*), which I earlier translated as 'god's house', can mean 'king's house' as well—but there are Andhrite and Keralite studies as well.[59] Across south India, deities reign like sovereigns over both court (temple) and kingdom (temple assets), and temple ritual is often said to be best understood as a species of political homage. Put differently, temple symbolism is sovereign symbolism, and sometimes it is sovereignty itself.

Anglo-Indian trust law would eventually accept and overextend this analogy between divinity and sovereignty by making the deity him or herself the *legal* owner of temple properties and thereby enabling, several decades later, an entire genre of bemused Krishna-goes-to-court journalism.[60] In the late twentieth century, for instance, litigation in the United Kingdom over a bronze image dubbed the Pathur Nataraja led the Queen's Bench to entertain what was, in all probability, its first divine plaintiff, in the form of the Hindu deity Shiva.[61] Much more recently (and more divisively) the deity Ram appeared as a litigant in his own cause during the long-running Ayodhya litigation, which centred on a plot of land alternately characterized as a mosque and as Ram's terrestrial birthplace.[62] But this kind of juridical status and property ownership, which had become true for temple deities across British India over the course of the nineteenth and twentieth centuries, had been true—more or less—ever since 1750 for the particular deity to whom Anizham Thirunal had given his kingdom.

In Travancore, as across south India, the colonial officials who came after native rulers found that in order, at first, to participate efficaciously in native life and, later on, in order to meaningfully regulate it, they too had to treat temples as venues for the redistribution of social and material power. Accordingly, the East India Company put temple deities on their coins, invoked divine blessings on their new ventures, and, in 1817, the Company enacted a statute—the Madras Endowments and Escheats Regulation—that made it the government's responsibility to oversee land and money endowed for 'pious or beneficial purposes'.[63] Some 130 years later, the vast bureaucracy that had grown out of this statute and that structured the administration of thousands of Hindu temples in south India—as well as Hindu monasteries, academies, and other charitable institutions in the region—was transferred to the brand new Indian province of Madras.

Politicized, bureaucratized, legalized temple governance is, for all these reasons, an especially *south* Indian story. All but one of today's five south Indian states were, at independence, partly or wholly governed by systems that descended from the 1817 Madras statute and commonalities between statutory parent and offspring abound.[64] But far more noteworthy than any specific inheritances is an undeniable family resemblance: the 1817 statute introduced a way of thinking about religion-state relations in general and about *temple*-state relations in particular that went on to inform, without much alteration, generations of regional statutory descendants. It is 'the duty of Government', the statute declared, 'to take over "the general superintendence of all endowments in land or money" and, thereby, to enter directly into the details of administering each and every religious institution'.[65] Travancore, despite never being part of British India, adopted temple legislation that broadly replicated the Madras Presidency's system as originally envisioned by the 1817 statute, and it is this legislation that governs Sabarimala now. Malabar, which *was* part of British India, operates under a much-modified version of the 1817 statute.

The administrative structures produced by these statutes are, predictably, also similar. In Andhra Pradesh, Karnataka, and Tamil Nadu, 'endowment' departments in the state government oversee public Hindu temples in conjunction with high courts and institution-specific boards, while in Kerala, public Hindu temples are governed by a 'devaswom' portfolio in the state government, a dedicated 'temple bench' at the Kerala High Court, and a complicated web of statutory bodies that is most easily thought of as the 'board system'.[66] Chapter 5 more fully describes the Keralite system and the ways in which its constituent parts interact with one another. But while the exact contours of this administrative infrastructure may be peculiar to Kerala, in its generalities, the Keralite system is similar to its cousins across south India.

Broadly similar tales can even be told about temples, governance, and temple governance from other parts of the country: the Kalighat temple in Calcutta and the Jagannath temple in Puri, for instance, share elements of the colonial-origin administrative and legal history I have described here.[67] The next section shows that, even in post-independence India, religious life continued to play a remarkable role in the conceptualization—and the customization—of what sovereign authority could look like in a democratic state. Anizham Thirunal's story is, in other words, remarkable only in its particulars: writ large, Travancore exemplifies the way in which sovereignty in south India, and to a great extent India itself, has been augmented, and often constituted, through involvement in temple life.

1.3 Keralite Temples, Indian Secularism

The statutes that most directly shape temple governance in Kerala today, the *Travancore-Cochin Hindu Religious Institutions Act* (1950) and the *Madras Hindu Religious and Charitable Endowment Act* (1951), do the important work of situating regional histories and administrative practices within a national legal framework.[68] The statutes are not sexy laws—unlike constitutional imperatives to ensure equality or prohibit discrimination, they translate between the specific and the general using language that is often distastefully, but deceptively, mundane—and consequently they are often overlooked in commentary, if not in case law.[69] Some of this oversight was corrected during the *IYLA* litigation, when most parties were drawn into a fairly extensive analysis of a third Keralite statute, the *Kerala Hindu Places of Public Worship (Authorisation of Entry) Act* (1965). But even so, the protests and the marches and the angry newspaper outpourings that greeted *IYLA* in 2018 were almost exclusively pitched at the level of India's national charter and were overwhelmingly concerned with the Supreme Court's successes and failures in living up to that object of national affection.

That charter came into force the same year as the *Travancore-Cochin Act* and it boasts a reputation for progressive principles that rivals Kerala's own. Indeed, India's Constitution has often been described as 'transformative', not only because it sought to change a colonial property into an independent nation but also because, in that process, it aimed to reconfigure the very individuals and communities who made up the nation.[70] Much, though by no means all, of this reconfiguration was focused on religion. Many constitutional framers believed that India's religious traditions would continue to permit, encourage, and even compel an impressive array of socially destructive and anti-democratic practices if they were left unrestrained by law.[71] The framers' anxieties in this regard, which encompassed everything from the spectre of immolated widows and child brides to caste segregation and human sacrifice as well as other evils, both mundane and spectacular, led these proto-parliamentarians to determine that, in India, the government would have to be actively involved in the task of changing people's preferences.

Some of the constitutional prose reflecting this worry neither confers a formal right to citizens nor imposes a formal responsibility on the state; it is, in other words, 'non-justiciable' through the courts and is located in a section of the Constitution that amounts to a national to-do list. 'The State shall *endeavour*', says Article 44, to develop a single code governing marriage, divorce, inheritance, and adoption for members of all religious communities—but, seventy years later, Indians continue to be ruled by different systems of personal law according to their natal or adopted affiliations.[72] 'It shall be the *duty* of every citizen', pronounces Article 51(A), 'to promote harmony and the spirit of common brotherhood' and 'to develop the scientific temper'.[73] But aside from a few atheistic rationalists who work through civic engagement and targeted litigation, a scientific temper, howsoever we may choose to understand that term, is no more to be found here than in the other national contexts, Irish or American as they may be, that inspired India's constitutional text.[74]

Where the transformative impulse of the Indian Constitution really shines through is in one of its most unusual provisions, Article 25(2), which circumscribes an otherwise conventional guarantee of religious freedom.[75] 'Nothing in this article', cautions 25(2), shall 'prevent the State from making any law—'

(a) regulating or restricting any economic, financial, political or other secular activity which may be associated with religious practice;
(b) providing for social welfare and reform or the throwing open of Hindu religious institutions of a public character to all classes and sections of Hindus.

Both elements of Article 25(2) occupy prominent roles in the debate over Sabarimala. Sub-part (b)'s applicability to the dispute over women's entry, at first glance glaringly obvious, became rather more nuanced—and more interesting—as litigants refined their perspectives about what, exactly, constitutes a 'class' or 'section' of Hindus. Nevertheless, and as is so often the case, sub-part (a) stole the show. This tiny bit of prose is part of the Constitution's original text, unlike many of the 145,000 words now making up India's magnum opus, meaning that its authorization of state action affecting 'any ... secular activity' existed before 1976, when the preamble was changed to designate India itself as a secular state. Article 25(2)(a)'s eighteen words have generated a judicial doctrine, a corresponding judicial test, and an entire body of jurisprudence, all of which are centred on distinguishing 'essential religious' practices from the 'other secular' activity with a view to giving back to people of faith some of the autonomy that Article 25(2) strips away. Should a ceremonial dance be exempt from proscriptions against unlawful assembly?[76] Should animal sacrifice be exempt from proscriptions against cattle slaughter?[77] The Essential Practices Doctrine can, we are told, help us arrive at an answer.

To be sure, religious reform is not the only way in which the Indian Constitution is said to be transformative. From its abolition of untouchability (Article 17) to its affirmative support for various disadvantaged populations (Article 15(3)–(5), Article 16(4)), its gradual limitation of property rights, and its inclusion, over time, of several positive entitlements (for instance, free and compulsory primary education), India's charter seemingly does the right things and recognizes the right target populations needed to facilitate a state-led revolution.[78] For its flexibility and longevity, the one probably flowing from the other, the Constitution is justifiably among the most celebrated national charters in the world.[79] For its accessibility, both practical and conceptual, it is greatly venerated at home. Indians can directly approach the Supreme Court and any of the upper courts for the vindication of their Fundamental Rights and the defence of the public interest. As a 'social document'[80] that 'quickly came to dominate public life in India',[81] the Constitution has undeniably been concerned with remaking far more than religious life in the new nation. But it remains the case that India's approach to religion-state relations, expediently dubbed 'Indian secularism', is among the most important, and certainly the most visible, elements of a constitutional framework that is often described as 'reformative'[82] or 'confrontational'.[83]

Indian secularism, it is worth saying, is every bit as secular as french fries are French. It is not simply that politics in India have steadily acquired a more saffron hue with the passage of time and the succession, at both regional and national levels, of one Hindu nationalist administration after the other. It is that, notwithstanding the aforementioned insertion of preambular language declaring the country to be a 'sovereign, socialist, secular' republic, India's Constitution and the legal system built around it have never been exclusively desirous of setting religion apart from public life and state action. How, one wonders while reading Article 25(2), could anyone think otherwise? And what does 'secularism' mean if it does not signal the desire, however varied and varyingly realized, to separate religion from the state, and from public life more generally? Big-tent concepts are tents nonetheless: someone must stand outside.

Difficult though it may be to name a liberal democratic politics that is neither secular nor theocratic, this is what we must do if we are to understand religion-state relations in independent India. That is because, alongside the provisions that actively insert the state into the definition and transformation of faith, the Indian Constitution also seeks, just as actively, to carve out domains of life into which the state may not intrude. Curiously enough, religion is one of these zones of desired autonomy. Article 25 declares that 'all persons are equally entitled to freedom of conscience and the right to freely profess, practice, and propagate religion'. Article 26 follows up with a specifically Indian spin on this blandly individualistic understanding of faith by stating that 'every religious denomination or any section thereof' shall have property rights, the right to establish and maintain institutions, and, most contentiously, the right 'to manage its own affairs in matters of religion'.[84]

Constitutional lawmaking, whether by courts or by legislatures, has regularly, if imperfectly, reflected this support for spiritual agency. Article 25(2)(a) may be a check on the religious freedom right conferred in Article 25, but the Essential Practices Doctrine was meant to function as a check on *that* check.[85] The doctrine counsels courts and warns lawmakers, in terms that are quoted ad nauseam throughout Indian jurisprudence, that 'what constitutes the essential part of a religion'—and consequently what lies, at least to some degree, beyond the purview of the state—'is primarily to be ascertained with reference to the doctrines of that religion itself'.[86] Chapter 3 explores the doctrine's rough dislocation from this originally boundary-marking purpose, but it remains that the intent behind this famous judicial principle was to limit governmental authority *and* that this intent was not merely the product of judicial idiosyncrasy. Alongside the impulse to reform religious life, there has always existed a recognition that religious life merits protection. Even the legislative action *most* emblematic of state intervention in faith, the four Hindu Code acts passed in the 1950s to modernize and standardize Hindu personal law, acted through generalization and selective retention rather than through transformation or whole-cloth creation. They were less about abandoning traditional principles (or about making good on nationalist-era promises of gender equality) than they were about governing the personal lives of Hindu Indians in a manner more befitting the newly democratic nation-state.[87] The Acts did not, in the concise words of one critic, 'introduce any principle which had not already existed somewhere in India'.[88]

This ambivalence towards state-led transformation is also often encoded in legislation that is less famously, but equally clearly, concerned with reforming religious practice. *The Kerala Hindu Places of Public Worship (Authorisation of Entry) Act* (1965) and the regulatory rules associated with it together provided a statutory hook for the writ petition that would eventually overturn Sabarimala's ban. The *Act* and the *Rules*, both distant descendants of Travancore's 1936 temple entry proclamation, were most obviously and most importantly meant to effectuate long-promised access rights, and so they contained an express guarantee of entry to all 'section[s]' and 'class[es]' of Hindus. But Rule 3(b) *also* contained—the past tense is intentional—a proviso allowing for the exclusion of certain populations when 'custom and usage' demand that they remain outside.[89] When the Supreme Court decided, via *IYLA*, that the custom and usage proviso was unconstitutional, it chose, for the moment, to rest on one side of a dynamic between reform and restraint that runs through the entire Constitution and through India's national imagination itself.

That dynamic, which periodically resolves itself in favour of one impulse or the other, only to then swing the other way, captures two very distinct—indeed, mutually exclusive—attitudes regarding the proper relationship between citizens and the state. Indian law and politics certainly embrace the transformative mission usually ascribed to them, and they do so in a way that must, at least in part, rest on the *state's* 'idea of India'.[90] A state that seeks to disabuse citizens' minds of prejudices and their behaviour of bad practices sets out to make them something other than what they previously were. It does *not* merely act as an agent of the citizenry but rather shares in sovereign decision-making just as much as the citizens themselves. Yet a state that recognizes the importance of religious freedom, that acknowledges both the individual and the collective nature of religious identity and grants rights accordingly—a state that places limits, however generous, upon its own reformatory zeal—*that* is a state that also recognizes its subservience to citizen-sovereigns.

Rather than commit to either of these extremes, the Constitution, in true Indian fashion, commits to them both. It intervenes in religious life, throwing open temples, reforming 'secular' activities associated with faith and restricting even essential activities when they conflict with other constitutional principles, just as it respects religious freedom by occasionally withdrawing itself from the consciences of individuals and the internal matters of denominations and sects. It is a constitution that espouses one vision of the nation, in which citizens are to be brought, intentionally and even unwillingly, into a community of equals, only to subsequently affirm an alternate understanding of nationhood (and of equality) in which citizens determine for themselves what they value and who it is they wish to become. In switching back and forth between these ideas of India, the Constitution and the courts that interpret it maintain a dynamic equilibrium between them. Sometimes—many times—that maintenance is messy.

***

Secular democracy, transformative constitutionalism, postcolonial politics, redistributive networks, temple governance, sovereign divinities (and occasionally divine sovereigns), communism, matriliny, literacy, and casteism: the Sabarimala dispute is about all of these and more. It is simultaneously Indian, Keralite, and Indian-because-it-is-Keralite.[91] Moreover, the dispute is neither contained in its entirety within petitioners' briefs and the judicial pronouncements issued in response to them, nor is it somehow independent of the technical arguments made within those legal documents. Without meaning to trade a statute- and citation-filled legal analysis for palm trees or peninsulas—an exchange that, as this initial foray well demonstrates, is both impossible and inadvisable—I want to suggest that this broader landscape matters for our understanding of the dispute over women's entry as well as its broader significance, indeed, it matters as much as (but not more than) the law itself.

When the Supreme Court released its *IYLA* opinion in September 2018, it did not merely affirm transformative elements in the Constitution or progressive elements in Keralite culture, although it certainly did both of these things. The Court also confirmed a long-standing and almost bewilderingly multifaceted relationship between state power and Hindu temples in Travancore and south India, and it departed, yet again, from the historically non-precedent-setting nature of that relationship. In the course of challenging pre-existing nationwide commitments to respecting spiritual autonomy, the Court exposed the ample rigidity and discriminatory tendencies characteristic of Kerala's religious life. None of this eventual significance was especially apparent back in 2009–11 when I was conducting my fieldwork on temple governance in Kerala, when the dispute over women's entry at Sabarimala seemed, even to many Keralites, like the particular problem of a very particular temple—a problem, moreover, that had disappeared into the black hole of India's overburdened judicial system. But as the reactions to *IYLA* made quickly and amply clear, even to an anthropologist professionally groomed to see the structural rather than the newsworthy, the dispute over women's entry activated multiple and often mutually contradictory interests. Those interests, and their articulation in the immediate aftermath of the *IYLA* decision, are the focus of the next chapter.

2
The Counterprotests

A *namajapam*, or 'name-chanting', can take many forms.[1]

Sometimes, it is a private and quiet ritual, a single person whispering a select few phrases to herself and counting her repetitions with the aid of prayer beads. Like their cousins the rosary, the chaplet, and the *tasbih*, Hindu *japamala*s ('chanting garlands'), which are usually made of either wooden beads or *rudraksha* seeds, are instantly recognizable in form and purpose. *Hare Rama, Hare Rama, Rama Rama, Hare Hare.*

At other times, a *namajapam* is a collective endeavour, a group of like-minded individuals brought together in the pursuit of divine blessings. It is accessible, inclusive religion. For the Ramnamis of Chhattisgarh and the Hare Krishnas of universal and enduring notoriety, chanting god's name proved to be so definitive a practice that the act itself came to label the community. Among the Ramnamis, chanting has traditionally provided an entrée to spiritual life for practitioners who cannot read or memorize long tracts of Hindi or Avadhi text but who can easily and enthusiastically inscribe divine nomenclature 'on their homes, their clothing, their possessions, and their bodies'—and, of course, in their minds through continuous repetition.[2] Among the Hare Krishnas, less commonly known as the International Society for Krishna Consciousness, chanting in public and in private simultaneously expresses, advertises, and saves. *Hare Krishna, Hare Krishna, Krishna Krishna, Hare Hare.*

Among Keralite Hindus, and perhaps especially among their expatriate clusters, a twenty-four-hour *akhanda* ('endless') *namajapam* is a moderately popular way to mark an important event. The installation of new temple images, the celebration of important community anniversaries, the beginning of a significant ritual: any of these may find assemblages of kurta-and-sock-wearing individuals participating in a kind of religious relay that incorporates, over the course of the day, a considerable percentage of their spiritual community.

The *namajapam*s that occurred repeatedly and throughout Kerala in response to *IYLA* exemplified none of these types. They were intended to be—and they emphatically were—shows of force, organized by critics of the Supreme Court's decision, sometimes facilitated by Hindu nationalist organizations, but always (and noticeably) peopled by women. In late 2018, dozens, hundreds, and frequently thousands of women marched as part of *namajapam*s that were arranged, through social media accounts and word of mouth, as a show of feminine disdain for a feminist victory. Women marched down main streets across Kerala, through some of India's major cities, and as far away as Nairobi, clapping their hands and shouting Ayyappan's name at the top of their lungs (this last part is not, even in the most enthusiastic *najamajapam*s, very ordinary practice). The photographs alone are intimidating.

While prayer as protest is all too familiar in India, the *namajapam*s triggered by *IYLA* nonetheless puzzled or dismayed many commentators, including many Keralites. Who were these women, with their strident religiosity and their declarations that they *wanted* to be excluded from a place of worship? Since when do Keralites of any gender parade in public defence of religious tradition? The imagined Kerala behind these reactions was, of course, just that: a land of uncomplicated gender relations and benign spirituality that has never existed except in the minds of eager tourists, determined politicians, and admiring development scholars. But the protests, which were indeed remarkable for their vehemence and their violence, as well as for the persistence that took them well into 2019, would have been noteworthy anywhere in India and, as such, were downright startling in God's Own Country.

2.1 *Aachaaram* Meets the Women's Wall

The marching *namajapam*s, like the blockades that soon appeared along the route to Sabarimala and the proliferating social media posts and newspaper editorials criticizing the Supreme Court decision, worked in defence of *aachaaram*. Much like any respectable umbrella concept pertaining to Hinduism, including the concept of Hinduism itself, *aachaaram* evades easy definition. A related noun, *aacharanam*, less complicatedly points to an observance, practice, or behaviour.[3] Another near-relation, the adjective *aacharaneeya*, suggests that which *should* be observed. By the time we get to *aachaaram* proper, however, we have arrived at something rather more than discrete observance or simple obligation: we encounter instead a 'massive, inter-connected, all-pervading web of practices, rituals, and ideas'.[4] *Aachaaram* is what produces small restrictions, like the conservative dress codes obtaining at many Keralite temples, and *aachaaram* is what produces great cruelties, like (to take just one intentionally upper caste example) the peremptory shunning of Nambudiri women who are suspected of so much as appearing within eyeshot of an unrelated man.[5] *Aachaaram* is rightness, cleanliness, purity, and circumspectness; things that are perpetually under siege and worth unapologetically protecting.

In the years leading up to *IYLA*, *aachaaram* had produced a great swelling of energy and enthusiasm among Keralite Hindu—especially upper caste Hindu—women, for whom the foundational assumptions of the PIL case constituted both misunderstanding and conceit. Shilpa Nair, a Dubai-based entrepreneur, founded People for Dharma in response to media coverage of the Sabarimala hearings; her organization—'supporting and defending Indian traditions and value systems'—would go on to become a prominent anti-entry voice during the hearings themselves as well as during the review petition process that followed *IYLA*'s 2018 release.[6] Anjali George, a self-declared 'Internet Hindu' based in Germany and a member of Shaktitva, a group whose name may not-unreasonably be translated as 'goddess-ness', led the #ReadyToWait campaign during the Sabarimala social media wars of 2015–16.[7] Both women appear, via the movements and organizations they led, in later portions of this book. They and their colleagues spoke in the established vernacular of female Hindu activists across India, demarcating religion as explicitly apolitical and themselves as its avenging, nurturing, technologically adept, and already-liberated mothers.[8] After the Supreme Court issued its opinion in September 2018, the considerable network that these women had established hustled to rhetorically and visually articulate a critical response that was characterized by a respect for *aachaaram*.

Supporters and critics alike had nearly three weeks in which to muster their initial reactions to *IYLA* because Sabarimala, which adds to its many idiosyncrasies by only opening during select periods of the year, was not accepting any visitors (of any gender) on the date, 28 September, when the opinion was released. Because that date was neither the Keralite New Year (which falls in mid-April), nor part of the annual pilgrimage season (November–January), and because it did not fall within the first five days of a Malayalam calendar month and was not linked to any of the small festivals observed at Sabarimala, the temple was closed and would remain so until 17 October. Even after Sabarimala reopened in October, however, and for a little over three months thereafter, reactions to the Supreme Court decision would remain merely contentious. There were marches, to be sure, as well as blockades, editorials, and vituperative tweets. But in a state that is habituated to collective displays of traffic-stopping indignance as a result of union strikes, student strikes, and political party strikes, among other things, the early demonstrations prompted by *IYLA v. State of Kerala* were a very mild and familiar annoyance for a slightly less familiar cause.

In the next phase, between 17 October and 31 December 2018, over twenty women tried, with varying degrees of failure, to visit Sabarimala. The *avarna* activist and schoolteacher Bindu Thankam Kalyani, who made the attempt on 22 October, was forced to turn back, then forced to vacate her residence, and finally forcibly transferred to another school after supporters of the ban harassed her landlord and her employer.[9] The Chennai-based progressive women's collective Manithi sent eleven of its members as part of a 23 December attempt; those women spent ten hours at a base camp on the way to Sabarimala's hilltop location before being chased back down towards the valley by scores of male devotees.[10] Kavitha Jakkala, a reporter from Hyderabad, and Rehana Fathima, a former telecommunications technician, were similarly rebuffed, and Fathima—who is the only Muslim woman I know of to have tried visiting Sabarimala during this period, besides being something of an agent provocateur—was fired by her employer and, seemingly, by her faith.[11] Yet another visit, from the media-savvy community organizer Trupti Desai (whom we will meet again in Chapter 6), received national attention. Nevertheless Desai, too, returned home after making an extended sojourn in Kochi International Airport that generated, in mid-November, an exciting day's work for scores of television reporters but little else. Thanks to this steady stream of female volunteers, as well as a veritable ocean of frequently female protestors, the Sabarimala dispute continued strong through the closing months of 2018. Nevertheless, it was not until New Year's Day, 2019, that the trouble well and truly began.

On 1 January 2019, my part of the globe woke up to the knowledge that several million women in another part of the globe had joined hands, quite literally, in support of gender equality. The *vanitha mathil* ('women's wall') ran for some 600 kilometres alongside Kerala's western coast, following the bustling National Highway 66 that connects Kanyakumari on the subcontinent's southern end with the outskirts of the Mumbai Metropolitan Region. After the manner of all things Keralite, the wall was simultaneously an expression of highly centralized state authority—it was organized by the Department for Women and Child Development—and also the product of grassroots efforts by local groups, over 150 of whom cooperated with the government to bring the wall into being.[12] In the northern district of Kasargod, as the first link in the chain, stood the Minister for Health and Family Welfare, K. K. Shailaja. As the last link, in Trivandrum, stood Brinda Karat, a member of the CPI(M)'s national Politburo and the former general secretary of its women's wing. Beside Karat stood Kerala's embattled Chief Minister, Pinarayi Vijayan, whose attitude towards the Supreme Court ruling had escalated from the determinedly bland ('Our government accepts the decision ... We have to make all required arrangements.') to the defiant ('I will not allow the Sangh Parivar to make Sabarimala into another Ayodhya.').[13]

At 4 p.m. on New Year's Day, 2019, Vijayan, Karat, Shailaja, and the millions of women in between them stretched out their hands in a Roman salute and recited words that commingled a touching idealism with a clumsy Eurocentrism and a rather hefty dose of snark:

> We are taking the pledge that we will uphold Renaissance values, we will stand for equality for women, we resist the attempts to make Kerala a lunatic asylum, and we will fight for secularism.[14]

The very next day, two women in the prohibited age range entered Sabarimala.

Bindu Ammini and Kanakadurga met online, brought together by a single-purpose social media account that had been started by a man named Shreyas Kanaran and that bore the modest title *Navothana Keralam Sabarimalayilekku* ('Renaissance Kerala goes to Sabarimala'). After a failed attempt to reach Sabarimala on 24 December 2018, the two women stayed for over a week in an undisclosed location, waiting for a second opportunity and reconsidering the logistics of their next attempt. Their second trip, on 2 January, was not only successful; it was, by all accounts, positively cinematic: a predawn departure, a decoy vehicle, discreet police protection, carefully rehearsed scripts and mannerisms, a brief, barely fifteen-minute, presence inside the temple itself, and an understated victory celebration in the form of a cup of coffee.[15] Ammini and Kanakadurga were inside Sabarimala around 3:30 a.m., while the rest of Kerala recovered from the excitement of previous day's *vanitha mathil*, and although it does not appear that they completed their visit entirely undiscovered, the hour was early enough that their observers were few, if any. Silver screen recreation is, I think, only a matter of time—and, were there any doubts on this score, the strikingly divergent backgrounds of the women themselves, should easily put them to rest.

Ammini, an *avarna* activist, lawyer, and law professor with a long history of involvement in gender rights advocacy and centre-left politics, is married to another political activist and has a child named after a German communist murdered by the Nazis.[16] During her attempts to visit Sabarimala, her husband knew where she was and supported her choice to be there.[17] Kanakadurga's Nair family, on the other hand, filed a missing person's report in between her two attempts to reach the temple; she replied to them via publicly released video but without announcing her location to them or anyone else. When she and Ammini finally returned from their safe houses after having entered the temple, her mother-in-law beat her thoroughly. When she returned yet again—this time from the hospital—Kanakadurga found, at first, that she had no home, and found later on (after a local court had affirmed her right to access the marital residence) that she had no family, because her husband and mother-in-law had decamped to another house with the couple's two children, while her own parents and siblings ignored her.[18]

But to say all this is to precipitously advance the narrative. A January 1st featuring 600-odd kilometres of women linking hands in the interests of gender inequality and a January 2nd on which two women entered a temple widely believed to be forbidden to them could only be followed by a January 3rd marked by considerable amounts of mayhem—and so they were. Hindu nationalist organizations called a statewide strike in Kerala, which so unnerved nearby Karnataka that it incurred a roughly ₹10 lakhs (1 million) loss by voluntarily ceasing all public bus service between the two states.[19] Bombs were hurled in Kannur (northern Kerala) and Nedumangadu (southern Kerala). Somewhere in the vicinity of 500–1,000 people were detained by the police in connection with the riots of that day, producing a secondary line of Sabarimala litigation. Shops were burned, injuries were incurred, and, although the Government of Kerala vehemently denies this, at least one person may have died.[20] Far away in Delhi, Keralite Members of Parliament protested *in* Parliament to, I have little doubt, the simultaneous amusement and chagrin of their northern colleagues.

Since the events of 1–3 January 2019, responses to the women's entry dispute have taken more than one surprising turn. After the news of Bindu Ammini and Kanakadurga's visit became public, Sabarimala's chief priest, Kandararu Rajeevaru, ordered a purification ceremony at the shrine. After news of the purification ceremony became public, Ammini petitioned the Supreme Court. She argued that the priest's actions created an equivalency between female fertility and *avarna* status in a way that was contrary to both the Constitution (which abolishes untouchability via Article 17) and to its own decision in *IYLA*. Kerala's CPI(M) government agreed: the Chief Minister and Devaswom Minister issued public rebukes of the chief priest, while another minister (who had formerly held the Devaswom Department portfolio) called the priest a 'Brahmin monster'.[21] Two statutory bodies, the Travancore Devaswom Board and the Kerala State Commission for Scheduled Caste and Scheduled Tribes, demanded that Rajeevaru explain his actions to them; a leisurely thirty-five days later, Rajeevaru simply declared that the ceremony had been conducted to address some other ritual impropriety.[22]

Less than four weeks into the year, the Government of Kerala disclosed to the Supreme Court, based on a list of names and identity numbers provided to temple authorities, that over fifty women in the prohibited age range had visited Sabarimala. One of these supposed entrants was a man who had incorrectly indicated his gender on his national identity card. Another—also a man—admitted to ferrying dozens of devotees to Sabarimala during the 2018–19 pilgrimage seasons but could think of no women between ten and fifty among his passengers. Several of the listed women who were, in fact, women were comfortably outside the prohibited age range, notwithstanding contrary indications on their identity cards. For Kerala's CPI(M) government, which had been steadfastly affirming (if not always actively facilitating) women's entry to Sabarimala, the identification blunders were an embarrassment. For the national Modi administration, which had staked so much on the necessity and viability of an all-India identity scheme anchored by a unique twelve-digit number, the Sabarimala misidentifications were, or should have been, an object lesson.

As 2019 wore on, the Kerala High Court continued to process the events of early January. Within a week of the first riots, and continuing on well into the spring and summer of that year, the High Court heard petition after petition from protestors who were seeking bail. Most of these individuals stood accused of garden variety offences—bus vandalism, road obstruction, minor altercations with the police—and were seeking bail after their arrests.[23] A few, like K. Sivadasan (involved in no fewer than six cases before the High Court), were charged with more serious wrongdoing, including bodily assault.[24] And a few others, like Sivan (accused of pelting police officers with stones), sought the peculiarly Indian benefit of *anticipatory* bail, which, as the name suggests, provides freedom from custody before custody is established.[25]

Like its more famous but also judicially created cousin, the public interest petition, anticipatory bail is a child of the political upheaval that characterized India in the 1960s and 1970s and that further involved the judiciary in matters of everyday governance.[26] If the 'right to life' enshrined in Article 21 was to have any meaning, India's national Law Commission determined, it would sometimes be necessary for courts to step in to protect individuals from the trauma of frivolous or politically motivated arrest as well as from the subsequent harms of pretrial custody.[27] Also like public interest litigation, anticipatory bail is sometimes blamed for simultaneously expanding judicial discretion and exploding judicial burdens.[28] It did neither of these things in the wake of the Sabarimala protests, given the ratio of traditional bail applications to anticipatory requests and the relatively formulaic nature of the analysis that was called for in all instances. But what the requests for anticipatory bail *did* achieve, besides handing the Kerala High Court yet another handful of remarkable petitions related to the Sabarimala dispute (including one concerning the 'publishing or transmitting [of] obscene material in electronic form'), was to demonstrate just how contentious and how unsettled the question of women's entry remained despite the existence of an ostensibly definitive and now several-months-old Supreme Court ruling.²⁹

Indeed, not even the *IYLA* petitioners were immune from the divisiveness and constant fluctuations that had already come to define the Sabarimala dispute by late 2019. The writ petition that started it all had been jointly filed by Bhakti Pasrija, acting both individually and in her capacity as the General Secretary of the Indian Young Lawyers Association, alongside Prerna Kumari, Sudha Pal, Laxmi Shastri, and Alka Sharma. On 3 January 2019, the *Huffington Post*'s India edition ran an article headlined: 'Only One of the 5 Women Petitioners Has Stood Her Ground.'³⁰ The article noted that while Sharma had never been very involved in the proceedings, Pal, Shastri, and especially Kumari had entertained doubts at various points along the path to a Supreme Court decision. In fact, Kumari had done much more: in 2018, after the hearings were concluded, she asked the Supreme Court to remove her name from the petitioner's list. In the weeks after the opinion was issued, Kumari wrote an opinion piece for the long-standing (albeit unofficial) mouthpiece of organized Hindu nationalism's *pater familias*, the Rashtriya Swayamsevak Sangh.³¹ She repeatedly supported the reasoning in Justice Indu Malhotra's dissenting opinion and announced her regret for having inserted herself into what was clearly a matter of Keralite culture and no type of discrimination after all.

Bhakti Pasrija, for her part, has remained steadfast in her opinions. When we met in Delhi in 2011, she acknowledged that the petition was largely her idea, but she insisted that all of the co-petitioners had been very enthusiastic at the time of filing.³² Certainly, the writ petition they produced did not lack for conviction: in addition to standard and legally potent terms like 'discrimination', 'freedom', and 'equality', the petition also readily deployed language like 'disgraceful', 'male chauvinism', and 'anti-Hindu' (the last of these with a frequency that is more common to Hindu nationalist prose). I spoke to her again in 2020, over the phone, by which point she had become Bhakti Pasrija Sethi and a seasoned attorney. Although it was now many years since she had effectively been transformed into the sole *IYLA* petitioner, as well as a couple of years in which she had officially been the sole respondent in the review litigation, she continued to be sure of the process she had initiated fourteen years earlier.³³ Sabarimala's admissions policies were demeaning to women, she argued, and for that matter, they were demeaning to Ayyappan too. She was hopeful that the review hearings would produce an outcome that was comparable to *IYLA* in its progressive flavour—something inspirational, something enlightening—and that I would write a book to match.

Bhakti's constancy in the face of time and considerable tumult is not exactly unusual in the context of the dispute over Sabarimala. She and a few others litigants—many of whom, like the chief priest and the Pandalam royals, are actually opposed to women's entry—have now maintained their positions, as well as the reasoning behind their positions, for over fifteen years. At the same time, and especially in the political realm, that kind of constancy has not been universal. Positions have been in considerable flux because the Sabarimala dispute set Keralite politicians against their colleagues at the national party level, set politicians from the CPI(M) against politicians belonging to the fabled and enfeebled Indian National Congress, and, additionally, because the dispute managed to draw the attention of a powerful, all-India, Hindu nationalist apparatus to a part of India that it had hitherto largely ignored. The Sabarimala dispute *did* all this, moreover, over some ten years of litigation and then again in the nine months before an anxiously anticipated national election. Some perspectival shifts were inevitable and some confusion understandable—but more than a little of both proved, ultimately, to be on offer.

2.2 A Gandhi in Wayanad

The Congress Party of today is a far cry from the eclectic movement that emerged in 1885, from the independence campaign that coalesced in the early twentieth century, and even from the political party that dominated India's first decades of nationhood. It is no longer powerful, having won less than 10% of all Lok Sabha seats in each of the last two general elections. It is no longer dynamic, having long since been transformed into an occupational scheme for generations of the Nehru-Gandhi family. And, now lacking both the obsessively idealistic developmentalism of Jawaharlal as well as the autocratic demagoguery of Indira, the Congress Party no longer has much in the way of an animating impulse. Indeed, for all of the twenty-first century and a good bit of the decades preceding it, the sole defining feature of the Congress has been that it is *not* something else. The occasional awkwardness this produces was on full display during the height of the Sabarimala protests.

At the national level, the Congress-led United Progressive Alliance remains, and one must be careful when bandying about such deceptively neat characterizations, the centre-left choice for Indians who are anxious to direct their votes away from the BJP. Accordingly, when the protests against *IYLA* reached across the news media and into Parliament itself, Sonia Gandhi (then Chair of the UPA) and Rahul Gandhi (then Congress President) both expressed their support for the ruling. 'Men and women are equal', declared Rahul, 'women should be allowed to go anywhere they want'.[34] However, neither of the Gandhis actively involved themselves in the chaos enveloping both Kerala and the Supreme Court, and inaction, when combined with the kind of cautiously and blandly progressive statement issued by Rahul, is more or less what one has come to expect of the Congress.

At the Kerala state level, however, the Congress-led United Democratic Front is a centre-right coalition. It pulls together Muslims, Christians, and a generous sprinkling of upper caste Hindus into what would be an unlikely alliance outside God's Own Country but that has proven to be surprisingly enduring within it. Indeed, the stability of Keralite political coalitions and constituencies is, like so much else about the state, an exception to the Indian norm: just as Congress and UDF supporters have remained relatively stable over the sixty-odd years of Kerala's existence, united by their disdain for a communist politics that is variously perceived as too anti-faith or anti-privilege, so too have the individuals—largely lower caste and *avarna* Hindus—who support the opposing CPI(M) coalition. It was, therefore, of no particular surprise to anyone more concerned with the reality of Kerala than with its popular image when members of the Kerala Pradesh Congress Committee (KPCC) came out immediately against the *IYLA* decision. Within days of the opinion's release, KPCC chief Ramesh Chennithala was encouraging the Travancore Devaswom Board to file an appeal, and within weeks he was leading a group of UDF representatives up the literal mountainside in order to demand a reinstatement of Sabarimala's old entry policies.[35]

Caught between the vehement critique of the state party and the tepid support of the national party stood a few Congress parliamentarians of

Keralite origin—although several of them did not, in fact, seem to view themselves as caught. Shortly after Bindu Ammini and Kanakadurga completed their visit, a handful of Kerala's seven MPs were seen distributing black armbands within the Lok Sabha as a protest against the women's infiltration. The MPs were quickly stopped and shooed away by Sonia Gandhi, who indicated that protests on the Sabarimala issue were well and good within the geographic boundaries of Kerala 'as part of their local politics', but that 'at the national level, the MPs should not protest against women entering the temple, because it would go against what the Congress stands for—gender equality and women rights'.[36] Gandhi's ideological NIMBYism is by no means accidental or incidental to the Congress Party's national self-presentation.[37] On the contrary, as one observer noted, her suggestion was in keeping with a broader Congress strategy born of 'confusion over how to counter the Bharatiya Janata Party's Hindutva'.[38] In their efforts to remain the party of Nehru and yet also a party of relevance, national Congress leaders have authorized 'state units to define their own positions on secularism, Hinduism, nationalism, gender justice, human rights and other great ideas Indians are forever conflicted about'.[39]

The Congress Party's internal tangle over Sabarimala, visible enough when it was spread across dozens of individuals, became impossible to ignore when it manifested in the person of a single individual *not* surnamed Gandhi. Shashi Tharoor, Member of Parliament for Trivandrum since 2009, is one of Kerala's favourite children. His style and his politics properly belong to a political generation whose heyday was largely over before he himself was born in 1956; like many of the Congress leaders who died off as he grew up—and, indeed, like many members of other existing or emerging parties of that time—Tharoor is urbane, literary, intellectually inclined, fashionable without being fashion focused, and carries more than a whiff of celebrity about him. He earned a doctorate at Tufts University before he was 25, has authored around twenty books (including several novels), and for several years served as an Under-Secretary General of the United Nations. His three marriages have been to exceedingly accomplished and cosmopolitan women, the last of whom died under tabloid-worthy circumstances in their five-star Delhi hotel room. His twin sons are successful, globe-trotting journalists, and authors who are themselves married to accomplished and cosmopolitan women.

None of this explains the content of Tharoor's response to the Sabarimala dispute or the consternation it caused in some quarters; the contrast between two of his most famous books are more suited to that purpose. In 1989, Tharoor published an irreverent and pun-riddled roman à clef, *The Great Indian Novel*, that superimposed the epic and literally 'great India[n]' story of the *Mahabharata* onto the events of the Indian independence movement and the early republic. It was the kind of book that made you giggle (*Kashmir* becomes *cash-mir* becomes *Manimir*, or *money-mir*) and that left you preening because of the historical and mythological allusions you were smart enough to grasp as well as the cultural bricolage you were sophisticated enough to enjoy. As a teenager suffering from severe cultural nostalgia and an overly abundant home library, I loved it.

Tharoor's (2018) book, on the other hand, was an earnest and deeply personal work of nonfiction whose title, *Why I Am a Hindu*, riffed off earlier works by the political theorist and anti-caste activist Kancha Ilaiah (*Why I Am Not a Hindu*), the philosopher Bertrand Russell (*Why I Am Not a Christian*) and, perhaps, the Indian revolutionary Bhagat Singh (*Why I Am an Atheist*).[40] Tharoor presented his book as an effort to 'resist the hijacking of Hinduism by Hindu nationalists',[41] and it received several positive reviews in India's English news media for being 'a timely reminder' of Hindu pluralism and an exemplar of Tharoor's 'vintage scholarly, conversational, and lyrical prose'.[42] The book also received sustained criticism from Kancha Ilaiah himself, who poked at 'Swami Shashi' for quoting the *Rig Veda* profusely while acting as if that text did not propound a system of spiritual, social, and economic stratification according to which both of them fared poorly—'as if', Ilaiah observed, 'he has no caste roots'.[43] For most reviewers, however, Tharoor's portrayal of Hinduism as having no doctrinal absolutism proved both intuitive and irresistible.

The witty, satirical Tharoor who played with Hindu tradition in *The Great Indian Novel* and the earnest, idealistic Tharoor who stumped for it in *Why I Am a Hindu* clashed mightily with the Tharoor who declared, in November 2018, that the 'Sabarimala issue leaves instinctive liberals like me torn.'[44] In an opinion piece published by *The Print*, one of India's most prominent online newspapers, Tharoor blamed the CPI(M) for being melodramatic, the BJP for being opportunistic, and the Supreme Court for failing to realize that 'abstract notions of constitutional principle also have to pass the test of societal acceptance'.⁴⁵ Without precisely stating that the Supreme Court was wrong to rule as it did, he *implied* that the Supreme Court was wrong to rule as it did. 'In religious matters', declared Tharoor, 'beliefs must prevail; in a pluralistic democracy, legal principles and cultural autonomy must both be respected'. He went on to add that the Court 'has a chance to consider all these issues'—as if it had not already done so—'when it hears the review petitions'.

Keralite voters responded to Tharoor's message and to Congress messaging by handing both remarkable successes in the 2019 Indian general elections. Whereas five years earlier Tharoor had only kept his seat by the relatively slim margin of 15,000 votes, he did so in 2019 by over six times as much.⁴⁶ The Congress Party, meanwhile, and although this constitutes no great achievement, did better in Kerala than it managed to perform anywhere else in the country. In the seventeenth Lok Sabha produced by the 2019 elections, fifteen of the Congress' fifty-two MPs came from tiny Kerala, compared to eight each from Punjab and Tamil Nadu and twenty-one from across fifteen states and union territories.⁴⁷ Congress also did better *within* Kerala than any other party: along with its UPA partners, it swept nineteen of Kerala's twenty parliamentary constituencies.⁴⁸ Rahul Gandhi, who left his presidency of the Indian National Congress in atonement for the party's overall dismal performance during this election, was only saved from having to leave Parliament itself by a Kerala constituency—Wayanad, in the far north—that he contested in addition to the established Nehru-Gandhi seat of Amethi, in Uttar Pradesh, which he lost.

Neither the CPI(M) nor the BJP could say that *IYLA* had similarly improved their fortunes, although perhaps they would not be too disappointed by this turn of events. True, the lone Keralite MP belonging to the CPI(M) represents the lone Kerala constituency *not* filled by a member of the UPA coalition, and that individual is one of just three almost equally lonely CPI(M) parliamentarians across all of India.⁴⁹ Nevertheless, the CPI(M) and its partners fared well enough in by-elections conducted just a few months later for Kerala's legislative assembly, the Niyamasabha, that the Chief Minister thanked his social media followers for showing that 'Kerala has once again rejected the politics of hate and reiterated its commitment to progressive politics'.⁵⁰ And for its part, the BJP, although it was unsuccessful at winning both state and national seats in Kerala during the 2019 elections, won the much larger prize of a second and stronger mandate at the central level. It won 303 of 542 available Lok Sabha seats on its own and controls another 50 through its alliance partners, making Kerala's lost twenty more of mild irritation than a cause for concern.

In truth, both Pinarayi Vijayan and Narendra Modi had reason to be annoyed by *IYLA* and its aftermath, at least as much as they had cause to be heartened by one or the other. Both leaders faced legislators who were determined to add statutory twists to the social upheaval and judicial confusion already created by the women's entry dispute. In the Niyamasabha, a first-time Congress MLA named M. Vincent tried to introduce a private member's bill contravening the Supreme Court ruling and declaring that Ayyappan devotees were a distinct religious community empowered to manage their own affairs in matters of religion.[51] The bill never made it past the assembly's secretariat, which by late November had informed the Speaker that it would be unconstitutional. In the Lok Sabha, a similar effort was put forward by N. K. Premachandran, whose party—the Revolutionary Socialists—has the doubtful pleasure of being allied with the Congress in Kerala and with the CPI(M) in West Bengal and Tripura.

Premachandran's bill, the *Sabarimala Sree Dharma Sastha Temple (Special Provision) Bill (2019)*, was the very first to be introduced in that parliamentary session. In a demonstration of the frequently topsy-turvy nature of responses to the Sabarimala dispute (and perhaps also of the perverse nature of divine humour), the bill won approval from the member of Pinarayi Vijayan's own cabinet who was responsible for temple affairs as well as criticism from a BJP Member of Parliament. Premachandran, however, remained unmoved by both support and critique and was similarly nonchalant while fielding subsequent accusations of publicity-seeking, of campaign misbehaviour (on the grounds that he appealed to voters' religious sentiments), and when faced with assertions that Parliament could not undo what the Court had done, especially while the Court itself stood poised to undo it.[52] That final concern—namely, that the Indian Supreme Court retains an unassailable authority over matters of constitutional importance—reflects a long-standing, if rapidly crumbling, deference to the country's apex judicial body that is, itself, a character in the dispute over Sabarimala.

2.3 A Diminishingly Supreme Court

The Supreme Court that decided *IYLA* had long been accustomed to thinking of itself as a powerful, progressive institution—and with good cause. (This is one of those rare instances where the lawyer's habit of referring to courts as if they are anthropomorphic entities with opinions that carry across time and space is, in fact, moderately justified.) Many of the Court's landmark moments support the justices' belief, once widely shared by India's legal intelligentsia, that the Supreme Court represents both a first point of appeal and a last line of defence against the inadequacies of political actors.

For instance, in the early 1970s, the Supreme Court held that Parliament did not enjoy an unrestricted ability to amend the Constitution over which the Court stood guard. Instead, as the multi-volume 1973 decision *Kesavananda Bharati v. State of Kerala* announced, there was a 'basic structure' to the nation's charter that could not be changed or destroyed via parliamentary amendment.[53] Whether or not an amendment met this standard was, of course, a matter for the Court to determine, and the exact contours of the Constitution's basic structure remain necessarily but also conveniently undefined. Even the thirteen justices behind the majority decision in *Kesavananda* could not agree on the component parts of basic structure—two of them included 'secularism', for instance, while three of them identified or alluded to a 'welfare state', and they all agreed on 'democratic governance'.

Also in the late 1970s, the Court decided that although Parliament was bound by the Court, the Court was not bound by well-established principles of the Common Law. Instead, and in the fulfilment of its mission to be 'an arm of the social revolution, upholding the equality that Indians had longed for during colonial days', the Indian Court was obliged to reach farther out and further down into the lives of struggling citizens than do most of its peers around the world.[54] India's upper judiciary was, in truth, *already* remarkably accessible: all twenty-five high courts and Supreme Court alike can directly receive petitions that allege fundamental rights violations rather than waiting to hear those cases on appeal.[55] Still, the Supreme Court wanted to do more. It developed a litigation technique that would allow some Indians to approach the courts on behalf of other Indians who were too poor, too uneducated, too ill, or too oppressed to speak on behalf of themselves. The same technique, the Indian Court figured, could also be used to protect a generic 'public interest' that, like the English commons to which it was conceptually related, would otherwise suffer tragedy because it was everyone's (and therefore no one's) business.

We will meet this litigation technique again in Chapter 3, where it plays a central role in the *IYLA* decision, but its significance for the Court's own institutional history and identity merits some immediate consideration. Public interest litigation has allowed an institution that had formerly been a bastion of aloof and elite conservatism to transform itself, rapidly and determinedly, into a stronghold of engaged, if still elite, populism. In the early days of PIL, Court watchers exuberantly declared that the country's apex judicial body was 'at long last becoming, after thirty two years of the Republic, the Supreme Court for Indians'.[56] The judges who developed this technique were hailed as individuals whose '[j]udicial creativity ... has enabled realisation of the promise of socio-economic justice made in the Preamble to the Constitution of India'[57]; as clairvoyants '[who] recognised the possibility of providing access to justice to the poor and the exploited people'[58]; and as original thinkers who gave rise to a 'distinctly Indian' legal phenomenon.[59] At home and abroad, the Indian Court began to enjoy a reputation for progressive, creative jurisprudence that has few analogues around the world and that is almost compulsively compared to the inadequacies of successive Indian parliaments.

Around 2010, the Court intensified its usage of a second litigation technique, one that frees jurists from being overly reliant on the existence of actual litigation in much the same way that the first technique, public interest litigation, freed individuals from being too circumscribed by the demands of legal standing.[60] *Suo motu* intervention (intervention 'on its own motion') exists outside India too, though elsewhere it largely occurs when courts seek to fix the effects of accident or of procedural carelessness in ongoing disputes.[61] Even then, it is usually viewed with some suspicion and as a genre of action that is unbecomingly forward for a branch of government that is usually and appropriately passive.

Within India, however, this kind of intervention has an altogether different flavour and purpose. When Indian courts act *suo motu*, they do not merely tweak procedural rules to see justice done in existing litigation: they *create* litigation (or, more precisely, adjudication) whole cloth by taking cognizance of an issue that no petitioner has brought before them. Like public interest litigation, *suo motu* intervention grew out of an impatient do-goodism:—a desire to make justice better, faster, easier, *now*. Small wonder, then, that one of the Indian judiciary's most insightful observers has, with a thorough absence of sarcasm, called *suo motu* intervention a kind of 'Cinderella law': 'the Court as good fairy appears, unbidden, to turn the tables on behalf of an obscure and resourceless victim'.[62]

Good fairy, powerful fairy, is the Court's preferred stance. An acceleration in *suo motu* interventions that started around 2010 was followed, a few years later, by yet another trend—this time in the mode of jurisprudence rather than litigation strategy—that promised to further burnish the Court's power and progressive credentials. In 2013, opinions issued by the Supreme Court began to conspicuously juxtapose the judicially crafted phrase *constitutional morality* with a second phrase, *public morality*, that actually appears in the text of the Constitution and that the Court has tended to equate with a majoritarian politics.[63] Like so much else in India's legal universe, *constitutional morality* begins with a bit of England and a hefty dose of Ambedkar. But unlike Ambedkar, for whom the term signalled 'an allegiance to a constitutional form,' the twenty-first-century Indian Court has generally treated constitutional morality as requiring 'allegiance to a particular [judicially-defined] substance'.[64] Constitutional morality is, in other words, the 'morality *of* a constitution'—and, not coincidentally, it tends to surface in cases that promote the kind of reformist jurisprudence for which the Court has become famous. There was *Joseph Shine*, which struck down the adultery provision of the Indian Penal Code; there was *Shayara Bano*, which outlawed an 'instantaneous' form of Muslim divorce commonly called 'triple talaq';[65] and, of course, there was *IYLA*.

But the Court that decided *IYLA*—and that, later on, reviewed it—was no longer the same court that had triumphantly announced the existence of a basic structure and a constitutional morality, or even simply the court that had expanded and accelerated access to justice for millions of Indian citizens. It was also, and much more recently, a court that had indignantly vetoed even the smallest infringements on its autonomy, as well as a court that had been damaged, over the last twenty years, by scandals or fraught circumstances that have been largely of the justices' own making.⁶⁶ The trajectory that produced this newer, less shiny iteration of the Supreme Court is part of the dispute over Sabarimala, every bit as much as the litigants and customs and Keralite politics that are more commonly associated with it—and any understanding of that trajectory starts with an acknowledgement that the Indian Supreme Court is an unusually powerful institution.

This is partly by design. The Constitution endows citizens with several important and complicated fundamental rights, and then charges the judiciary with protecting those rights against any infringement by state law. Via Article 124, the Constitution also explicitly grants the Chief Justice of India a role in the appointment of his (and thus far, as well as for the near future, it is indeed *his*) colleagues on the apex court, as well as in the appointment of his subordinates on the high courts, too.⁶⁷ The Indian Supreme Court, in other words, was always meant to be heeded by the other branches of government because India was always meant to exemplify constitutional rather than parliamentary sovereignty.

But the Indian Supreme Court's immense authority and autonomy also derive from its own concerted efforts over a span of several decades. This is exemplified by nothing so well as the battle between the Court and the central government over the matter of judicial appointments, most notably appointments to the Supreme Court itself. Through a series of opinions during the 1980s and 1990s, the Court developed a 'collegium system' for managing appointments to itself and to the high courts that largely prioritized the opinions of current Supreme Court justices over those of other potential decision-makers, and that prioritized the Chief Justice's perspective over them all. The collegium system, which provides no mechanism for investigating candidate backgrounds and has the dubious felicity of eliciting consensus among 'academics, lawyers, political commentators and a large section of the judiciary', who all believe it to be broken, would have been changed by the 99th Amendment to the Constitution that was passed by Parliament in 2014.⁶⁸ But the Court, in 2015, determined that the 99th Amendment undermined judicial autonomy and therefore also undermined the basic structure of the Constitution that it had, itself, identified back in 1973. And, it should be noted, the Court did this despite the fact that the amendment proposed a multi-stakeholder process that was similar to the systems obtaining in some global south countries also influenced by the Common Law (like South Africa) and that was markedly less political than the systems obtaining in other countries that are influential comparators (like Canada and the United States). No matter, said the Indian Supreme Court: anything that took away from the collegium's authority was anathema to the courts and therefore to Indian democracy itself.

Unfortunately, the parties most responsible for undermining the collegium and the Court have, more often than not, been the justices themselves—and none more so than the Chief. The Chief Justice of India is the powerful head of a powerful institution. As 'master of the roster', he can both ignore the Court's own customary practices regarding case assignments *and* override the automated system for randomly distributing cases, all in order to assign specific matters to specific justices. The same power also means that the Chief Justice can accelerate or delay the hearing of a politically sensitive matter, and that he can punish colleagues who do not conform to his preferences by handing them bad case assignments or by withholding good ones. Meanwhile, through his status as the head of the collegium, the Chief exercises more influence over appointments to the entire upper judiciary than any other person in India. Adages about the corrupting effects of absolute power are not quite in order here, but there is, as we will shortly see, precious little to be done when a Chief Justice of India behaves badly, and there is even less to be done when he attempts repair.

Despite this enormous influence, or perhaps fortunately in light of it, Indian chief justices are radically evanescent beings: thanks to a mandatory retirement age of sixty-five and a career path that conventionally winds its way through years of law practice and service on multiple high courts before reaching its judicial zenith, a majority of chiefs spend scant months in the most important legal appointment of their lives. U. U. Lalit, who served as Chief for some seventy-four days in 2022, is a bit on the low end, but D. Y. Chandrachud, who should do so for almost two years, is somewhat unusually high. At the same time, chief-designates *know* that they are designates with a certainty even greater than that of an American legal luminary whose preferred political candidate has successfully clinched the presidency. A Chief Justice of India is what he is by virtue of the date of his elevation to the apex court and, in the event of a tie, by virtue of several subsidiary factors, including the exact hour of his swearing-in.[69] Barring death, voluntary retirement, or (least likely of all) involuntary removal, an appointee to the Supreme Court knows, from the moment his oath is administered, if, when, and for how long he will be chief. In the summer of 2020, India's legal mediascape began buzzing with excitement at the possibility that the country could—in far off 2027—have its first female chief justice if B. V. Nagarathna, then sitting on the Karnataka High Court, were to be elevated to the apex court within the next six months.[70]

Immediately after *IYLA* was handed down in September 2018, Ranjan Gogoi came to occupy the Chief's role. Thanks to those aforementioned elevation and retirement rules, Gogoi would have known—ever since his appointment to the Court in April 2012, and with a confidence that few of us enjoy regarding our professional lives—that this day was coming. Equally, he would have known the date on which his tenure would end: 17 November 2019. In between the two lay the period of his Chief Justiceship, 411 days in total, during which he could, as Master of the Roster and first among (questionable) equals, establish his legacy. Gogoi inherited from his predecessor a Court that was at once flush with accolades for effectuating progressive social reform and dizzied by accusations of disrespect and paternalistic interference, all stemming from the same, now merely five-day-old, opinion. He also inherited some fifty review petitions asking, quite bluntly, that the Court change its mind with respect to Sabarimala. After spending the first few months of his term encountering angry *namajapam*s, blockades, and scathing editorials, Gogoi spent the next few months managing a professional crisis that was as momentous as it was of his own making, and that made his ultimate response to the women's entry dispute painfully unsurprising.

On 19 April 2019, a former staff clerk of the Supreme Court filed a complaint of sexual harassment against Gogoi and forwarded the complaint to the home addresses of twenty-two sitting Supreme Court justices.[71] From then onwards, until nearly mid-May, and despite the fact that a highly contentious national election was being conducted at that same time, India's legal elite remained transfixed by the 'CJI Scandal'.[72] First came the revelation that, in the absence of any independent oversight, Gogoi had hand-picked *and joined* the very jurists assigned to hear the complaint against him during a special and hastily arranged Saturday session of the Court. Next came news that his name had been mysteriously redacted from the record of those proceedings, as if he had not, per the indignant media chorus, sat as 'a judge in his own cause'. A series of closed-door hearings followed, with the complainant making increasingly desperate requests to be accompanied by, first, an attorney and, later on, by any support person at all, only to be repeatedly rebuffed by the country's highest echelons of justice.

When the complainant finally disassociated herself from the hearings, the Court continued on without her. When the Secretary General of the Supreme Court issued a three-sentence public announcement reporting that an in-house committee had absolved Gogoi of any wrongdoing, Delhi (and several other cities) erupted in protests. At one of these protests, held on 7 May 2019 in front of the Supreme Court building, the Court-side of the street featured water cannon, Delhi police personnel, and RAF (Rapid Action Force) facing a few dozen overwhelmingly female protestors who were still milling around and chatting when I arrived to watch. I learned later on from conversations and media reports that over four dozen protestors, including several relatively senior women, had been detained that morning.[73]

The commotion of the CJI Scandal ensured that, by November of that year, Ranjan Gogoi would have been in search of a redeeming—or at least, a distracting—finale. The *IYLA* review petitioners, for their part, were in need of some closure. It had been over thirteen months since Sabarimala's admissions policies had been declared unconstitutional, over six months since the CJI Scandal occupied Indian headlines, and a little less than that since the national election had concluded. Following a practice that is rapidly becoming traditional for departing chief justices, Gogoi arranged to have himself preside over and release a handful of politically and legally significant decisions in the days immediately before his retirement. He wrapped up a decades-long dispute over the erstwhile Babri Masjid in Ayodhya, dismissed a petition alleging corrupt dealing by the Modi government, and granted review in the battle over women's entry.

Review petitions are a peculiar phenomenon; whenever I try to explain them to lawyers unfamiliar with the Indian legal system (and sometimes even to lawyers familiar with it) I am met with amusement, incredulousness, or simple confusion. Unlike an appeals process, which has the potential to change outcomes previously won through litigation in lower courts, review petitions in India set out to *undo* outcomes. They are, in other words, more annulment than divorce, and consequently they unsettle one of the assumptions that is foundational to most hierarchical legal systems: that, roughly speaking and regardless of the specific nomenclature, a supreme court is supreme because its decisions are final, and that a decision is final when it is made by a supreme court. Because review petitions disturb this background principle and because that disturbance is unnerving for law and litigant alike, the grounds for permitting a review petition to go forward are extraordinarily narrow.

Chief Justice Gogoi (now Member of Parliament Gogoi, thanks to a presidential nomination) did not much trouble himself over any of this. Perhaps looking backwards at the CJI Scandal and the 2019 Kerala protests, and looking forward to his post-retirement life—at any rate, *not* looking at the law—Gogoi decided to keep the review petitions pending; his majority opinion on the issue, *Kantaru Rajeevaru v. Indian Young Lawyers Association*, appeared three days before he left the judiciary. The logic of that decision, as well as its subsequent journey, are things to which we will return in due course.

But if Ranjan Gogoi's choice to prolong the women's entry dispute emerged in the aftermath of contentious protests and a tumultuous tenure in the chief's seat, the judicial circumstances leading up to the decision at the heart of it all, *IYLA*, were no less dramatic or troubling. Some of those circumstances—protests, marches, and social media campaigns not entirely unlike the unrest that greeted *IYLA*'s release—are discussed towards the end of this book. One of them, however, has little to do with the lay individuals mobilizing for or against the ban on women, and everything to do with the jurists, one more than others, who determined that the ban was unconstitutional.

Dipak Misra, the forty-fifth Chief Justice of India, presided over the Supreme Court bench that issued *IYLA* in September 2018. At least until his successor came along, Misra's tenure seemed to establish new and unbeatable lows for the Chief's office. During the 'Judge Loya investigation', Misra ensured that a politically sensitive public interest case would be heard by a junior and therefore presumably impressionable colleague. This was no ordinarily contentious lawsuit: it concerned the death of a special tribunal judge who, at the time of his passing, was hearing a murder-in-custody case in which a primary defendant was Amit Shah, then-President of the BJP. Similarly, during the 'medical admission scam', Misra seemingly arranged for a medical college that had been temporarily de-accredited to approach and possibly bribe a sympathetic high court judge, before subsequently hampering India's premier investigating agency in its efforts to catch the judge participating in a bribery scheme. When a civil society watchdog inquired into the matter, Misra saw to it that the organization was fined 'exemplary costs', a kind of punitive measure, of ₹25 lakhs (₹2,500,000). There were other scandals too, including a property scam dating back to the 1980s, but ultimately, despite the plethora of suspicious circumstances surrounding him, it was the way Misra exercised his powers as Master of the Roster that inspired the most critique.[74]

On 12 January 2018, four senior justices—the members of Misra's 'collegium'—took the unprecedented step of speaking directly to the public about the Court's internal affairs. It is hard to overstate just how astonishing this was within the insular and rigorously tight-lipped world of India's legal elite. 'This is an extraordinary event in the history of the nation,' admitted Justice Jasti Chelameswar, one of the four jurists who spoke up. 'It is with no pleasure that we are compelled to call this press conference. But the administration of the Supreme Court is not in order and many things which are less than desirable have happened in the last few months.'[75] Four months after the justices' press conference, Misra inspired another first: in April 2018, opposition parties submitted a notice to the Vice President and chair of the Rajya Sabha that they would be initiating impeachment proceedings against the Chief Justice. Over seventy parliamentarians signed on to the motion, which was far more than the fifty required to begin proceedings. And, although the Vice President ultimately dismissed the motion, speculation began to grow that Misra's management of the Court reflected some kind of obligation to the central government.

None of this, by itself, explains the content of the *IYLA* decision, which was in keeping with Misra's own fairly progressive track record, including the decriminalization of both adultery and sodomy, and was also consonant with recent trends in Indian jurisprudence towards highly individualized notions of autonomy and equality. It does not even wholly account for the timing of *IYLA*'s release during the last week of Misra's tenure; that tradition was foreshadowed by the forty-third Chief Justice (T. S. Thakur) and observed by the forty-fourth (J. S. Khehar) so that by the time Misra stood ready to vacate the Chief's office it was expected that he would issue a few prominent decisions as a final act.[76] Although it is inadvisable to wholly exclude institutional actors from individual stories, as many accounts of the Sabarimala dispute have tended to do, it is no more helpful to suggest that what happens in a specific instance like the *IYLA* litigation is entirely determined by orthogonal events at an entity like the Supreme Court. Causality, as both ethnographers and torts professors will attest, is always difficult to pin down.

And yet, it is not possible to understand this phase of the women's entry dispute without acknowledging the particular histories of the institution and the individuals behind it. The review petitions were not advanced for further consideration by just anyone; they were advanced by a Chief Justice besieged by protests, fresh from a sexual harassment scandal, and retiring under the aegis of a decidedly anti-access national government that was still celebrating the electoral trouncing of its political rivals. The opinion that prompted those review petitions had not, for its part, been decided by just anyone: it was presided over by a Chief Justice almost equally known for his rights-enabling jurisprudence as for his troubling attitude towards institutional norms and legal form. The technical contours of the *IYLA* opinion, to which we now turn, reflect these layered and complicated histories as well as a decades-long process of refining and recalibrating conflicting impulses in the Indian Constitution.

3
The Case

Anthropologists not being used to working on the cusp of the news cycle, the commotion that followed *IYLA*'s release caught me by surprise. It should not have. In retrospect, the circumstances and particulars of the women's entry dispute were combustible in the extreme. The Supreme Court's declining stature, the onset of an election year, the satisfying if questionable characterization of the dispute as a clash between (Western) feminism and (subcontinental) tradition—all of this, by itself, ensured that *any* outcome from the litigation would have generated heat. Unfortunately, however, the outcome that emerged was not all that promised to provoke. Instead, the opinion at the heart of it all, the one that either liberated or desecrated depending on one's perspective, was also *constructed* in such a way as to ensure a good deal of dissatisfaction.

This was not quite because of the prose, although it could have been. Many of the Court's splashier judgements are lexically obese; some, like the landmark *Kesavananda Bharati*, have unleashed the better part of a thousand written pages upon the world. A good deal of this length is owed to the generous inclusion of still more generously proportioned quotations, blocks of texts that are mostly cribbed from earlier opinions and are frequently so voluminous that even the most carefully trained reader is apt to emerge, foggy and disoriented, at their conclusion. What prose does not emanate from elsewhere regularly violates basic principles of authorial decency: a 2016 opinion by Dipak Misra, for instance, featured a second sentence consisting of 228 words, 17 *and*s, and 6 commas.[1] *IYLA* itself is no great pleasure to read. Its pages are littered with awkward phrasings and gently indented columns of quotations, and early on in many of its constituent parts, opinions beget opinions with a determination no less dogged or anesthetizing than the biblical patriarchs. But if *IYLA* contains rather more multi-page excerpts than was necessary or lengthier sentences than is seemly, these qualities actually place it squarely within the mainstream of contemporary Indian constitutional jurisprudence.

Nor are *IYLA*'s shortcomings owing to the actual outcomes sought by any of its five authors. Chief Justice Misra, along with Justices Khanwilkar, Nariman, and Chandrachud, all of whom held that Sabarimala must allow women aged ten to fifty onto its premises, possessed ample grounds for concluding as they did. So too did Justice Malhotra, who dissented. The Indian Constitution being what it is, with its dual, simultaneous, yet mutually exclusive understandings of democratic sovereignty and citizen-state relations, the Court would have been well within its rights to conclude either that Sabarimala's admissions policies lay beyond its reach or, conversely, that they were comfortably within it. Neither outcome was inevitable, neither was impossible.

The problem with *IYLA*, as the rest of this chapter shows, is that despite its nearly 200 pages, its prodigious references, and the entirely reasonable conclusion arrived at by a majority of its bench (as well as the equally reasonable view espoused by its lone dissenter), the opinion's reasoning simplified that which is exceedingly complex. Indeed, it did so thrice over: with respect to a constitutional principle, a judicial rule, and a set of social practices. And, although it may seem counterintuitive to say so, the cost of this simplification is not to be measured in protests and petitions; absent a serious excursion into counterfactual conditions, we must assume that such responses were likely always forthcoming. Instead, the true cost of *IYLA*'s shortcomings is broader and deeper than any main street march, even if it is also less spectacular, because it amounts to nothing less than the accelerated erosion of a balance that has been carefully created and is only very tenuously maintained. It takes care and great courage, neither of which were noticeably on display in this instance, to maintain the twin visions of sovereignty set forth in India's Constitution.

3.1 Anatomy of a Case

When the Indian Supreme Court hears cases, it mostly does so in benches of two or three justices. Since benches of equal size cannot overrule one another, and since the Court's currently sanctioned strength—over thirty members—makes it comparable to a respectably sized chamber orchestra, this means that the interpretations of law emanating from the vicinity of Tilak Marg are often polyvocal and are occasionally cacophonous.[2] Harmony, when it appears, is most often generated by internal observances of deference to one's senior judges, to the actual or supposed inclinations of the Court's powerful Chief Justice, and even, occasionally, to precedent. Less frequently, harmony is imposed by means of a 'constitution bench' of five or more justices whose analysis of an issue is binding on all benches of smaller size.

Before it began receiving serious consideration by a three-judge bench headed by Dipak Misra, the *IYLA* petition spent around ten years in pleading purgatory. Nearly a decade of pleadings, though it may seem unacceptable to outsiders and be unacceptable to litigants, is neither very unusual nor very unreasonable given the immense workload of the Indian higher judiciary. India's most powerful jurists simply appear in court more often than many of their counterparts worldwide (around five times as often as their American peers in particular), and their caseload almost doubled in the first ten years of the twenty-first century.[3] Moreover, the back and forth process of requests, explanations, briefs, and reschedulings that American lawyers tend to dismiss as 'motion practice' is both a feature and a bug of the Indian judicial system. Lawyers use the pleading process to delay or redirect their cases based on the anticipated sympathies of the judge to whom they are initially assigned. Judges and justices, for their part, use pleadings to delay or decipher cases, or to engage in the kind of judicial experimentation that has earned India's apex court its glowing international reputation. Indeed, the Court's most high-profile innovation not only emerged from the theoretically interminable pleading process but seemingly *capitalized* on it by encouraging judges to conduct ongoing reviews of the litigants' behaviour with an eye towards protecting the public interest.

At the beginning of 2016, the *IYLA* petition finally emerged from pleadings into substantive if sporadic hearings. Nearly two years later, at the end of 2017, Misra's three-judge bench asked that the case be referred to a larger bench and provided a set of questions for that bench to consider. The request was both instructive and deceptive—the one because it signalled the smaller bench's estimation of the dispute's importance and, perhaps, the need to overturn Supreme Court precedent in the course of resolving it, the other because the three-judge bench was effectively making the request to itself. By virtue of his status as Chief Justice, which he had assumed in August 2017, Misra was the most senior member of the three-judge bench, and therefore, in keeping with the conventions of the Court, his benchmates were extremely likely to defer to his wishes. That same status as Chief Justice granted him the power over the Court's roster and, thus, the ability to convene constitution benches as well as determine their composition. Accordingly, in January 2018, Misra appointed himself to a bench alongside four other justices, only two of whom would ultimately be part of the Sabarimala decision and none of whom had participated in the extraordinary press conference critiquing his leadership just three days earlier.[4]

Besides the original petitioner (the Indian Young Lawyers Association, via Bhakti Pasrija) as well as the key respondents (the Travancore Devaswom Board and the State of Kerala), the *IYLA* bench faced a tangle of additional litigants. Not one of them, to my knowledge, was a female devotee of Ayyappan between the ages of ten and fifty who wanted to visit Sabarimala. That this was possible—that a small but voluble village could assemble in India's highest court to debate institutional practices that either did not impinge on them personally or did not apply to them at all—was made possible by the Court's own development of that special type of legal technique first mentioned in Chapter 2. Officially known as 'public interest litigation', it is, to the everlasting delight of pun-loving academics, far more commonly reduced to the unfortunate acronym 'PIL'.

The great innovation of public interest litigation is precisely that it allows individuals who have not themselves suffered harm to approach the courts for certain kinds of redress. A legal action filed as a PIL petition does not need to explain why the petitioner herself possesses *locus standi* ('standing to sue') nor does it need to observe various intricacies of convention and process that usually apply to all petitions. This is because the harms for which a PIL petition seeks redress are of a specifically public nature—they must involve the Fundamental Rights section of the Constitution—and because the party who might directly benefit from the petition is, for whatever reason, unable to approach the courts herself. The earliest PIL proceedings reflected an almost literal interpretation of this mandate to expand access to justice on the part of petitioners and jurists alike, and those proceedings exposed behaviours that were almost theatrically horrifying. Courts granted compensation to women raped by on-duty Indian soldiers, forced negligent town councils to provide slum dwellers with basic sanitation facilities, and released individuals whose pretrial detentions exceeded the maximum penalty for their alleged crimes—all of which is to say that early PIL cases exemplified legal innovation, progressive politics, and judicial independence in a way that was endearing at home and exciting abroad.

India's Supreme Court developed this rather quirky form of litigation in the late 1970s, so the story goes, as a kind of comprehensive *mea culpa* for its spectacular failure to withstand the anti-democratic machinations of Indira Gandhi's government during the Emergency period, which lasted from 1975 to 1977. For around thirty years after PIL petitions made their debut, the apology was warmly and widely accepted. The Indian higher judiciary, and especially those judges who are elevated to the Supreme Court, have built up so much goodwill among domestic and international audiences alike that, as I have already suggested, it has taken the efforts of several chief justices and decades of defensive manoeuvring to seriously tarnish the Court's reputation for principled and erudite populism. Much of that rapidly disappearing goodwill is derived from PIL.

All good things come to an end, however, and for the better part of twenty years PIL has been viewed less as a force for good than a tool to enforce good behaviour.[5] Now, the archetypical PIL petitioner is no longer a benevolent and civic-minded member of India's elite—the lawyer who reveals prisoner abuse or the professor who speaks on behalf of the mistreated residents of a women's shelter—but a representative of India's nebulous middle class whose advocacy predictably redounds to the benefit of a public to which they, in some easily identifiable sense, belong. These new petitioners are indignant neighbourhood associations seeking to tidy up their particular patches of earth, as well as indignant television watchers and newspaper readers and social media users seeking to prescribe the boundaries of acceptable speech. They are also, of course, indignant secularists and indignant people of faith, each seeking to promote their particular idea of India through, among other things, the management of religious institutions.

None of the goals attributable to the 'new PIL' are inherently unreasonable, just as none of them are self-evidently improper uses of the judiciary. In a country where roughly 40% of the lower house of parliament has faced criminal charges and where a ranking of 78th on Transparency International's Corruption Perception Index is cause for celebration rather than dismay, courts still offer one of the best paths to participatory governance for many citizens, even if that path no longer is and was never meant to be an especially straightforward one.[6] Moreover, at a time when the central government has been steadily imbuing both public discourse and public institutions with a virulent shade of saffron, it cannot be in the least bit surprising that a dispute over religion-state relations drew a noticeably colourful cast of secondary characters, none of whose ambitions could be easily characterized as the improvement of access to justice.

There were, among others, individuals like the college student Nikita Azad, the erstwhile king of Pandalam, the chief priest of Sabarimala, his grandson, and the Ayyappan devotee Usha Nandini; there were caste or interest-based organizations like the Nair Service Society and People for Dharma; and there were political entities like the CPI(M)-affiliated All India Democratic Women's Association.[7] As crowded as this roster was—as many as thirty-four separate parties applied to participate in the litigation, although not all were admitted by the Court[8]—it paled in comparison with the number of petitioners who sought inclusion in the review process that would begin less than twenty-four months later. Even for someone like me who has spent as much time studying this case as some of its participants, and likely more than time than many, the plethora of perspectives is occasionally overwhelming. Consequently, instead of either summarizing the views of every litigant (like a good Indian lawyer) or articulating and analysing every argument that was put forward (like her good American counterpart), my synopsis below emphasizes key elements in the opinions written by the five Supreme Court judges.

What follows is an unabashedly legal analysis of a legal artefact. Other parts of this book explore other aspects of the dispute over women's entry—a dispute in which, it is worth reiterating, the *IYLA* opinion constitutes just a single moment, if an important one. That importance stems in no small part because of how the four opinions comprising the decision known as '*IYLA*' confirm, contest, or ignore concepts that are internal to law. We must sometimes, however reluctantly, read law in order to talk about it.

Readers should note that, going forward, I will refer to the Chief Justice's opinion as the 'plurality' and the opinions of Justices Nariman and Chandrachud as *other* 'majority' opinions. Thanks to the Supreme Court's practice of hearing cases in benches, majority outcomes (like the invalidation of Sabarimala's ban) without true majority opinions (as in *IYLA*) are not uncommon in India. American scholars would probably refer to the opinions by Justices Nariman and Chandrachud as *concurrences*, but I have not found this to be a common usage among Indian lawyers and scholars and consequently do not follow it here.

3.2 *IYLA* Redux

After summarizing the arguments of the various petitioners, respondents, intervenors, and amici—no small feat, in a case where there are over half a dozen—Chief Justice Misra, writing for himself and Justice Khanwilkar, begins by stating that Ayyappan devotees do not constitute a religious denomination separate from Hinduism. If they did, they would be entitled to manage their own religious affairs in keeping with the group rights afforded by Article 26 of the Constitution. And even though the Chief Justice starts with Article 26, lurking not so very far in the background of his discussion is the Essential Practices Doctrine more often associated with Article 25; the interplay between these constitutional provisions, often at issue in disputes within a faith community, proved especially significant in the Sabarimala litigation.

The Essential Practices Doctrine was established via a landmark 1954 Supreme Court case called *Shirur Mutt*, and it was meant to guide judges confronted by the vexing task of determining the scope of individual and group religious freedom rights under the Indian Constitution. Article 25(2)(a), remember, stipulates that the state may regulate any 'economic, financial, political or other secular activity which may be associated with religious practice'. As they are trying to decide whether a given practice is merely *associated* with religious practice or is *essential* to it, the Doctrine reminds judges that 'what constitutes the essential part of a religion is primarily to be ascertained with reference to the doctrines of that religion itself'.[9] It is, in other words, a kind of judicial approximation of the divide-and-choose principle: religion first demarcates a core and a periphery, after which law chooses (the latter) for itself. To be sure, neither religion nor law work in the way the Doctrine imagines, and several academic disciplines, anthropology being just one among them, stand ready to tell us why. But none of this entirely deserved criticism can gainsay the fact that the Essential Practices Doctrine *is* an effort at fair constitutional cake-cutting or that constitutions are cakes that *must* be cut.[10] Thanks to the Doctrine and the test it inspired, which involves nothing more or less complicated than asking whether a given religious practice is essential, *Shirur Mutt* has become one of the heavyweights of Indian constitutional jurisprudence—what lawyers love and anthropologists increasingly hate to call canonical.

But *Shirur Mutt* also gave rise to a second, less widely discussed test that is used to decide the applicability of group (and *only* group) religious freedom rights under Article 26.[11] This 'denominational' test is used to decide whether a community qualifies as a 'religious denomination or section thereof' such that it should be allowed to enjoy various property rights, to establish and maintain religious and charitable organizations, and, especially, whether the community should be allowed to 'manage its own affairs in matters of religion'.[12] In the *Shirur Mutt* formula that has achieved widespread acceptance, a denomination is characterized by its possession of a name, a faith, and an organization in common.[13]

The Chief Justice begins, as I said, by determining that Ayyappan devotees do not qualify as a religious denomination. Although individual pilgrims to Sabarimala are called 'Ayyappans' for the duration of the pilgrimage, the Chief Justice notes that devotees at large are not called Ayyappans (the way, for instance, followers of the Sikh faith are called Sikhs).[14] Nor do Ayyappan devotees have a shared faith, whether this means a 'new methodology' or 'any common religious tenets peculiar to themselves'.[15] They certainly do not have a common organization if that is understood to be an exclusive religious community with an authoritative ecclesiastical hierarchy—say, like the Catholic Church—although there are, it should be noted, many devotional associations dedicated to Ayyappan. Put together, the plurality opinion declares, Ayyappan devotees are not a distinct denomination and consequently the Court's task in adjudicating the Article 25(1) rights of individual devotees who favour the ban is to determine whether excluding women between ten and fifty from temples is an essential practice of *Hinduism*. At the end of a series of passages that is almost as suspenseful as the alphabet song, the Chief concludes in the negative.[16]

Finally, the Chief Justice examines specific provisions of the *Kerala Hindu Places of Public Worship (Authorisation of Entry) Act* (1965), as well as the statutory Rules meant to give effect to that Act. Notwithstanding the tendency of religious freedom cases everywhere to traffic in the more ethereal stuff of constitutional principles, the *IYLA* litigation has, from its inception, been alive to the highly statutory nature of temple governance in contemporary India. The original PIL petition filed in 2006 challenged the validity of one of the statutory Rules governing Keralite temples, and subsequent participants in the litigation added to this line of argumentation. Both in the litigants' materials and in the judgement itself, the statutory discussion ultimately focused on three segments of the *Kerala (Authorisation of Entry) Act*. Section 3 of the Act provides that places of public worship that are 'open to Hindus generally or to *any* section or class thereof, shall be open to *all* sections and classes of Hindus'.[17] Section 4 stipulates that although trustees of public places of worship may make regulations to maintain 'order and decorum and the due performance of rites and ceremonies', these regulations may not discriminate against any Hindu on the grounds he belongs to a particular section or class.[18] However, Rule 3(b), formulated under the power granted by §4, states that temple authorities may exclude '[w]omen at such time during which they are not by custom and usage allowed to enter a place of public worship'.

In most instances, 3(b) is understood to permit the exclusion of women during the few days they are literally menstruating. During the *IYLA* litigation, however, supporters of Sabarimala's ban argued that 3(b) permitted the exclusion of all women aged ten to fifty because they are likely to be fertile—to be in between menarche and menopause—regardless of their menstrual status at the time of visiting Sabarimala.[19] Fertility, argued these supporters, made women in the prohibited age range dangerously appealing to Sabarimala's celibate deity, but it did not make them a 'section or class' of Hindus eligible for the protections afforded by §3 and the proviso to §4 because *all* women are not banned from Sabarimala at any given time and *no* individual woman is banned for all time. The Chief Justice, however, disagreed and concluded on behalf of himself and Justice Khanwilkar that Rule 3(b) violates §§3–4 of the

Kerala (Authorisation of Entry) Act as well as the religious freedom rights of female Ayyappan devotees under Article 25(1) of the Constitution.[20]

The first twenty paragraphs of Justice Nariman's majority opinion are a duty roster of Indian precedent regarding religious freedom. He reviews case after widely read case addressing the interplay between the freedom guaranteed by Article 25(1) and the qualifications allowed by Article 25(2), as well as case law addressing the relationship between Articles 25(1) and 26. He then moves on to a brief synopsis of *IYLA*'s predecessor opinion from the Kerala High Court, *S. Mahendran v. Secretary, Travancore Devaswom Board*.[21] And, agreeing with the plurality on the matter of denominational status, he states that since *non*-Hindus may worship at Sabarimala without ceasing to be practitioners of their own faith, it follows that Hindus who worship at Sabarimala also do not cease being Hindu.[22] But the true core of Justice Nariman's opinion—even if it appears briefly and very near the end—is his discussion of the religious rationales for Sabarimala's ban and, in particular, his discussion of the idea that menstruation is ritually polluting.

In the space of just eight paragraphs, or a mere five pages, Justice Nariman conducts a whirlwind tour of major belief systems, which he groups into 'older religions' (Hinduism, Judaism, Islam, Christianity, and Zoroastrianism) and 'new religions' (Sikhism and the Baha'i faith). He quotes from the Book of Leviticus, the Gospel of Mark, the Qur'an, the Bundahishn, and the Zadspram, as well as from the Bhagavata Purana and the Dharmasutra of Vashistha. After canvassing these religious texts with a kind of palpable nonchalance, as if the task occupied only part of his Sunday afternoon, he concludes that '[a]ll the older religions' view menstruation as ritually polluting, while 'the more recent religions' take 'a more pragmatic view'.[23]

Justice Nariman's brisk sprint through several collegiate courses' worth of material is, of course, only partly relevant to the dispute over women's entry, which as we have already seen is concerned with fertility as much as with menstruation. It is also unusual, but not for its methodological approach: philosophically inclined and textually infused discussions of religion, or what jurists believe ought to be considered religion, were once an unremarkable feature of Indian constitutional jurisprudence. The exemplars of this genre, Justice Gajendragadkar's musings on 'the distinctive features of Hindu religion'[24] (citing the Bhagavad Gita and the philosopher-statesman Sarvepalli Radhakrishnan) and Justice Aiyyar's enquiry into the necessity of image worship among Hindus[25] (citing the Agamas), continue to be reprised with dependable regularity in religious freedom cases. (Other instantiations exist too but they are less likely to find a place in the lineage recitations of contemporary judicial analysis.[26]) Indeed, the foundational premise of Justice Nariman's opinion, namely, that scriptures reflect true religion such that courts must necessarily engage with them, has a pedigree older than the Republic itself. Colonial officials and the courts over which they presided were famously dependent on sacred texts that might aid the adjudicative process—and, rather infamously, they were also dependent on the resident pundits, muftis, and maulvis who were adjured, although never entirely expected, to provide accurate and neutral interpretations of those texts.[27]

Consequently, what makes Justice Nariman's forays into textual exegesis unusual is not method or purpose, but timing: Indian judges, never noticeably loath to pronounce upon the nature of true religion, have become decidedly more comfortable with viewing themselves and *not* texts as the arbiters of religious authenticity. Through a handful of prominent religious freedom cases from the 1960s, a spate of temple-administration cases from the 1990s, as well as individual opinions between and after, the apex court in particular has shown itself to be less and less interested in what religious texts have to say or with what non-judges think they have to say.[28] Instead, the justices of the Supreme Court have become more eager to rely on their own notions of what true religion is—notions that, by and large, are marked by a rationalism and a high modernism that is fortuitously consonant with the Constitution. For those of us who have spent far too long poring over the judicial pronouncements of yore, Justice Nariman's decision to consult texts, howsoever briefly and breezily, is likely to trigger nothing so much as nostalgia.

After conducting his global tour and accepting, for argument's sake, that menstruation is ritually polluting for many Hindus—and that preventing this sort of pollution from compromising the temple is an essential aspect of faith for Ayyappan devotees—Justice Nariman asks whether either Article 26 or Article 25(1) provides constitutional protection for the ban on women. Like the plurality, he finds that Ayyappan devotees do not qualify for Article 26 protection, and, also like the plurality, he finds that Rule 3(b) violates §3 of the *Kerala (Authorisation of Entry) Act* as well as the Constitution. Article 25(1) serves supporters no better in his analysis: '[t]he fundamental right claimed by the Thanthries and worshippers ... must necessarily yield to the fundamental right of such women' who wish to visit Sabarimala between the ages of ten and fifty, just as 'the right to practice religion, as claimed by the Thanthri[e]s and worshippers, must be balanced with and must yield to the fundamental right of women'.[29]

Before he concludes, Justice Nariman swiftly disposes of two of the respondents' objections, one of which is fascinating and the other of which should be. First, he notes the argument that the Indian Young Lawyers Association is not an appropriate petitioner, 'inasmuch as no woman worshipper has come forward with a plea that she has been discriminated against'.[30] Outside India, this reasoning might have been so self-evident as to be uninteresting, but within India—within the very edifice that produced public interest litigation, no less—it reads rather like quixotic and ineffectual quibbling on the part of the respondents. One of the hallmark characteristics of PIL petitions, after all, is their relaxation of *locus standi* requirements. Justice Nariman's response, that the dispute presented 'far-reaching' constitutional matters such that 'this technical plea cannot stand in the way of a constitutional court applying constitutional principles to the case at hand', is entirely predictable if nevertheless decidedly dismissive.[31]

Second, Justice Nariman acknowledges the critique that the Supreme Court should have engaged in fresh fact-finding when it heard *IYLA*, but his engagement with this objection is even more fleeting than with the first. He writes that 'a writ petition filed under either Article 32 or Article 226 is itself not merely a pleading, but also evidence in the form of affidavits that are sworn', a statement that has the dubious benefit of being neither more nor less than the truth.[32] Following this, he declares that '[t]he facts, as they emerge from the writ petition and the aforesaid affidavits, are sufficient to dispose of this writ petition'.[33]

Admittedly, the documentation produced by the Sabarimala dispute, whether in its *IYLA* or its *Mahendran* phases, was never miniscule. The *Mahendran* court heard at least seven witnesses regarding the nature and necessity of the ban on women, while the barrage of petitions and supplementary materials filed during the initial *IYLA* hearings (to say nothing of the review process that followed) ought to elicit some concern for the ocular health of the justices involved. But the absence of standing in PIL cases is perhaps only matched, reputationally, by the existence of a non-adversarial process in which judges are all too willing to order ongoing hearings and request additional information. For a Supreme Court justice to say 'no, thanks' to further fact-finding while entertaining a PIL petition on a matter of great importance and greater visibility in the months preceding a national election, and following just 1.5 years—a veritable blink of the judicial eye—of sporadic hearings, is, suffice it to say, odd. Both of these objections would also be considered by Justice Malhotra, but between her remarkably streamlined dissent and Justice Nariman's moderately proportioned majority opinion lies the magnum opus contributed by (now Chief-) Justice Chandrachud.[34]

Even from afar, there is something rather magnetic about Justice Chandrachud. It is not the name, although that name is imposing enough: the current Justice Chandrachud's father was yet another Justice Chandrachud, and was India's longest-serving Chief Justice into the bargain, while the current Justice's sons are dashing lawyer-scholars who write books with the kind of insouciance the rest of us might exhibit when cooking dinner. But in the highest echelons of Indian law and especially on its more rarefied benches, the absence of a famous name is cause for more comment than is its presence.

Nor does Justice Chandrachud's appeal stem in any straightforward manner from the aura of scholarly rigor that hangs around his persona and his jurisprudence. In the Justice's universe, peopled by expensively educated clerks and colleagues, neither a Harvard LLM nor a fistful of honorary degrees are any longer the singular achievements they might have once been. And, while his unrepentantly lengthy opinions boast a signature alpha-numeric organizational matrix, as well as scholarly references that are both current and classic, this academic fluency also does not explain the entirety of his appeal.

It may have something to do with his generally progressive inclinations, a judicial quality whose value is in no way diminished by being more or less expected in India. Since he ascended to the apex court in 2016, Justice Chandrachud's opinions have, among other things, affirmed a right to privacy (*Puttaswamy*[35]), dissented against the arrest and silencing of activists (*Romila Thapar*[36]), decriminalized adultery (*Joseph Shine*[37]), and chastised the Indian armed forces for limiting the job security and advancement of women officers (*Babita Puniya* and *Annie Nagaraja*[38]). Or, perhaps, Justice Chandrachud's appeal owes something to his leadership style, which seems to sit at the crossroads of the awe-inspiring and the *au courant*: his clerks report being invited to tea—the hallmark of benevolent condescension among a certain age and class of Indian elites—and also report being encouraged to share their legal opinions, no matter how critical, alongside movie and music recommendations. Whatever the reason, or perhaps due to all of them, it remains the case that several decades ago Indians got into the habit, not altogether inexplicably, of admiring their Supreme Court jurists, and (despite the tumult that has recently engulfed his court and several of his colleagues) Justice Chandrachud still makes it relatively easy for them to do this.

His *IYLA* opinion runs for over 60 pages divided into 14 parts or 119 paragraphs; it is around twice as long as any of the other opinions and, as usual, is a book as much as it is a judicial opinion. Several parts engage with issues that were also considered by the plurality and by Justice Nariman: the origins and development of essential practices jurisprudence (Parts F and G); whether or not Ayyappan devotees constitute a religious denomination (Part H); and the statutory and constitutional validity of Rule 3(b) (Part J). To be sure, Justice Chandrachud's analysis of these issues is not identical to that of his colleagues. On the matter of denominational status, he takes the unusual approach of arguing that since the *Mahendran* record demonstrates that Sabarimala's ban has not enjoyed perfect observance, *and* since the need for the ban forms '[t]he basis of the claim that there exists a religious denomination of Ayyappans', it follows that where there is no uniformity, there is no denomination. Similarly, he makes an astute and (within the bounds of the *IYLA* opinions) unique observation about shifts in essential practices jurisprudence, although he does not seem to heed the lesson of his own teaching. We will return to both his observation and his capitulation shortly.

But beyond some areas of common interest, Justice Chandrachud also ventures into topics that are clearly part of the documentary record yet were, for whatever reason, largely or wholly overlooked by the other judges in the majority. He considers whether gendered exclusion based on ritual pollution constitutes a form of untouchability and is hence prohibited by Article 17 of the Constitution (Part I). He asks whether the ban was an uncodified 'custom or usage' that existed before independence and, as such, enjoys some immunity from the Constitution (Part K). He explores the extent to which the ban is premised on a sexual stereotype of women as too weak-willed to complete the forty-one-day penance or too physically weak to climb to Sabarimala's mountaintop location (Part G). And, finally, he speaks to whether or not a deity can be said to have constitutional rights (Part L).

Although Justice Chandrachud's perspectives on these issues do not create precedent, they acknowledge gaps in the plurality opinion. He alone engages with the brief kerfuffle that arose during the *IYLA* hearings, when a dynamic young attorney representing the advocacy group People for Dharma proposed that Ayyappan himself could sue to protect the ban under Article 25.[39] The attorney's arguments were probably a revelation to many Indian observers about one of the more idiosyncratic aspects of their legal system, just as the degree to which his logic tickled fancies inside (and, if I am being honest, outside) the courthouse is its own revelation about the peculiar tastes cultivated by legal education.

Ayyappan, the attorney correctly noted, is a juristic person. Most countries recognize non-human persons in the form of corporations, and some have even bestowed person-like rights on abstract entities (as with Mother Earth in Bolivia) or natural formations (as with a river and a forested area in New Zealand).[40] Yet few, if any, have ventured into the realm of the divine, and certainly none have done so with the same population-exploding implications as India. It is not quite true that *every* one of Hinduism's supposed 300 million deities is a person—only those given consecrated material representation qualify—but this not-very-stringent requirement would likely still vault India into first place among the world's populations. Roadside altars, corner shrines, neighbourhood temples, regional and national pilgrimage sites: India is almost as full of gods as it is of people, and even small gods are (small) people.

Like a human being or a corporation, Ayyappan can initiate and sustain litigation, have financial obligations, and own property.[41] Indeed, Indian deities have won cases against donors and their wasteful heirs, against corporations, and even against each other—and they have lost, too, in favour of human property owners and income tax tribunals, to name just a few of their victorious opponents.[42] There was nothing to definitively show, said People for Dharma's attorney, why the same deity who enjoyed many of the rights and obligations accorded to human persons by statute could not also lay claim to some of their freedoms as enumerated under Section 3 of the Constitution. He was right, of course, and the argument was inevitable given well over one hundred years of case law identifying and expanding the legal capabilities of Hindu deities—but so too was Justice Chandrachud's response, which blandly observed that having statutory rights did not perforce endow one with constitutional rights.

While none of the other justices devoted word space to the analysis of Ayyappan's rights, two of them joined Justice Chandrachud, however briefly, in considering whether Sabarimala's admissions practices violated the abolition of untouchability mandated by Article 17 of the Constitution. Justice Nariman disposed of this possibility in a footnote, while Justice Malhotra considered it at some length before rejecting it.[43] It is not hard to see why the justices varied in their responses: Article 17 places the word *untouchability* within quotation marks, an otherwise innocuous punctuation practice that never fails to convince lawyers that something funny is afoot, and that it is both their burden and their privilege to say what:

> "Untouchability" is abolished and its practice in any form is forbidden. The enforcement of any disability arising out of "Untouchability" shall be an offence punishable in accordance with law.

Jurists, legal scholars, and treatise-writers, who are on occasion all contained within the same person, have often viewed these four pairs of small scratches as indicating that untouchability ought to be understood in its particular historical sense—and, moreover, that this particular historical sense denotes practices concerned with caste. Justice Malhotra quoted several legal luminaries to this effect and not a little of the Constituent Assembly Debates on the drafting of Article 17. But as Justice Chandrachud and *other* luminaries have proclaimed, neither text nor transcribed debates are as forthright as they may appear.[44] The Constitution itself is completely vague regarding the meaning of untouchability, saying simply that '[it] and its practice' are abolished. What *is* clear, says Justice Chandrachud, is that this vagueness was intentional rather than being either accidental or an exemplar of the strategic evasion in which legislators are all too apt to indulge. And what *makes* this clear is the fate of an amendment specifying that untouchability is a practice relating to 'religion or caste'. That amendment was criticized by Ambedkar and rejected by the Assembly, the latter of which heard rationales for a narrower understanding of the term and even heard a statement that 'at certain periods women are regarded as untouchables' and nevertheless opted to keep the more commodious and unqualified phrasing. Indeed, to the extent that there are *any* qualifiers in Article 17, those qualifiers arguably expand the scope of its protection, inasmuch as the text forbids the practice of untouchability 'in any form' as well as the enforcement 'of any disability' arising out of it.

If this explanation sounds suspiciously spheroid—crudely, *Article 17 is broad because the Debates say so; the Debates support breadth because Article 17 says so*—it is. Nevertheless, it remains that Justice Chandrachud's rationales for an expanded reading of Article 17, one that would have rendered Sabarimala's admissions practices impermissible because they constitute a kind of untouchability on the basis of gender, rest on impeccable sources and not-unreasonable interpretations even if they did not ultimately appeal to any of his colleagues.

Justice Malhotra's dissent is not markedly shorter than the opinions authored by Chief Justice and Justice Nariman, but it is quite devastatingly to the point. After expeditiously summarizing the parties' submissions, she moves on to question the appropriateness of the lead petitioners and of their choice to present *IYLA* as a PIL petition. Ideally, she argues, a petitioner who directly approaches the Supreme Court regarding a violation of fundamental rights should have personally suffered that violation.[45] Neither Bhakti Pasrija, who represented the IYLA, nor any of her colleagues, nor any of the parties who joined them in seeking to overturn Sabarimala's ban had professed to be Ayyappan worshippers with a hankering to visit the temple. Failing an actual experience of harm, Justice Malhotra goes on, whenever an Article 14 (equality) violation is articulated via a PIL petition, and with respect to religious practice, the petitioner should at least be a member of the community whose practice is being questioned.[46] Again, neither Pasrija nor her colleagues nor their co-litigants met this requirement. Had they done so, however, they may still have failed to satisfy Justice Malhotra, who notes rather pointedly that '[p]recedents under Article 25 have arisen against State action, and not been rendered in a PIL'.[47] (She does not note, unsurprisingly, that all but one of the precedents in her list were decided *before* the Supreme Court developed the very concept of PIL.[48])

Justice Malhotra's critiques are nothing short of astounding. Unharmed parties are the archetypical PIL petitioners, and the non-necessity of personal standing is one of the technique's defining features; to say that it should be otherwise is not unlike criticizing the proverbial square peg for being insufficiently round.[49] A 'sincerity' requirement, to use the language of American constitutional lawyers, and even a lesser 'membership' requirement, effectively removes religious freedom disputes from the purview of PIL. Nothing in existing PIL jurisprudence suggests the kind of hierarchy of cases this would create, a sorting of Fundamental Rights provisions into those that are eligible to be brought as PIL petitions and those that are not. Creating such a hierarchy is most certainly within the powers of the Court (what the justices gave, the justices may also take away), but it would, at the very least, be strange. In a country where religion is a key axis of division and the judiciary is still for the most part a key source of governance, Justice Malhotra's suggestion that the courts should voluntarily stay out of many religious disputes appears remarkably out of place.

And yet, much like the traditional perspectives on Article 17 with which Justice Chandrachud took issue, there is both more and less than meets the eye. Justice Malhotra's concern, palpable throughout this part of her opinion, is precisely that PILs targeting religious practices sit uncomfortably with the history and contemporary reality of Indian politics. The Partition that divided the subcontinent into India and Pakistan in 1947, the Sikh pogroms following Indira Gandhi's assassination in 1984, the violent destruction of the Babri Masjid in 1991, the horrific Godhra train massacres of 2002, the beatings of actually and ostensibly beef-eating Muslims in the late 2010s, and the literally innumerable killings of various minorities because they looked, spoke, walked, smiled, ate, or loved in a way that was unacceptable in some way to someone else—Indian nationhood is not simply *constructed* out of religious violence: in a very real if nonetheless partial sense it *consists* of religious violence. In this context, Justice Malhotra all but shouts, to enable any individual to bring suit on behalf of anyone else—or even on behalf of no one in particular—and, in the process, to allow the state to restrict, alter, or forbid a religious practice, is to steadfastly ignore the country with which one is concerned.

Justice Malhotra's views on fundamental rights vindication via PIL petitions constitute an unusual perspective as well as a foundational parting of ways with her colleagues, but she also diverges from the majority on the narrower questions of the case. On the denominational status of Ayyappan devotees, the validity of Rule 3(b), and whether the ban relates to an essential religious practice, she simply disagrees with her colleagues.[50] She also draws on the Constituent Assembly Debates concerning the drafting of the Indian Constitution to argue that Article 15's prohibition of discrimination on the basis of, among other things, sex and Article 17's prohibition of untouchability were never meant to apply in situations like Sabarimala's ban on women.[51]

But among her most striking arguments are two observations specifically concerned with religion: that courts should not weigh religious practices against constitutional understandings of rational behaviour, and that '[t]he form of the [Hindu] deity in any temple is of paramount importance'.[52] The first point, which would have been impressively banal coming from an American judge, is a shockingly self-limiting statement for a member of the Indian Supreme Court. Since when, one imagines generations of scholars and lawyers asking themselves incredulously, since when exactly is 'delineat[ing] the rationality of ... religious beliefs or practices ... outside the ken of the Courts'?[53] For decades now, Indian judges faced with religious freedom disputes have, seemingly, done little else.

Justice Malhotra's second point about Hindu deities is an important one and a response to an argument contained in both the plurality opinion and in some of the petitioners' filings: namely, that Sabarimala's ban was not essential to Ayyappan worship because other Ayyappan temples did not have a similar ban.[54] She notes that Ayyappan-at-Sabarimala has a different personality and preferences than Ayyappan-elsewhere and suggests that since '[w]orship has two elements—the worshipper and the worshipped'—the right to worship Ayyappan-at-Sabarimala 'cannot be claimed in the absence of the deity in the particular form in which he has manifested himself'.[55] What her observation overlooks is, of course, the potential for disagreement as to the nature of the restrictions imposed by a deity's 'particular form'. Even granting that Ayyappan-at-Sabarimala is a celibate manifestation of the deity, whereas, say, Ayyappan-at-Achankovil is married to Purna and Pushkala, it does not follow that we all agree on the former's preferences concerning female visitors.

Still, Justice Malhotra's point about the differing personalities of Hindu temple deities is significant, especially given the well-known religious *and* legal salience of deity personas. Temple ethnographies and other studies attest to the unique habits and proclivities of deity X as manifested at temple Y. Deities play tricks, go on holiday, have sex, and wage war, but all of their manifestations do not do all of these things, or at least they do not do them all in the same ways.[56] The considerable documentation on this front, which went unacknowledged by the plurality's analysis, offers no mean support for Justice Malhotra's view that, when it comes to Hindu temple deities, it simply does not make sense to employ generalizations along the lines of 'what *Ayyappan* wants'.

The distance between Justice Malhotra and the majority (but especially the plurality) on differentiation within Hinduism is not small, is not new, and is not limited to members of the judiciary. The politics of Hindu nationalism, which increasingly characterize the rhetoric of Indian nationalism, also makes much of the Oneness of Many. Hindus are One despite divergences of caste, language, philosophy, and lived experiences. Hinduism is One despite disagreements spanning theology, ontology, and epistemology. It follows that Hindu deities are One, both among themselves—Vishnu, Shiva, Brahma—and within themselves—Ayyappan at here, there, and elsewhere. But while the Chief Justice's opinion builds on this creeping sameness to achieve its admittedly progressive ends, Justice Malhotra's focus on difference is an appeal for the Court to remember the many-ness of Many. Neither the plurality nor the other justices in the majority ultimately heed this call.

3.3 Sovereign Citizens | Sovereign State

If this dizzyingly quick tour of *IYLA* has been unbecomingly doctrinal by anthropological lights, what follows is likely to figure as unbecomingly critical among scholars of Indian law, who have generally found much to approve of in the decision if not necessarily in the Court that issued it. Nevertheless, the critique is warranted, although not because *IYLA* is unjustifiable, in either outcome or reasoning, according to the jurisprudential universe of which it now forms part. In fact, and as I have already noted, it is neither.

The core finding in *IYLA*, that Sabarimala must welcome women of all ages, is so decidedly within the realm of the plausible that for many Court watchers it must have seemed very nearly inevitable. India's Constitution has substantial anti-discrimination and equality protections that could easily support such an outcome, and the Supreme Court's recent jurisprudence involving those protections as well as other several constitutional provisions has a markedly expansive and progressive flavour. Whether one has nine justices or more than thirty, some cases are easy to call.

Nor, barring a few of the more intriguing and iconoclastic lines of argumentation discussed above, is the *reasoning* in the plurality or majority opinions inexplicable. The Indian judiciary, as generations of scholars have observed in alternating modes of pride and despair, experiences few qualms when extending the state's power over religion. The exact manner in which that power is allowed to manifest itself may vary, ranging from administrative infrastructures that direct the daily lives of religious institutions (like the Travancore Devaswom Board) to judicial pronouncements regarding the significance of religious beliefs (as with *IYLA*). But both Indian judges who predate *IYLA* as well as those who are yet to come have asserted and will continue to assert that the state has a role in shaping the religious lives of its citizens, and they will be entirely justified in doing so.

One cannot, after all, have a truly transformative constitution that is also *wholly* devoted to the concept of citizen sovereignty—to the idea that the locus of democratic authority lies solely with citizens and is merely exercised on their behalf by the state—not, at least, if the citizenry itself is the object of transformation, which in India it undoubtedly is. The same Constituent Assembly Debates that reflect a careful decision to leave untouchability undefined for the purposes of Article 17 also convey, in no uncertain terms, a sense that the state requires immense discretion to effectuate important reforms. Conceptualizing sovereignty as being divided between the people and the state provides this discretion; it enables the state to undertake the kind of broad and often unpredictable reforms that are inescapable in the construction of a more equitable society. *This* is the vision of religion-state relations, and of democratic sovereignty, that *IYLA* attempts to realize, but it stumbles profoundly in the process.

That is because, whether as social scientists or as theologues, the justices fall short. Individuals either *are or are not* Hindu; beliefs and practices either *are or are not* essential; communities either *are or are not* exclusive denominations. Admittedly, inasmuch as its goal is to sort Ayyappan worship into any of these buckets, the plurality's conclusions are not unreasonable. It is undeniably true that not all Ayyappan temples exclude fertile women (in fact, it is quite likely that *no* other Ayyappan temples do this). It is equally true that being a devotee of Ayyappan places few proscriptions or prescriptions on one's everyday existence; the forty-one-day penance is a special observance rather than a way of life. And it is also the case that worshipping Ayyappan—whether at home, at Sabarimala, or at one of the other 'thousand' Ayyappan temples scattered throughout India—does not preclude worshipping other deities or even belonging to other faiths. But this kind of binary analysis, which is as popular in law as it is in computer science, produces conclusions that are problematic and beside the point—or, more accurately, that are problematic *because* they are beside the point. Such an analysis ignores, among other things, the politics behind naming conventions, the always-changing nature of religious practice, the possibility of multiple and overlapping religious identities, and the impossibility of absolute consensus regarding religion (and, indeed, almost anything).

To a degree, these problems are the problems inherent in any governmental actor defining any religion, and, as such, they can be mitigated but not avoided.[57] Nevertheless, the *IYLA* majority inhabits the gap between legal form and lived reality with disconcerting ease. The plurality, for instance, requires that Ayyappan devotees think of themselves as 'Ayyappans' throughout the year instead of only when they are on pilgrimage—and since they do not, it ignores the fact that they *do* think of and refer to themselves as Ayyappans while on pilgrimage. The plurality's approach also requires that Ayyappan devotees have unique methodologies or tenets but ignores their view that Ayyappan-at-Sabarimala has different traditions and preferences than Ayyappan-elsewhere (this was the point made by Justice Malhotra in her dissent). Justice Nariman and Justice Chandrachud are not much less exacting than the plurality, with one demanding airtight communities of believers and the other demanding airtight observances within communities. Over and over again, the four majority justices demand consistency and exclusivity, and, where they encounter none, they discount whatever points of distinction they do find.

None of this is mandated by the Constitution or even by the Essential Practices Doctrine, which, Justice Chandrachud notes, long ago shifted from protecting *essentially* religious (as opposed to secular) practices to protecting the much smaller and more difficult-to-determine circle of practices that could be considered *essential to* religion.[58] The move from *essentially* to *essential* was not accidental, inasmuch as anything jurisprudential can be the result of accident, and it did not by itself eviscerate the Doctrine's fair-cake-cutting impulses. Nevertheless, it has worked to annihilative effect when paired with a second transformation that downgraded the persuasive authority accorded to religious doctrine from being determinative to being merely indicative. Justice Chandrachud acknowledges this second transformation, too; in fact, he describes it in terms that are even stronger than my own. '[T]he Court', he admits, 'began with the *Shirur Mutt* formulation that what is essential to religion would be determined by the adherents to the faith', but it gradually 'moved towards a doctrine that what is essential "will always have to be decided by the Court"'.[59]

IYLA thus makes clear, for those who still entertained doubts on the matter, that the Essential Practices Doctrine is now really the Judicial Preferences Doctrine. In this latter instantiation, the Doctrine deserves almost all of the criticism that is routinely heaped on it by lawyers, scholars, and—mark the irony—by the Supreme Court itself. But, as Justice Chandrachud himself suggests, it did not need to be this way.

Perhaps none of this matters: perhaps Ayyappan devotees would not have won under the Court's original and more expansive understanding of the Doctrine, either. Even an *essentially religious* practice would have been '[s]ubject to public order, morality and health and to the other provisions' of the Fundamental Rights section. Even then, Ayyappan devotees would have still struggled to show that the ban cohered with other fundamental rights that, by the very terms of Article 25, took primacy over religious freedom. There was, however, no chance at all of Ayyappan devotees succeeding under the Doctrine's current manifestation. The shifts in its application, at once described and exemplified by Justice Chandrachud's opinion, have transformed what was once a jurisprudential innovation for balancing competing constitutional impulses into a popular scapegoat for scholars, lawyers, and laypersons alike.[60] And regrettably, that newer and virtually unwinnable version of the Essential Practices Doctrine is by now so thoroughly entrenched in Indian jurisprudence that it would have been more surprising if Justice Chandrachud had *not* ultimately gone along with the reformulated version that he himself had just carefully exposed as an incidental rather than conceptually required.[61]

The majority opinions' biggest failing is both cause and consequence of their attitude towards religious identity and the Essential Practices Doctrine. They forget—the plurality forgets most severely of all—that there *are* conflicting impulses at play in India's founding charter. The goods of societal well-being, which we might call *communal* (as Hindu nationalists often do) or *confrontational* or *transformative* (as many scholars do), are not the goods of Indian politics in their entirety. There are also other goods—the primacy of the people over the government, or of the individual over the group—that are most readily associated with liberal democracy of a generically North Atlantic type. Opinions like *IYLA* that omit even a pretence of accounting for devotee perspectives in the course of ruling on devotee practices ride roughshod over the balance between these contrasting visions of citizen-state relations. That the majority justices should seek to effectuate a theory of the state centred on transformative governance is well and good; that they should fail to meaningfully acknowledge any alternate conceptions while doing so is decidedly otherwise.

* * *

Unlike the proverbial hard case, the writ petition behind *IYLA* did not make bad law so much as unfortunate judicial writing. True, the plurality opinion assiduously avoided the nuances of lived Hinduism, the original, workable, formulation of the Essential Practices Doctrine, and any recognition of the Constitution's conventionally liberal democratic impulses— and the other majority opinions were not much less dexterous. And yet, neither the outcome in *IYLA* nor the core arguments advanced by the majority opinions were unreasonable or unpredictable. They advanced exactly the kind of rationalizing, equalizing, secular humanist vision of Indian society for which India's higher judiciary, and especially its Supreme Court, have become famous, and for which there is ample legal as well as historical support. There were, in other words, two possible imaginaries to draw on: one characterized by constitutional mandates to reform, another by constitutional mandates to resist reformation. The coexistence of these worlds, and of the distinct citizen-state hierarchies they signal—more specifically, the shifting balance between one possible world and the other—*this* is the dynamic equilibrium at the heart of Indian constitutionalism. But it is not, unfortunately, at the heart of *IYLA*.

Ten or fifteen years earlier, a decision like *IYLA* would have likely occasioned even more in the way of adulation and triumph than the not-insignificant celebrations it actually summoned in 2018. That *IYLA* was *also* received with all the protests, politicking, and review petitions described in the previous chapter is, moreover, only minimally attributable to the jurisprudential failings I have described in this one. Neither supporters nor critics were reacting to the opinion and the opinion *alone*. The declining credibility of the Court, and of PIL, the entrenchment of Hindu nationalism, along with a thousand other inscrutables, mean that the universe in which *IYLA* began, in the early 2000s, was markedly different from the one in which it began to conclude. The events underlying the origins of the case belong, now quite literally, to a different generation, and it is to those events, as well as to the writ petition they inspired, that we now turn.

4
The Scandal

The late 1980s were, it seems, rife with actresses surreptitiously visiting Sabarimala. Two other film stars put in appearances at the temple within a year of Jayamala's now infamous 1987 pilgrimage, and although one of these visits also generated a court case, neither of them captured anyone's imagination half so well as the visit that eventually inspired *IYLA*. In the ruthlessly hierarchical universe of Indian cinema, this is not altogether surprising. Jayamala's reputation may not have been made in the prestigious Tamil film industry that dominates south India—and, in 1987, that reputation may have already been on the wane following her maritally induced exit from the industry two years earlier—but she was still the most famous of the actresses to have, ostensibly, visited Sabarimala. She was also the only one to express any regret. Sudha Chandran flatly denied having danced on Sabarimala's famous eighteen steps as part of a film shoot, saying that her portions of the scene had been completed on set. Girija Lokesh declared, somewhat mysteriously, that she had simply been indulging in a little last-chance tourism. 'I was 36 years old then', Lokesh stated, adding 'that was the last year that the shrine permitted women to visit, so I took all the women in our family and went there'.[1]

Perhaps, on the other hand, Jayamala's visit garnered as much attention as it did because the circumstances surrounding it as well as the events leading up to her confession were cinematic in themselves. On 16 June 2006, a four-day *devaprasnam* ceremony began at Sabarimala.[2] A *prasnam* is a question or a concern; *devaprasnam*s, which allow for relatively focused interaction with the divine, are consequently more office hours than public lecture, and they are precipitated either by a desire to ascertain the deity's mood or in response to a specific unfortunate event.[3] By all accounts, the *devaprasnam* of June 2006 was of the first, general type, and so the independent astrologer who had been hired to perform the ceremony reported back to Sabarimala's administrators on a wide range of matters. His comments touched on everything from the appropriate timing of festivals, to the type of flowers to be used in temple ceremonies, to the provision of free food to all pilgrims. He argued in favour of greater functional distinction between Sabarimala's two types of priests, and against the continuation of a foot-washing observance accorded to the Pandalam family's representative during the annual pilgrimage season.[4] Somewhere among all this divine feedback was a pronouncement that Sabarimala's precincts had been desecrated within the last twenty years due to the presence of a woman in the prohibited age range. When the *devaprasnam* concluded on 19 June, with various TDB officials agreeing to action and atonement, there was little to suggest that 'women's entry' would emerge as the unquestionable focal point of the whole endeavour.

A good many of the developments that followed turned on the respective positions of the hired astrologer and Sabarimala's priests—a few middle-aged men, in a sea of middle-aged men, disputing over young and middle-aged women. The astrologer, who had earned fame and no inconsequential fortune in the early 2000s by assuring the former Chief Minister of Tamil Nadu of her (inevitable) return to power, was a freelancer hired for the occasion by the temple board.[5] Since *devaprasnam*s are astrological rites as well as religious ones, they are largely the province of individuals like the astrologer, who are at once more specialized (in terms of procedure) and less specialized (in terms of affinity to a particular institution or deity) than regular temple priests. They are also—again, in a departure from regular priests at elite institutions like Sabarimala—often non-Brahmin, a fact that the astrologer did not hesitate to publicize during the uproar that followed his performance.

Regular priests, at least in Kerala, tend to come in two varieties: *santhi*s and *tantri*s. While a reliable distinction between *santhi*s and *tantri*s is hard to articulate and their roles may be interchanged or combined depending on the size of a temple's staff, *santhi*s are generally viewed as having more to do with quotidian administration and rituals than with special ceremonies or the overall *aishwaryam* ('prosperity') of the temple.[6] The *melsanthi* (chief *santhi*) of a major public Keralite temple like Sabarimala is likely to be chosen annually through a state-administered vetting process, although some *melsanthi*s of public temples are still hereditary appointees. Their prominence is highly variable: at Sabarimala, although the selection of each new office holder is assiduously covered in the newspapers, *melsanthi*s themselves are not particularly influential. Newspaper accounts of the 2006 *devaprasnam* almost never noted the name of Sabarimala's *melsanthi*, or whether he was even present during the ceremony, although they went to considerable trouble to name all of the hired astrologer's assistants. And the same accounts frequently mentioned the leader of Sabarimala's other type of priest, its chief *tantri*—a position that, at Sabarimala, rotates annually between the male-line descendants of a single family. In June 2006, that role was held by Kandararu Mohanaru.

The chief *tantri* of Sabarimala is one of the most powerful priests in Kerala. He is, ritually and legally, the father of the deity. He is said to have ultimate authority over ritual practice at the temple (and, as the next chapter shows, he sometimes actually possesses this). And, in the pantheon of individuals responsible for administering Sabarimala, the chief *tantri* oversees all other priests, including both other male members of his own family and everyone in the otherwise parallel hierarchy of *santhi*s. When journalists or lawyers or scholars talk of 'chief priests'—particularly in Kerala, particularly with regard to Sabarimala—they always, always mean the chief *tantri*.

Part of this immense authority derives from the authority accorded in contemporary India to *any* chief priest in regard to his temple. Part of it also derives from the special orthopraxy of Keralite *tantri*s, who are always Nambudiris and are therefore, as Chapter 1 suggested, not just your garden-variety Brahmin. But, equally, part of the authority accorded to Sabarimala's chief priest derives from circumstances that are entirely unique to his family. Sabarimala's chief priestship is inherited through the male line of the house of Thazhamon, one of two Nambudiri lineages at the apex—or more correctly, at the *apex's* apex—of Keralite caste hierarchy. As Mohanaru's father told me in 2011, and indeed as any news-reading Keralite could have probably explained after the excitement of 2006, the families of Thazhamon and Tharananallur come by their names and their positions thanks to nothing less than divine intervention.

Parasuraman, the warrior-sage incarnation of Vishnu who is often credited with having created Kerala by reclaiming it from the sea, once saw two Brahmins standing across from him on a riverbank. Since Hindu celestial beings, whether they are gods or sages, let alone divine sages, are notoriously incapable of resisting a chance to test human beings, Parasuraman promptly made the river waters rise and asked the Brahmins to cross over to his side. The elder Brahmin took a plantain leaf and used the powers he had derived from long years of ascetic penance to cross the river standing on the leaf. This Brahmin became the head of the Tharananallur family (*tharanam* meaning 'to cross' or 'to overcome') as well as the chief priest of the Padmanabhaswamy temple in Trivandrum. The younger Brahmin used his powers to part the waters and walk to the other side on the river bed; he became the head of the Thazhamon family (*thazha* meaning 'bottom', and *mon* meaning 'soil') as well as the chief priest of Sabarimala. Both families are also recognized as the *tantri*s of hundreds of other temples inside and outside Kerala.

Thazhamon's orthopraxy is worthy of its origin story, and the significance attached to it by a remarkable range of actors emerges through a thousand details, great and small. Even the State of Kerala, progressive and occasionally communist as it may be, nonetheless makes much of this *tantri* family's elite credentials: the Travancore Devaswom Board's official website describes the multiyear process by which Thazhamon boys are initiated into their family legacy by male relatives and external instructors.[7] (Of course, Kerala being what it is, the description ends by noting that 'even the women of the family have to follow certain practices' like eating medicated *ghee* during the second and third trimesters of their pregnancies.) More tellingly, in a family that is every bit as reliant on the production of male heirs as the beleaguered occupants of the Chrysanthemum Throne, Thazhamon *disowned* one of its eligible sons in the early twentieth century on the grounds that his mother was a non-Nambudiri woman.[8] True, Thazhamon no longer observes the dictum that only the eldest son in a Nambudiri family may marry and thus produce legitimate Nambudiri children—a practice that left younger sons to engage in contractual alliances with, among others, Nair women that produce Nair children. Instead, *all* of its sons may now marry, so that none of them need produce the lower caste offspring who, like my paternal grandfather, often grew up resenting the Nambudiri men who had sired them. Still, marrying a *non-Nambudiri* was a step too far for Thazhamon, and the child of this particular non-conforming brother was excluded from the family birthright.

The family's commitment to ritual education and caste purity are enhanced by an especially determined, if not especially unique, patrilineality. Thazhamon, like other Nambudiri families, traces descent through the father, rather than matrilineally, as most Nairs do. The practicing *tantri*s of Sabarimala thus continue to exclusively be the sons of Thazhamon fathers and Nambudiri mothers, the latter of whom, in a practice that has more or less fallen by the wayside across the rest of Kerala, still often adopt as their surname the rather forbidding descriptor *Antharjanam* ('one who dwells inside'). Thazhamon wives are a far cry from the isolated, unempowered Antharjanams of historical truth and artistic representation—when I first connected with the family, I did so by calling Devaki Antharjanam on her cell phone—but technology and education have not affected kinship calculations or the considerable cachet they can bestow. In the aftermath of the *IYLA* decision, when his antics became too controversial for their taste, the family's three practicing *tantri*s issued a statement disowning their nephew and cousin, Rahul Easwar, and reminding the public that Easwar, son of a Thazhamon *mother*, was no Thazhamon at all.

During the summer of 2006, Thazhamon's immense prestige enabled Mohanaru and his relatives to quickly and definitively dismiss the most astonishing outcome of the *devaprasnam*. On the second day of the ceremony, 17 June, the Executive Officer in charge of Sabarimala received a faxed confession that was addressed, curiously enough, to the astrologer. In that fax, Jayamala declared that, in the late 1980s, she had sworn to accompany her husband on a trip to Sabarimala if he were to recover from a major leg operation. The crowds at Sabarimala were immense (this part, at least, remains uncontroversial), and as a result of their movements, she was inadvertently pushed into the temple's sanctum sanctorum, where she fell, blissfully, at Ayyappan's feet and was handed a flower by a nearby priest before leaving the premises. Jayamala went on to write that it was not until 1999 that she learned about Sabarimala's ban on women and, consequently, of her own unknowing misdeed. It was a relicf to finally acknowledge the guilt she had been carrying for almost a decade.

Thazhamon promptly objected. There was no way a young, beautiful woman would have been permitted inside the temple complex, no way she could have been fallen *up* the eighteen golden steps leading to the sanctum, and no way, had these impossible feats become somehow possible, that she would have been permitted within arm's length of the deity. She was delusional—or, just as likely, she was in cahoots with the astrologer for reasons that were beyond the *tantris*' comprehension but that very likely had to do with publicity-seeking.

This narrative, once uttered by the chief priests of Sabarimala, did as much to shape the tenor and the tenure of the events that followed as did Jayamala's relative celebrity and the unusual circumstances surrounding the *devaprasnam*. The temple board requested a government investigation into Jayamala's claim, and, in early July, some of the board's representatives interrogated Jayamala at her home in Bangalore.[9] The Pandalam family went further by requesting a wholly new *devaprasnam*.[10] Instead of becoming a quick blip on Kerala's collective screen, as it had been with Girija Lokesh, or a moderate to-do in Kerala's courts, as with Sudha Chandran, the Jayamala phase of the longer women's entry dispute escalated.[11] It lurched from being a minor controversy over ritual breach to a six-year saga imbricating everything from the interaction of fundamental rights and criminal law jurisprudence to the cultural significance of the ban itself.

4.1 Separate but Equal

In this book, as in almost all of my earlier writing on Sabarimala, I have called the temple's relevant admissions policies a 'ban' or, at the very least, a 'prohibition' on women. In doing so, I have kept ample and largely respectable company: the writ petition filed by the Indian Young Lawyers Association talks about 'entry denied to women'; the brief authored by a Court-appointed *amicus curia*, or friend of the court, references the 'prohibition'; the plurality opinion written by Chief Justice Misra criticizes Sabarimala's 'exclusionary practice'.[12] India's news media, in a throwback to colonial-era debates over the 'women's question' (which variously meant widow immolation, widow remarriage, child marriage, polygamy, and the age of consent) usually refers to the Sabarimala dispute as a question of 'women's entry'.[13] Almost everyone who has described, defended, or decried Sabarimala's admissions practices has done so using a framework that emphasizes their limiting effects on women.

Almost but, of course, not all. Anthropological writing on Sabarimala, to the astonishment of no one remotely familiar with the discipline, skews heavily towards the temple's annual pilgrimage season, and is therefore characterized by a focus on transformation, togetherness, and, especially, on hyper-masculinity rather than on feminine exclusion.[14] In other words, anthropological writing on Sabarimala has not, until very recently at least, been framed in terms of a ban on women. This is likely because Sabarimala's pilgrimage offers exactly the kind of spectacular, immersive, ritual-filled, boundary-pushing experience that haunts anthropological dreams. The pilgrimage season occurs between late November and early January, over the course of one *mandalam*, or the forty-one-day period between one full moon and the eleventh day after the next full moon. Pilgrimage activities extend even further, up until the observance of a special lamp (*vilakku*) lighting ceremony on the festival of Makara Sankranti, which marks the sun's transition from Sagittarius to Capricorn and almost always falls on 14 January. In 2010–11, I was in Kerala—though not, it goes without saying, at Sabarimala—for the tail end of the *mandalam-makaravilakku* season.

By virtue of its size and duration, Sabarimala's pilgrimage season is a defining event in Kerala's annual calendar. Anywhere between 6 and 25 million people visit Sabarimala during this period, making the pilgrimage solidly larger than the average Hajj (under 5 million) and smaller than the average Kumbh Mela (over 30 million).[15] As a graduate student conducting fieldwork, I came exceedingly close to dispatching my non-Hindu and non-Indian (although conveniently Indian-presenting) husband to make the trip on my behalf, so great was the temptation to gather some of the ethnographic riches that it promised. As a professor reading the *IYLA* opinion from my home office in the United States, I suggested—and my husband agreed—that we should attempt the pilgrimage together, now that it appeared feasible to do so. It was not, of course, and it is not still. Perhaps one day we will go with our son.

In the meantime, I continue to rely on accounts by fellow anthropologists, who are quite literally *fellow* anthropologists and were therefore fortunate enough to have undertaken the pilgrimage themselves.[16] Their stories are filled with all the painstakingly assembled detail one might both expect and fear from anthropological narratives, ranging from pre-departure rituals meant to cleanse and equip the hopeful pilgrim, to obligatory riverside defecations (and then riverine baths), to arduous barefoot scrambling up and down the forest hills in which Sabarimala is situated, to the pilgrim's triumphant return home, laden with *prasadam*, offerings that have been blessed by the deity, along with small trinkets for waiting women-folk.[17] These narratives document how pilgrims, for the duration of their journeys, will be called *swami* ('lord') or simply *Ayyappan* because they go to Sabarimala *as* the deity in addition to *with* him or in order to *see* him; 'everybody', noted one anthropologist-pilgrim, 'became an Ayyappan for us'.[18]

What emerges from these narratives is a journey that is equal parts spiritual transformation and buddy film. The exhaustion and the frustration, the petty humiliations, the limbs that are stretched, scratched, burned, and cut—all of these are encountered at once in isolation, as a pilgrim struggles to overcome himself, and within 'a collectivity of men'.[19] Men go in groups that are usually led by a *guruswami* (literally 'holy teacher', but more prosaically denoting a veteran pilgrim) and they go in their particular roles *as men*—as the material providers for their families, as the concerned husbands of childless or pregnant wives, as the paternal guardians of children—always, in other words, as men seeking to acquire or protect the trappings of a 'successful mature male householder'.[20] For days or weeks, depending on how strictly one is keeping pre-departure vows of abstinence and the particular route by which one ascends to the temple, a pilgrim's world becomes a sea of unshaven, black waist-cloth wearing men, all named *swami*, all carrying identical cloth bundles of votive offerings (*irumudikettu*), and all chanting the same entreaty to a youthful bachelor god born of two male deities: *Swamiye Saranam Ayyappa!* ('Oh Lord Ayyappa! You are my refuge!'). Hyper-masculinity indeed. 'The mature self which is consolidated and evoked at Sabarimala is', said another anthropologist-pilgrim, with what can only be characterized as commendable understatement, 'a gendered self'.[21]

Anthropological accounts of the pilgrimage are, I should note, not the only narratives to present Sabarimala as a venue that is hyper-masculine rather than anti-feminine. Popular biographies of Ayyappan himself often seem specifically constructed so as to demonstrate that the deity and his most famous temple are not misogynistic just because they prefer to exclude women for a majority of their lifetimes. Some of these biographical stories connect Ayyappan with a minor local deity who was cursed to remain an eternal bachelor for having interrupted the divine coitus of Shiva and his consort. Others suggest that Ayyappan avoids female company in order to conserve, through celibacy, the powers on which his devotees rely to help them in their troubles. But by far the most popular explanations of Ayyappan's many idiosyncrasies—and of the unusual admissions practices associated with those idiosyncrasies—serve to render them more conceptually manageable by separating them into two distinct personas. The creative interplay between these personas, and the way in which that interplay is resolved through the composite figure called 'Ayyappan', is central to the task, undertaken with increasing urgency in recent years, of reframing the Sabarimala dispute in terms of men rather than women.

First, courtesy of his affiliation with Vishnu, Ayyappan's asceticism is not infrequently explained by linking him to the Buddha. The Vishnu-Buddha connection is long-standing and far-reaching, surfacing everywhere from seventh-century inscriptions to twentieth-century children's magazines, and, as with so much else that comes into contact with Hinduism's suffocatingly welcoming embrace, it is usually unidirectional.[22] Buddhism, in these accounts, becomes another off-shoot of Brahmanical Hinduism, and the Buddha one of the ten avatars of Vishnu.[23] To be sure, any sort of absolute statement fares as poorly here as in discussions of Hinduism more generally, since there are Buddhist Vishnus as surely as there are Vaishnavite Buddhas.[24] But readers of Sanskrit *puranas* and English comics alike will readily recognize the Buddha's habitual inclusion within a wider Hindu canon.

With Ayyappan, however the connection flows in reverse: for much of its existence, Sabarimala is said to have been a Buddhist shrine rather than a Hindu temple.[25] The temple is only supposed to have ceased being a Buddhist institution when Adi Shankara, the ninth-century Keralite philosopher, brought Hinduism back to prominence in south India after sectarian wars had left it vulnerable to the theological onslaught of Buddhism. The deity who was installed at this newly Hindu temple in a remote part of southern Kerala symbolized the resurgent regional strength of a unified faith community. Instead of *one* of the old pantheon—say, a Vishnu or a Shiva—Sabarimala was dedicated to the literal manifestation of this newfound unity, to Ayyappan, whose most commonly used name reiterates his status as the child of *both* Vishnu

(Ayyan) and Shiva (Appan). Nevertheless, the story goes on, shadows of the temple's Buddhist past can be seen in the temple's egalitarian ethos, which calls for men of all castes and all faiths to be welcomed equally, as well as in its annual pilgrimage, when devotees chant *Swamiye Saranam Ayyappa!* instead of *Buddham Saranam Gacchami!* ('I take refuge in the Buddha!'). The *most* telling indicator of Sabarimala's Buddhist past is, however, said to be Ayyappan's ascetic celibacy. He is not merely, like a generous handful of other Hindu deities, unmarried, but is also, like a good Buddhist monk, vehemently abstinent in accordance with his status as a *naishthika brahmachari*, or permanent celibate.

Alternatively, the peculiarities of both Ayyappan and Sabarimala are sometimes explained as the product of encounters between Vedic traditions and folk histories. In this version of Ayyappan's biography, the temple at Sabarimala, though always Hindu, was originally solely dedicated to the puranic deity Sastha, who was the product of Vishnu and Shiva's union. Sabarimala's original identity as a shrine to Sastha (rather than to Ayyappan) is said to be borne out not only by its first, and still prevailing, official denomination as the 'Sabarimala Sree Dharma Sastha' temple, but also by the fact that the image atop the temple's iconic gold flagstaff is one of *Sastha's* mount (a horse) rather than of Ayyappan's tiger. In contrast to the puranic Sastha, Ayyappan is said to be a heroic human warrior—perhaps a prince of the local Pandalam family, perhaps not—whose mission was to subdue the petty chiefs resisting Pandalam's authority. As a warrior, he was uninterested in domestic life and refused to marry, unlike Sastha who had two wives named Purna and Pushkala. In time, as Ayyappan's fame grew, he came to be seen as divine and his identity became indistinguishable from that of the deity whose temple sat in the hills under his protection. Today, this narrative concludes, the name 'Ayyappan' encompasses both the puranic and historic figures.

Anthropologists of a generation before mine would have been at pains to discover the origins and significance of these popular biographies, while contemporary scholars of Hinduism would be knee-deep in analysing the certitudes, platitudes, and elisions of power and history that they mask. But what matters is not that these stories are true, to any degree that such stories can be so, but that they are told. The very act of telling is an act of interpretation and an act of power—a way of saying to whom Ayyappan belongs and how we should view his preferences. No less than the judicial, journalistic, and scholarly analyses that speak of the 'ban on women', these biographies, by explaining Ayyappan's celibacy as the remnant of other faiths or other gods, present Sabarimala as the especial yet unremarkable domain of men instead of as a place that is forbidden to women.

One of the foremost proponents of the view that Sabarimala is 'pro-men' rather than 'anti-women' has been the nephew and cousin of the temple's current *tantri*s, Rahul Easwar. Easwar, who proved extremely gracious as an interlocutor and more than a little well-connected, is fascinating in the way that only someone who is both your likeness and antithesis can be. We are roughly the same age, we were married within a year of each other, and we attended universities of international repute—although, it appears, we did not both graduate from them.[26] His wife and I even share the same name, as, indeed, do both of our mothers. When Easwar and I first met in Trivandrum, in June 2011, he was relatable. Not infrequently, as when he combines Sikh, Muslim, and Hindu expressions of faith in a single utterance, rejects BJP proposals to bar non-Hindus from Sabarimala, or defends the right of a Hindu woman to convert and marry a Muslim man, he is disarming.[27] And yet, his published views on everything ranging from homosexuality to women's entry place him firmly, if peripherally, on India's powerful Hindu Right.[28] His personal website describes him as a 'right of centre voice', while his Twitter profile calls him a 'Hindu Activist'.[29] He has led multiple marches and rallies in connection with Sabarimala, first to advocate for its unusual admissions practices and later in protest of the Supreme Court decision that outlawed them—and finally, notwithstanding that decision, as part of an effort to block women between ten and fifty from accessing the temple. He often wears the awkward if transparently symbolic combination of Nehruvian jacket over a saffron or camouflage kurta, and in May 2020, he drew ire and amusement in equal measure for mistakenly having a *hakenkreuz* tattooed on his wrist in lieu of a *swastika*.[30]

For over a decade now, Easwar has argued (and interviewed, and litigated, and protested) in favour of the ban on women on the basis of three assertions: first, that *all* women are not excluded from Sabarimala; second, that any exclusion is based on the deity's particular manifestation at that location; and third, that such an exclusion is rendered acceptable by the fact that there are women-only sacred spaces in India, too.

The first of these declarations is both unquestionably true and questionably accurate: at no point in time are *all* female persons excluded from Sabarimala because girls under ten and women over fifty were permitted to visit the temple even before the Supreme Court released *IYLA*—but, by the same token, *all* women will be banned from Sabarimala for an extended period of their lives. Moreover, verbal and conceptual slippage runs rampant on both sides of this dispute. Just as critics of the ban frequently confuse the very large fraction for the whole, the ban itself as well as Easwar's support of it are predicated on the elision of fertility, age, and attractiveness. Especially during high-traffic periods, the Kerala State Police enforces the ban using a two-step process that begins with an informal visual assessment and that often ends with a request for official documentation establishing an aspiring female pilgrim's age.[31] Youthful sixty-five-year-old women and physically mature eight-year-old girls thus invite scrutiny that is not strictly required, while a prepubescent twelve-year-old might well escape it.

Easwar's second argument, that the ban reflects the particular preferences of Ayyappan-at-Sabarimala in contrast to those of Ayyappan-elsewhere, was of course made by intervenors in the *IYLA* litigation and deemed persuasive enough by Justice Indu Malhotra to warrant mention in her dissent.[32] Nevertheless, it is likely Easwar who articulated the point first and certainly Easwar who has done so most frequently. 'Every temple', he states, 'has a unique *"pratishta sankalpa"*'—meaning, 'the choice of a particular aspect of a particular deity for worship'.[33] Whereas Sabarimala venerates Ayyappan as eternal celibate, the deity is married in two of his other four most prominent temples. To force fertile women upon a manifestation of the deity who has undertaken to permanently avoid female company despite—or even because of—the deity's willingness to receive women elsewhere is thus, in Easwar's eyes, and in the eyes of at least one member of the Court, to ignore an inescapable feature of temple Hinduism. In Easwar's view, it is no more correct to say that *all* forms of Ayyappan reject women than it is to say that *this* form of Ayyappan rejects *all* women.

Whereas his first two arguments question the extent to which Sabarimala is truly anti-women, Easwar's third line of reasoning explicitly and unapologetically affirms Sabarimala as a masculine space. The temple, he contends, is like any other sacred venue inasmuch as it is 'designed to create a specific spiritual experience'—an experience that happens to be emphatically male.[34] This singular focus on celebrating and celebratory masculinity does not make Sabarimala any more guilty of misogyny than the exclusion of men makes women-only places of worship misandristic. Here, too, Easwar's argument is true enough as far as it goes—but that may not be very far. Easwar's standard point of comparison is the Attukal *devi* (goddess) temple in Trivandrum, which every year hosts a ten-day festival involving millions of women (and no men), who gather to honour the goddess by preparing *pongala*, a sweet rice porridge. No one, Easwar likes to point out, complains that the *Pongala* festival discriminates against men. We each of us have our special places, our sacred places, and the enjoyment of one place by one gender does not imply the inferiority of the other gender.[35] The problem, of course, is that every other day of the year, Attukal is open to all men.

Easwar's 'separate but equal' gloss on Sabarimala's overwhelmingly masculine ethos invokes and reframes themes that are contained in both anthropological accounts of the pilgrimage season and in popular biographies of Ayyappan. Nevertheless, 'separate but equal' is no less jarring in India than it is in America because India has never truly warmed to the idea that its constituent parts could find equality in separation. On the contrary, whether the fault lines between citizens were of caste, religion, language, or gender, and whether citizens transcended these divisions or built upon them, inhabitants of the new nation were presumed by many of India's early political leaders and constitutional framers, to achieve parity through their *shared* identities as Indians.[36] To argue, as Easwar has continually done, that Indian men may reserve a place of worship largely to themselves because other places (or at least, other festivals) have been reserved for Indian women is to do more than simply repackage Sabarimala as a space of joyfully masculine spirituality. It is, instead, to appeal to notions of political belonging that have never enjoyed much purchase in India, on the grounds that these ways of belonging are more authentically Indian.

In the end, there was little question as to whether or not Jayamala herself belonged at Sabarimala because, in 2006, Sabarimala was unequivocally a space open to all men and accessible to very few women. Virtually no one—from Easwar and his Thazhamon relatives, to the Pandalam family, to the astrologer and even Jayamala herself—entertained any misgivings on this issue. 'I Pray the almighty', concluded Jayamala's electronic *mea culpa*, 'to pardon me for the sin I did without my knowledge'. Nor, for that matter, was there much question as to whether Jayamala had *in fact* breached the temple's boundaries, climbed the eighteen steps, or entered the sanctum. This was, to be sure, because Thazhamon priests publicly questioned her story, but so too did the Devaswom Minister and, more remarkably, so did Jayamala's second husband, who supposed her recollection to be the product of a sincere but overactive faith.[37] Very soon all that remained undecided was a determination as to the consequences, if any, that should flow from the actress' improbable claim.

4.2 'Doing a Jayamala'

After an initial frenzy of several weeks, Jayamala and the astrologer largely disappeared from public conversation.[38] Sabarimala and its chief priest, on the other hand, remained in the thick of media speculation throughout the summer of 2006 for reasons still more salacious than a wandering film star. Within days of the last news articles quoting a despondent but increasingly harassed-sounding Jayamala, fresh stories began to surface of an alleged kidnapping, a prostitution ring, compromising photographs, and extortion conspiracies, all centred on Mohanaru, who was still in his rotation as the temple's *tantri*. The images (which I have not seen) are everywhere described as standard extortionist fare: Mohanaru in a strange venue, in strange positions, with a woman who is in various stages of undress. Mohanaru himself first claimed that he had been kidnapped, forcibly photographed, and blackmailed, then later revised his story to say that he had been ambushed after voluntarily going to the apartment (where the photographs were taken) for the unremarkable, if unblinkingly elitist, purpose of collecting a new servant.[39] The Travancore Devaswom Board quickly removed him from the priestship rotation on the grounds that he had filed a false police complaint alleging that he had been attacked.[40]

Although many of his relatives have regularly sparred with the TDB and the Government of Kerala over the specifics of temple administration, Mohanaru stands apart for the explicitly legal and often nearly criminal nature of his engagements with the state. The '*tantri* attack' scandal, which could not have been better constructed for daytime consumption had it been commissioned by *Stardust*, would not be Mohanaru's last. In 2019, the Kerala High Court ordered him to pay ₹30 lakh as restitution to his widowed mother, who had accused Mohanaru of draining her bank accounts and of secretly selling off her car.[41] That judicial directive came less than a year after Mohanaru had finally been returned to the priestship rotation, which, in the years between 2006 and 2018, had circulated among his cousin, his father, and (during the last years of his father's life) his own twenty-something son. Because of this long absence from the position of ultimate ritual authority, Mohanaru is the Thazhamon priest least associated with a lawsuit whose genesis lies in a writ petition that was, in fact, filed during his tenure.

Admittedly, beginning in the second half of 2006 and for nearly three and a half years afterwards, *no* Thazhamon priest was required to trouble himself very much about the actress or the astrologer, both of whom had seemingly vanished into the triplicate lumberings of Indian bureaucracy. A year after the *devaprasnam*, in June 2007, the powerful Nair Service Society (NSS) attempted to revive the scandal by publicly demanding to see documentation that, it claimed, the Kerala State Police had long since submitted to the government.[42] What had the investigators found, the NSS demanded—and what did they intend to do?

What was to be done with Jayamala depended, of course, on what *she* was held to have done, and this changed for the police just as, albeit somewhat more slowly than, it has changed for the public. Curiously enough, the FIR filed in 2007 suggested that Jayamala was not responsible for defiling the temple whose premises were said to have been compromised by her presence. Instead, the document omitted Jayamala's name altogether and charged the astrologer and one of his aides with violating §120(B) ('criminal conspiracy') of the Indian Penal Code, and §295, which prohibits the destruction, damaging, or defilement of 'any place of worship, or any object held sacred'.[43] Almost anyone who touched the divine image would have defiled it—temple deities only entertain physical contact from a highly circumscribed set of individuals—but Jayamala would have been especially unwelcome since she was in her late twenties when she ostensibly stumbled into Sabarimala's inner sanctum and fell at Ayyappan's feet. Within just four days of the NSS outcry, the Kerala Police had filed the initial step in a criminal investigation, the ubiquitous First

Information Report.[44] Matters thus seemed poised for a revival—but, for the time being, the Jayamala scandal remained dormant.

Then, between September and December of 2010, for reasons I have sought but never discovered, the police acted again. They submitted a second FIR in which they replaced one of the original three accuseds (a Sabarimala administrator) with Jayamala herself, and, perhaps bowing to the widespread conclusion that Jayamala could not have actually visited Sabarimala, they altered the substantive charge from §295 to §295(A). Even if the actress and the astrologer had not *actually* defiled the temple, these new charges implied, they had nonetheless acted with the 'deliberate and malicious intention of outraging the religious feelings of any class of citizens of India'.

Section 295(A), an early twentieth-century addition to a mid-nineteenth-century penal code, shares with many Indian statutes a reputation for being the misguided calcification of once-relevant norms. But whereas some of India's dated statutory provisions invite ridicule—the *Factories Act*'s spittoon mandate is a perennial favourite[45]—§295(A), like the now-circumscribed anti-sodomy provision contained in §377, more often prompts fear or sadness in certain, increasingly silenced, corners of India. In relatively recent memory, Hindu sentiments have been wounded by proposals to cut through an underwater pebble bridge said to have been built by the god Rama, by unwed couples celebrating Valentine's Day, by the paintings of M. F. Hussain, the fiction of Perumal Murugan, and the academic writings of, among others, Wendy Doniger, James Laine, and A. K. Ramanujan.[46] Moreover, because hurting religious sentiments need not involve any underlying offences like trespass or theft, which tend to involve specific sequences of behaviour and easily identifiable victims, §295(A) facilitates legal actions that require courts to speak to otherwise non-criminal acts.

The 2010 charges against Jayamala and the astrologer were followed by a complicated game of jurisdictional ping-pong that, although occasionally followed by the news media, was decidedly overshadowed by a stampede that killed over 100 pilgrims during Sabarimala's 2010–11 *mandalam-makaravilakku* season. When I began observing sessions at the Kerala High Court in January 2011, the Government of Kerala had just granted the police permission to proceed with its investigation of the Jayamala incident despite the thorough disregard this would involve for any plausibly applicable statute of limitations. During the roughly five months I attended hearings at the High Court, as well as the months when I was conducting archival and other research elsewhere in Kerala and India, the parties sparred over the precise moment at which the police ought to have brought their charges, and the venue of their disagreement moved from the state government to the High Court to a magistrate judge and back to the High Court. The sheer number of times the Jayamala scandal died, was revived, and died again would be striking and not a little indicative of its underlying appeal in the context of *any* judicial system, let alone India's profoundly overburdened one. And yet, notwithstanding this impressively phoenix-like activity, the final stages of the debacle involving the actress and the astrologer garnered little more than a few perfunctory articles in the regional news media. Keralite journalists were far too busy following a parallel struggle between the High Court, state government, TDB, and the police, over the cause and consequence of the January stampede—a process that had itself been transmogrified from a sober bureaucratic endeavour into a spectacular judicial event.[47]

Precisely the opposite of this happened during the tail end of the Jayamala scandal—although, in keeping with the determinedly regenerative nature of disputes over women's entry at Sabarimala, it happened twice. In April 2011, the Kerala High Court dismissed the charges against Jayamala in light of the Kerala State Police's leisurely approach to mounting them. A magistrate judge then resuscitated the proceedings that June, after which, in July 2012, the Kerala High Court quietly dismissed, for the last time as it turned out, all charges against the actress. Justice Satheesachandran sounded not a little weary of the statute of limitations debates that had preoccupied earlier stages of the litigation and at least two of his fellow judges. Instead of asking, once again, whether the police had acted with sufficient speed, Satheesachandran focused on whether the 2010 FIR laid out factual allegations that were sufficient to support a charge under §295(A) and concluded that it had not. *However* probable it was that her faxed admission was a complete falsehood, and Satheesachandran certainly supposed it to be so, and *however* indisputable it was that this falsehood had hurt the sentiments of Ayyappan devotees, falsity and feelings by themselves did not satisfy §295(A)'s requirements. Since the Kerala State Police report gave no indication that Jayamala had *intended* to hurt the religious sentiments of

Ayyappan devotees, neither she nor the astrologer were subject to prosecution under a provision that spoke only of intentional conduct. In this way, a full six years after the *devaprasnam* had occurred and the *IYLA* petition had been filed, the Jayamala scandal came to an abrupt conclusion.

But before that finale could come to pass, Jayamala's travails raised one more issue that, like the *IYLA* litigation itself, would eventually carry unanticipated significance. In the latter half of 2011, the matter of her prosecution was still bouncing around between the Kerala High Court, the Ranni Magistrate's tribunal, and the Home Department of the Government of Kerala. After the Ranni Magistrate demanded her appearance, Jayamala petitioned the High Court for relief yet again.[48] Besides the usual arguments about delayed prosecution, she offered an additional explanation as to why the charges against her should be dismissed: she was guilty of no wrongdoing, stated her petition, because in 1987 Sabarimala's ban against women had not acquired any legally protected status.[49] That would only come four years later, when the High Court began hearings in a public interest case that eventually culminated in the *Mahendran* opinion and its recognition of Sabarimala's ban as an essential religious practice.

Jayamala's arguments were simultaneously inventive and perplexing, since §295(A) does not suppose that religious sentiments can only be hurt where religious beliefs or practices already enjoy specific legal recognition. Indeed, the recent past of §295(A) litigation is dominated by peoples' propensity to have feelings about things that could not possibly be the subject of essential practices jurisprudence. Moreover, Jayamala's suggestion that *Mahendran* did not establish the ban as an *always already* essential element of Ayyappan worship flew in the face of what *Mahendran* itself claimed to have done.

Neither of the two High Court judges who, in 2011, were on the receiving end of this particular argument engaged with it in their interim or final dispositions of her case, so we know even less about their views on its merits than do most lawyers dealing with most judicial pronouncements. Nevertheless, the questions that Jayamala's argument raised—namely, when, and with what consequences, does a specific religious practice become legally 'essential'—asked the judiciary to *own* its powers of definition when it comes to the religious lives of Indian citizens. In

2012, the Kerala High Court would decline to do so in Jayamala's case, but in 1991, when it had been confronted with a dispute explicitly about the nature and extent of Sabarimala's ban, the High Court had proven far less reticent.

* * *

It is in the nature of things, both anthropological and legal, that the Jayamala episode should have come to be largely omitted from analysis of the Sabarimala dispute. Anthropologists, once notorious for their fascination with ritualistic minutiae, are now equally bewitched by the routine and the ordinary in ways that do not easily accommodate a tabloid-worthy scandal extending over half a decade and peopled by priests, actresses, astrologers, and politicians. Lawyers, meanwhile, continue unabated in their particular regard for that, and only that, which moves the precedential needle or, at the very least, for that which expands the documentary record. The Jayamala episode satisfies neither of these necessary conditions: it was directly responsible for only a few short judicial orders that are scattered across legal databases like so much electronic detritus and are rarely if ever authoritative according to the canons of Indian jurisprudence.

Nonetheless, Jayamala's story ought to figure importantly in the dispute over women's entry. It prompted the Indian Young Lawyers Association to file the public interest petition critiquing Sabarimala's ban and eventually resulting in its official, if not entirely successful, prohibition. It surfaced, for the first time since *Mahendran*, and sometimes for the first time altogether, arguments that would be more fully developed during the *IYLA* litigation, including the view that the ban reflected the unique preferences of Ayyappan-at-Sabarimala and that the custom was pro-men rather than anti-women. It made amply clear that Sabarimala's ban was not to be dismissed as the unusual practice of an unusual temple in a still more unusual state—that it was, in both impact and interest, an all-India affair. Above all else, the Jayamala episode aired questions that hang uneasily over all phases of the women's entry dispute and, indeed, over all disputes over essential practices. On whose authority is essentiality identified? Is essentiality retrospective? And what exactly is the nature of the protection afforded by designation as an essential religious practice— or, which is to ask much the same thing, what are the consequences of violating a practice that has been deemed essential? Jayamala's story, though it answered none of these questions, ensured that they would live on into the next phase of the women's entry dispute by connecting the *IYLA* case with the *Mahendran* litigation that had occurred some twenty-five years earlier.

5

The Rule

Krishnaswami Sundara Paripoornan was a one-man event in the recent life of Keralite temples. Paripoornan, who began his career as a civil and tax attorney, was appointed to the Kerala High Court in 1982, went on to become Chief Justice of the Patna High Court in 1994, and eventually sat on the Supreme Court between 1994 and 1997. A quick search on one of the electronic databases housing Indian case law might suggest that he spent his time on the bench writing nothing but tax law opinions and his time off the bench appearing—as the petitioner—in land acquisition cases against the state of Kerala. In fact, however, he was widely known for his interest in and knowledge of Hinduism.

When I met Paripoornan in Kochi, in 2011, he had been living in remarkably active retirement for almost fifteen years. Both the Kerala High Court and the Indian Supreme Court had periodically appointed him to lead commissions to or oversee administrative tasks related to the management of religious institutions, and in the course of fulfilling these roles, he had produced comprehensive reports on temple governance in Kerala that I was instructed to acquire and read. His assistants reverently referred to him as *S[w]ami* ('lord') and chuckled appreciatively or clucked indignantly, as appropriate, in response to everything he said regardless of whom it was said to. Paripoornan himself held forth on the subject of temple governance with a fluency and a sly humour that were only a little marred by my periodic attempts at asking him questions. He offhandedly dismissed one of his own reports ('bad English'), abruptly telephoned the High Court registrar and instructed him to give me access to yet another one of his reports ('the Chief [Justice] will give permission'), and creatively misquoted Sir William Blackstone's *Commentaries* on the nature and types of perpetual minors in order to support one of his arguments.[1]

In between these diversions, Paripoornan conveyed, in no uncertain terms, that it had been both his privilege and his great pleasure to whip

Kerala's system of temple administration from a state of unmitigated corruption into something approaching acceptability. He happily reminisced how, during the last five to six years of his tenure at the Kerala High Court and at the request of the court's Chief Justice, he 'was regularly interfering in many matters' relating to temple governance.[2] He chuckled as he observed that his reports now bind the temple boards 'hand and foot'.[3] Over and over again, Paripoornan recounted how he had used the High Court's limited and statutorily defined powers to bootstrap its authority into other aspects of temple governance. And although his expansive understanding of judicial responsibilities and prerogatives would, even in India, now likely meet with critical reception—to say nothing of how that attitude would fare in countries where disavowals of activist adjudication are required political theatrics—Paripoornan's views were once commonplace inside and outside Indian courts.

From their inception in 1950 until Paripoornan's involvement in 1984–85, Kerala's temple boards were merely (and, one imagines, inconsistently) subject to a financial audit by the High Court. Because he viewed this minimalist intervention as 'absolutely a show' and because he believed that 'he who controls the purse controls everything', Paripoornan worked to extend judicial oversight to virtually everything involving public Hindu temples in contemporary Kerala.[4] Indeed, although Keralite temples are subject to three distinct forms of state oversight, and although the balance of power between these various authorities shifts with time and personnel changes, ties often go to the High Court. This is largely the product of Paripoornan's efforts.

In the first of these three regulatory systems, five geographically defined statutory boards oversee the daily operations of several thousand public temples in Kerala, institutions that range in size from roadside altars to influential pilgrimage centres like Sabarimala. (Private temples often also have administrative boards, but although these may interact with the state, they are not themselves statutory bodies.) The public temple boards are rich—richer than any other statutory body in the state—and they are influential because of the control they wield over valuable state contracts and temple jobs. Three of these boards (Travancore, Cochin, and Malabar) are named for the erstwhile political divisions of Kerala, while the other two, Guruvayur and Koodalmanikyam, are each responsible for a single major temple along with some subsidiary shrines. By far the most prominent of the boards is the one discussed most often throughout this book: the Travancore Devaswom Board, which, by itself, controls over 1,000 temples. Sabarimala, the highest earning temple within the TDB's purview, earns about as much as all forty-two public sector undertakings operated by the State of Kerala.[5]

Second, the state government includes a cabinet-level temple portfolio. This person, the Minister for Devaswom Affairs, oversees a statewide Devaswom Department and liaises with the temple boards. The Minister exerts much less influence over the TDB, with which he jointly supervises some subsidiary offices, than he does over the other boards, although the power-sharing dynamics of all these collaborations are also constantly shifting.[6] For example, a 'Devaswom Commissioner' was for some time appointed by the TDB with the High Court's approval, but later on the TDB circumvented the court and appointed the commissioner in conjunction with the state government.

Beyond these quick sketches, it is hard to say much with certainty about either the boards or the ministry. The task of ascertaining exact figures or institutional dynamics in the world of Keralite temple management is sometimes Borgesian and sometimes Orwellian, but it is always one or the other. I have, for instance, long since stopped trying to determine exactly how many temples are subject to the TDB's authority: this figure, as it appears on the board's website, in scholarly estimates, in reports commissioned by the High Court, and in the comments of a former Devaswom Minister, varies by as much 300 temples. Similarly, when I was circulating within the High Court in 2011, lawyers who were then representing or who had previously represented four of the five boards told me that neither the Cochin nor Malabar boards had much control over temples within their jurisdictions and, by way of partial explanation, gave me to understand that both these boards were smaller and poorer than the TDB. But just one year later, in 2012, the *Times of India* reported that Malabar was the largest board in terms of the absolute number of temples under its authority, and that both Malabar and Cochin had revenues of at least ₹50 crores (500 million), which is not quite $7 million in 2020 American dollars.[7] Admittedly these figures pale in comparison with some of the other boards and even with some individual temples—before the coronavirus pandemic, Sabarimala alone earned around ₹200 crores annually—but they nonetheless fit awkwardly with the image of cash-strapped, limited governance in Cochin and Malabar that I encountered during my fieldwork.

The third and final layer of state oversight is, of course, judicial. The Chief Justice of the Kerala High Court appoints two colleagues—usually one junior and one senior judge, as with division benches of the Supreme Court—to the 'temple bench', which sits twice weekly to hear matters for all public temples in the state. During our first meeting, Paripoornan noted with some disappointment that the High Court's involvement in temple management had quietened down, but to me it appeared both active and varied.[8] On a single day of hearings—9 March 2011—the temple bench considered matters ranging from the exceedingly minute (approving a replacement chauffeur for the TDB's president) to the administrative (determining whether local police may lease office space within temple grounds) to the quasi-religious (assessing the relative monetary share, from devotee offerings, of a junior priest who also performs the duties of a senior priest) to the ontological validity of religious beliefs (investigating whether phenomenon associated with Sabarimala's pilgrimage season is man-made or an exercise in divine communication).

The breadth and depth of this judicial involvement in Keralite temple affairs is, as I have already said, due in no small part to Paripoornan's efforts. His determination to impose discipline on corrupt or ineffectual government officials was considerable, and it extended beyond temple administration and even beyond his tenure at the Kerala High Court. A judicial colleague who had worked alongside him in both Kochi and Delhi recalled how Paripoornan 'introduced to the high court the practice of summoning government secretaries directly to the court if orders are not implemented'.[9] The colleague went on to note, somewhat wistfully, that 'secretaries used to be afraid to appear before him'—before adding, more wistfully still, that 'summoning of government officials to court proved to be very effective during [Paripoornan's] time'.[10]

Paripoornan would have been tremendously pleased by this recollection, blunt though it was. He himself did not tend towards being mealy mouthed: one of the last reports he authored (the one that was insufficiently attuned to the Queen's English) accused the TDB of 'mismanagement, maladministration, nepotism and proven incompetence and indiscipline'.[11] He may even have been pleased by the markedly different interpretation of his judging that was articulated by my courthouse guide, Mangot, an interpretation that was punctuated by words like 'arrogant' and 'dangerous'.[12] At one point or another over a fifteen-year judicial career as well as another fifteen years of nominal retirement, Paripoornan may well have merited either or both of those epithets in his drive to render the internal functions of Keralite temple boards standardized, transparent, and accountable to another branch of government. Certainly, these qualities were not altogether absent from the 1991 opinion, issued by a two-judge bench on which Paripoornan sat as the senior member, that first declared Sabarimala's ban on women to be an essential religious practice.

5.1 Babies, Bundles, and Books

S. Mahendran v. the Secretary, Travancore Devaswom Board began its life like very many other constitutional disputes in late twentieth- and twenty-first-century India: as an informal communication that was converted into a PIL petition. The named petitioner, Mahendran, sent a complaint to Paripoornan alleging that women in the prohibited age range were visiting Sabarimala and that the wives of VIPs were being given 'special treatment'.[13] He included as proof a newspaper photograph dated 19 August 1990; the photograph showed a former Devaswom Commissioner, S. Chandrika, at Sabarimala along with her daughter, infant grandson, and several female relatives for a rice-feeding ceremony marking the baby's first intake of solid foods. Mahendran asked Paripoornan to do something about the blatant violation of temple custom.

Paripoornan acted with what amounts to lightning speed in the Indian judicial system. Less than five weeks after the photograph in Mahendran's clipping had been published, his complaint came up for hearing at the High Court. Not ten days after that, Chandrika, the TDB, and Mahendran himself all appeared in person. Within a further three weeks, on 26 October 1990, a second hearing was held at which an *amicus* was appointed to act for Mahendran. Nine witnesses were called to speak at this hearing regarding temple custom, and seven were actually heard. As the case progressed, it collected a handful of intervenors: a temple advocacy group joined Mahendran on the petitioner's side, while the Kerala branch of the Indian Federation of Women Lawyers (IFWL) joined

Chandrika, the TDB, and the State of Kerala on the respondent's side. The *Mahendran* opinion itself was issued within an impressive eight months of the newspaper article's publication.

Because I was unable to access the litigation materials submitted by the *Mahendran* litigants, the summary of arguments that follows is based on the final opinion issued by Paripoornan and his colleague, Balanarayana Marar. As such, this discussion necessarily reflects little of the perspectival multiplicity favoured by anthropologists or the copious documentation favoured by lawyers, although I have tried to approximate both as best I can. Moreover, judicial opinions are no more dispassionate statements of law and fact than the litigation materials on which they draw, and this one—for the reasons I have just articulated as well as some that are still awaiting discussion—may well demand more than usually generous saline seasoning for the analysis below.

Chandrika, who was, of course, no wife of a VIP but a VIP in her own right, argued that she had neither violated any customs nor abused her own authority. All female commissioners are over fifty years old at the time of their appointment, she noted, so she herself was outside the prohibited age range. Her daughter *was* within the range but had enjoyed no special favour: other women, who were presumably not the children of VIPs, had been conducting similar ceremonies for their babies on the very day that Chandrika's family had visited Sabarimala. For good measure, Chandrika added that not one of them had violated temple custom because they had all been present in August and the prohibition against women applied only during other, select periods—during the pilgrimage season in November–January and on Vishu, in April.

Paripoornan and Marar appear to have either accepted Chandrika's arguments as to her own and her daughter's wrongdoing or to have lost interest in the specific circumstances that gave rise to the PIL petition because the rest of their opinion is concerned with far more abstract issues, including the nature of the ban and its constitutionality in light of Articles 15, 25, and 26. Although this means that the opinion in *Mahendran* has less to do with the specific violation of a norm that prompted the High Court's enquiry than with the evaluation of that norm writ large, this distance between origin and outcome does not make *Mahendran* unusual. Indeed, Chandrika's disappearance from the litigation is of a piece with well-established trends in Indian adjudication: for decades now, scholars have noted, the PIL petitioner has been disappearing from PIL cases.[14] The 'public-spirited individual' of the 1970s and 1980s rapidly became 'merely an informant' who was able to speak *of* the people but not *for* them, before transforming yet again into just one more of the many 'impediments to justice' plaguing the country's judges.[15] From the mid-1990s onwards, PIL petitioners were often simply displaced, supplanted by lawyers who would serve as *amicus curiae* and who would continue on with the cases even after the petitioners themselves might have wished to end them.

Overall, the respondents—Chandrika, the TDB, the State of Kerala, and the IFWL—made four arguments. Thirty years later, these arguments range from the curious and largely forgotten to the immediately recognizable. Indeed, two of the *Mahendran* respondents' arguments did much more than merely survive into the *IYLA* phase of the dispute: they went on to define it.

First among these was the objection, widely considered standard in essential practices cases and given pride of place in the *IYLA* majority opinions, that a practice cannot be so very essential if it has not always been observed, with the *always* referring to both duration and consistency. This standard is nearly, albeit not categorically, impossible to meet. Many things, according to Indian courts, have indeed persisted 'since time immemorial', including entire villages, some usufruct rights, and even select practices for the draining of household waste water, so that it seems to follow quite inevitably that essential religious practices, in order to be *essential* religious practices, ought to have done likewise.[16] Notwithstanding the potential inappropriateness of applying a single standard to waste water and faith traditions, the expectation of unbroken eternity is now baked with crisp perfection into in the Essential Practices Doctrine.

Other religious communities have discovered this to be true after legal travails even more spectacular than those of Ayyappan devotees. The adherents of Ananda Marga ('Path of Bliss'), for instance, a spiritual organization that originated in the mid-twentieth century and is headquartered in West Bengal, learned over the course of a multi-decade litigation process that essential practices must have existed *and* must have been essential to a religion since time immemorial or since the religion's founding, whichever occurred first. The practice that Ananda Margis were fighting to preserve was their *tandava* dance, in which practitioners re-enact the vigorous, cosmic dance of Nataraja (a depiction of Shiva) while carrying a human skull, a live snake, and a trident. Much of the time, Ananda Margis perform their *tandava* in private, but on occasion they process publicly and *en masse*, to the consternation, several years ago, of polite Calcuttan society, and consequently the group received an interdiction by Calcutta's Commissioner of Police.

After the Supreme Court held that the *tandava* dance was not an essential practice of the Ananda Marga faith and so could be proscribed (at least in public) by the Commissioner, the community's founder revised its seminal text, the *Carya Carya*, to describe the dance as such.[17] The Court was not amused. It noted that Ananda Marga had existed as a religious community for over a decade before the *Carya Carya* was altered and added sternly that 'subsequent alterations' to religious texts or doctrine would reduce the judicial process 'into a useless formality and futile exercise'.[18]

During the *Mahendran* litigation, the respondents adopted precisely this kind of logic to argue for the non-necessity of Sabarimala's ban. They suggested that a total prohibition of women aged ten to fifty could not really be essential to Ayyappan worship at Sabarimala because women in that age range had been openly visiting the temple for some considerable length of time. Indeed, there was documented proof—in the form of TDB receipts for rice-feeding ceremonies—that the authorities *knew* women aged between ten and fifty were visiting Sabarimala and had even charged them fees for the services they had procured there.[19] The respondents also argued that the last queen of Travancore was known to have visited the temple in the year 1115 M.E. (1939–40).[20] And indeed, stories of female Travancore royals visiting Sabarimala are common enough that it is easy to imagine how, for much of the twentieth century, it was possible for some women in the prohibited age range to openly enter the temple.[21] The *Mahendran* respondents, like the *IYLA* petitioners who came after them (and the four justices on the *IYLA* majority), maintained that any such deviations from continuous and exhaustive observation signalled the ban's ancillary nature to the core of Ayyappan worship.

Second, the *Mahendran* respondents argued that various legislative enactments made access to temples a particularly strong default rule subject only to some limits that either did not or should not apply to Sabarimala. This was the statutory law that, during the *IYLA* phase of the dispute, received particular attention from both the plurality opinion written by Chief Justice Misra and the majority opinion authored by Justice Chandrachud. In 1991, as in 2018, the discussion of statutory law turned on two points: how to rank order the plural and often mutually conflicting elements of a single statute, and how to understand the phrase 'section or class of Hindus'.

In *Mahendran*, the High Court emphasized a proviso over a rule, and a rule over a proviso. First, the court held that §3 of the *Kerala (Authorisation of Entry) Act*, which allowed all Hindus into places of public Hindu worship, was overridden by one of its provisos, which empowered denominational institutions to restrict access as they saw fit. Because the process of statutory interpretation is a bit like reading a children's choose-your-own-adventure gamebook—one choice often and not always pleasantly leads to the next—it should come as no surprise whatsoever that the Supreme Court, which arrived at a different conclusion about the ban, also arrived at a different conclusion on the first of these issues. After all, §3 could not possibly be superseded by a proviso empowering denominational temples if, as the *IYLA* plurality maintained (and the other majority justices believed but did not assume), Ayyappan devotees were not a denomination unto themselves.

At the same time, the *Mahendran* court held that §4 of the *Authorisation of Entry Act*, which enabled trustees of public temples to make regulations for the observance of rites and ceremonies, did not give way to one of *its* provisos forbidding discrimination against particular sections or classes of Hindus. It may be less self-evident that the Kerala High Court and Supreme Court should disagree on the matter of §4, but in fact this is no more surprising. Section 4 and its proviso turn on one's view of women, or more specifically on one's view of Hindu women who might wish to visit Sabarimala but are constrained against doing so, and still more specifically, they depend on one's view as to whether these women constitute a 'section or class' of Hindus. The *Mahendran* judges looked to the definition of 'section or class' in §2(c) of the *(Authorisation of Entry) Act*, saw that it encompassed 'any division, sub-division, caste, sub-caste, sect, or denomination whatsoever', and decided that none of these accurately described Hindu women aged ten to fifty desirous of visiting the temple. The *IYLA* majority looked to the same definition in §2(c) and decided otherwise. Statutory interpretation is not always so thoroughly in the eye of the beholder, and, as some of the *IYLA* justices observed, other elements of the *(Authorisation of Entry) Act* support their interpretation of exactly how the *Act* should be applied to Sabarimala's admissions policies.[22] Nevertheless, to the eternal consternation of people who are not professionally obligated to worry about things like comma placement in book-length statutes or the myriad implications of the word *notwithstanding*, this kind of interpretive divergence is almost as reasonable as it is common.

These two arguments, on the consistent observation of essential practices and the interpretation of statutory prose, went on to command significant attention during the *IYLA* litigation. However, the *Mahendran* respondents also made two other arguments that received considerably less traction in subsequent phases of the dispute. The respondents' third contention, regarding transformations in customary practice (rather than the non-observance of customs) itself appeared in two iterations.[23] On the one hand, the *Mahendran* respondents maintained that Sabarimala's original policy had, at least until 1950, been one of universal entry. A major fire that year prompted both renovations to the physical infrastructure of the temple and changes in the ritual practices observed there—including, the respondents suggested, the rules governing female pilgrims. In the alternative, the respondents argued that Sabarimala's ban had been motivated by practical concerns about the difficulty of visiting the temple, and those concerns were obsolete in an era where better roads and transportation simplified the once-arduous trek to its hillside location.

Finally, the *Mahendran* respondents argued that even if (and contrary to the first and third arguments) the ban was a long-standing custom motivated by essential religious concerns, it was never meant to be in effect year-round. Chandrika, the TDB, and the State of Kerala all agreed that the ban only applied during the pilgrimage season and Vishu because those were the only times of year when worshippers were required to undertake the forty-one-day penance that enabled them to carry the *irumudikettu*, the bundle of votive offerings tied on at the beginning of the pilgrimage. At other times of year, no bundle and no penance were required, and therefore neither was any exclusion of women aged ten to fifty.

Someone seems to have gone even further by suggesting to the High Court that, even during the pilgrimage season and Vishu, the *irumudikettu* and the penance that it signalled only limited devotees' access to the eighteen golden steps leading up to the front entrance of the temple. The steps are visually and ritually integral to Sabarimala. In the absence of many other architecturally compelling features that are common to south Indian temples, most photographs of Sabarimala feature the metallic brilliance of either the steps or the temple's gold-plated roof. More importantly, the ascension of each one represents a specific stage in the devotee's spiritual evolution on the way to reaching Ayyappan himself. Nevertheless, the respondents apparently argued, another entrance—the 'northern gate'—was available for those with bare, because bundle-less, heads. The forty-one days of ritual penance that stood between women in the prohibited age range were neither required all year nor required at all entrances.

The petitioners, who now officially included Mahendran and the president of the *Kshethra Samrakshana Samithi* ('Temple Preservation Association'), and who unofficially included the Raja of Pandalam, appearing as a witness, as well as the *amicus*, Balagangadhara Menon, acting for Mahendran, simply reiterated their normative stance. Whatever might be descriptively true of the practices obtaining at Sabarimala, they maintained, the prescriptive standard was one of total prohibition. Women's entry was not one of the areas in which ritual practice had changed after the 1950 fire. The rationale for excluding women ages ten to fifty was a religious objection to their fertility. And, finally, the objection to fertile women was not subject to carveouts based on either time or temple architecture. Deviations, in other words, did not imply dispensations.

Neither side drew support from sacred texts, a fact that is likely to be far more intriguing to historians of colonial India than to either anthropologists, who generally do not work with texts, or to scholars of religion, who know their limitations too well. The genesis of 'Hindu Law' as a concept, a collection of texts, and an analytic framework is by now so ingrained in the historiography of South Asia as to need no revisitation here; so too is its constitutive role with respect to colonial governance. From Warren Hastings' somewhat unusual opinion that Hindus possessed ancient written laws forming a coherent and contextually preferable system of governance, to William Bentinck and Thomas Macaulay's views on the relative paucity of native lifeways (and law-ways), Hindu Law was instrumental in the construction and manifestation of a theory of governance in British India. In turn, sacred texts were instrumental in constructing a theory of Hindu Law that has been largely adopted by the postcolonial state.

To colonial judges, a defined corpus of authoritative texts promised the kind of soothing uniformity that was missing from the chaotic diversity of Hindu customary practices. A stable textual canon would enable British judges to standardize their own practices when resolving native disputes, thus realizing a Common Law maxim of treating like cases alike for reasons of both fairness and expediency. Not coincidentally, a canon would also allow judges to rid themselves of the pesky, because untrustworthy, native courtroom advisors on whom they were otherwise reliant. Adding to all this, colonial officials and the philologists on whom they relied generally saw themselves—at least during this earlier, more 'Orientalist' period—as revivifying true religious norms that had been corrupted by centuries of poor enforcement and Eastern decadence.

But the works that were deemed 'Hindu Law texts' mostly belonged to the relatively small circle of Sanskrit *dharmasutra* and *dharmashastra* writings that were cited by native courtroom advisors, to the exclusion of hundreds of vernacular texts. Those Sanskrit canons, moreover, were classified, weighted, and used in ways that differed sharply from the very traditional practices that colonial officials were ostensibly concerned with preserving and reinvigorating.[24] Whereas, for instance, the British favoured *smriti* (tradition, 'remembered' texts like the *Laws of Manu*) over *shruti* (revelation, or 'heard' texts like the Vedas) and *nibandha* (annotated digests of *smriti* texts) over both, classical traditions tended to advise the opposite. And whereas the British favoured the direct application of *smriti* prescriptions to real-life circumstances, native practices emphasized *aachaara* ('customary law') that was applied in light of *dharmashastra* jurisprudence without necessarily being subject to its substantive and procedural dictates.

Setting aside, as one can only do in an academic context, the political, material, racial, and religious considerations behind these colonial manoeuvres, there is a kernel of fundamental difference between 'Hindu' and 'British' thought regarding the relative merits of oral versus written communication.[25] Hindu traditions have by and large accorded great status to oral preservation and transmission and, indeed, have often viewed oral communication as more exacting, more eternal, and more foundational than its written counterpart. This is how it comes about that the *Mahabharata*, which is loved, is being constantly reimagined and reinscribed in a multiplicity of languages, while the *Rig Veda*, which is revered, was kept safely and with remarkably little variation in the heads of those who committed its more than 350,000 words to memory even when Hindus 'had used writing for centuries'.[26] As an epistemic stance, this embrace of oral knowledge is just about as far away as one can get from contemporary and generically Western theories of knowing, according to which writing something down is an act of both memorialization and of validation. Moreover, colonial-era transformations to dispute resolution have left written knowledge as influential as its oral counterpart—and usually more so.

Given this legal and epistemological baggage, it may seem somewhat surprising that neither the petitioners nor the respondents in *Mahendran* sought support from sacred texts, but in fact their choice is easily explained. Put simply, the Sanskrit texts that might have otherwise figured prominently in the *Mahendran* hearings as well as in the High Court's final analysis simply do not exist with respect to Ayyappan and there are few 'if any' comparable vernacular texts.[27] What does exist amounts to a few indirect references in some of the major *purana*s, and even these allude merely to Sastha, or to the encounter between Shiva and Vishnu-as-Mohini that are integral to most variants of the Ayyappan story.[28] Absent the kind of unimpeachably Sanskritic authority to which Indian courts have habitually turned, and absent even very many vernacular texts that could stand, albeit inadequately, in their place, both the parties and the judges quite naturally turned to oral and personal testimony.

Just as surprising, but just as easily explained, is the opinion that was ultimately produced by Paripoornan and Marar. First, and seemingly in contravention of a long-standing preference for the old over the new in matters of religion, Paripoornan and Marar concluded that the length of time a religious practice had been observed conveyed nothing about its legitimacy. Second, and notwithstanding the fact that women aged ten to fifty had seemingly been visiting Sabarimala openly and with varying degrees of official acceptance for almost fifty years, the judges announced the ban on women to be an essential religious practice. Indeed, they did much more than this. Not only did Paripoornan and Marar affirm the ban's validity for the annual pilgrimage season and Vishu, they also officially extended it to cover *all* days on which the temple is open. That is, almost none of the jurisprudential conventions that I have just described—conventions that usually carry the day in disputes over religion—seemed to resonate with the *Mahendran* Court.

But despite its superficially perplexing approach to considerations of duration and consistency, the Kerala High Court's analysis actually reflects several long-standing practices in Indian jurisprudence. Like the colonial-origin corpus of Hindu Law that informs it, *Mahendran* subscribes to the notion that religious authenticity is best located not in observed behaviour, but by something—a text, a priestly utterance—that can be considered prescriptive. Thus it was that a declaration by then-*tantri* Kandararu Neelakantaru, to the effect that women aged ten to fifty should never have been visiting Sabarimala, overcame observations by parties (on both sides of the dispute) to the effect that women in the prohibited age range *had* been visiting Sabarimala.[29] And, like those same colonial-origin Hindu Law traditions, as well as like legislative efforts at both state and central levels, and—not least of all—like the work that Paripoornan himself had been pursuing throughout his judicial career, *Mahendran* also reflects a commitment to consistency and predictability. The governance structures discussed at the beginning of this chapter as well as the statutes discussed in Chapter 1, along with the case law and constitutional principles discussed throughout this book, are all testaments, variously motivated and variously successful, to a preference for uniformity that has long characterized Anglo-Indian jurisprudence on religion. That preference, it should be noted, also manifested itself to striking if opposite effect in *IYLA*.

Finally, *Mahendran*'s outcome reflects established jurisprudential preferences inasmuch as it worked to demarcate some aspects of social life as being beyond governmental influence—although much like the mid-century Supreme Court opinion to which it was most beholden, *Mahendran* managed to expand state authority in the course of restricting it. *Shirur Mutt*, which had first articulated the limiting principle of the Essential Practices Doctrine in 1954, did so *en route* to upholding the statute behind Madras State's massive infrastructure for temple governance. Similarly, in an apparently unasked-for show of judicial largesse,

Mahendran established new and expansive parameters for the very practice that had been determined to be so essential to Ayyappan worship at Sabarimala that the state could not interfere with it. The High Court's decision to standardize and universalize the ban to all times of year may seem like nothing more than further evidence of the impossibility of true religious freedom—assuming, of course, that freedom is understood in its conventionally liberal and negative sense as freedom *from*.[30] Expanding religious privilege, after all, is an exercise of authority no less than contracting it. Perhaps this means that the first of *Mahendran*'s achievements is how the opinion places yet another log on the pyre of liberal-democratic pretensions to religious neutrality by demonstrating, once more, that non-involvement in religious life is unrealizable within the nation-state framework.[31]

But granting constitutional validity for Sabarimala's ban, as *Mahendran* did, was intended to demarcate religion as a zone of citizen autonomy, and that intent—the *IYLA* petitioners would themselves later argue—compels acknowledgement. To be sure, the autonomy protected by the Kerala High Court was the autonomy of religious collectivities rather than of individual persons. Article 25(1) subjects individual claims to religious freedom to other fundamental rights, but the collective claims created by Article 26 make no similar concession.[32] It 'necessarily' follows, the High Court reasoned (albeit in carefully abstracted prose), that a woman's right to visit Sabarimala gives way to the right of the community saying she should not go. That community had affirmed the ban's essential nature, went the argument, and the community's views, in the eyes of the High Court, enjoyed 'complete autonomy'.

Even though few things in law *necessarily* follow from others, and even though *Mahendran* subordinated individual freedom to collective freedom, the High Court's analysis is worth marking. By mobilizing the Essential Practices Doctrine as it did, the Court proved itself responsive to a constitutional impulse that is sometimes weak and that is always overshadowed, but that nevertheless remains persistently present: the impulse to affirm the sovereignty of citizens in a democratic polity and to recognize their authority to, at least occasionally, hold the state at bay. *Which* citizens are affirmed and *how much* resistance they may engage in are worthy sources of debate and dissatisfaction; moreover, as the next chapter recounts, battles over inclusion and access that are now most commonly fought over gender were once regularly fought over caste.³³ But imperfect mobilization is mobilization all the same— and, as *Mahendran* suggested, intra-religious disputes are prone to zero-sum analysis. *Mahendran*'s shortcomings, like *IYLA*'s, were flaws of execution—not intent.

5.2 Invisibility, Then and Now

Among the scholars, lawyers, journalists, and general citizenry who are most concerned with the women's entry dispute, *Mahendran* has not aged well. *IYLA*, on the other hand, notwithstanding the utter failure of its intended impact on the world, has been generally well received. Consequently, and in obedience to my own contrarian inclinations, I have spent much of my time explaining the one and critiquing the other. Anthropological aversions to overt normativity can, like furtive glances from an angry parent, only impose so much restraint on even the most well-behaved practitioners, and considerably less on the rest of us.

And yet, none of this is to say that *Mahendran* is a good decision, while *IYLA* is a bad one. The core outcome in each of these moments— exclusion first, entry thereafter—was entirely reasonable in light of competing constitutional and administrative impulses. The nuances, in each case, were problematic. The Kerala High Court seemingly granted more than the petitioners had asked for by extending the ban year-round. The Supreme Court may have granted less than the petitioners had asked for, inasmuch parts of the opinion appear to emphasize the right of entry for *Hindu* women aged ten to fifty, while men of all faiths and all ages remained free to visit.³⁴ (What *exactly* the *IYLA* majority opinions made possible will undoubtedly become of greater interest when, in fact, any of it becomes possible.) Both opinions ignored lived practice, the one when it disregarded the persistent presence of women at the temple and the other when it discounted devotees' spiritual traditions and identity markers.

Some of these problems may not even be problems, since we do not know exactly what the *Mahendran* petitioners requested and we cannot, at least yet, know what the *IYLA* petitioners will ultimately receive. To the extent that they *are* problems, they do not take away from the fundamental reasonableness of either decision. Constitutional adjudication in India as elsewhere, indeed in India rather more than elsewhere, is a matter of forests over trees. These forests were, both of them, thick and green with possibility. The Indian Constitution *does* value a community's ability to define and administer itself, although in practice the lack of ministerial hierarchy often requires the state to play umpire. The Indian Constitution *does* value the dissolution and reform of proclivities that are as cruel as they may be culturally ingrained. The 'person' whose freedom of religion is protected by Article 25(1) is both the person seeking change and the one seeking stasis. This, in the proverbial nutshell, is what both *Mahendran* and *IYLA* forgot.

To put matters somewhat differently, those individuals who believe in the religious necessity of excluding some women from Sabarimala are as glaringly absent from *IYLA* as the women being excluded were missing from *Mahendran*.[35] *IYLA* transformed Ayyappan devotees into little more than the grounds of a (new and valuable) discourse on equality. To the extent that individual devotees actually figure in Chief Justice Misra's plurality opinion, they are 'just Hindus'[36]—people whose beliefs are insufficiently idiosyncratic to distinguish them from the breathtaking diversity of traditions expediently styled *Hindu*. *Mahendran*, by contrast, simply and literally renders women absent. The catalyst for the entire affair, Chandrika, is herself only named seven times in the entire opinion (five of those being on the first page) and is only indirectly referenced another two, perhaps three, times.[37] The only woman to appear in the opinion besides Chandrika is the attorney for the Indian Federation of Women Lawyers, who surfaces just three times.[38] There are no female witnesses cited—against the ban or otherwise—although no fewer than seven witnesses were heard and many of them were explicitly relied on by the High Court.[39]

Some of this imbalance in *Mahendran* was inevitable since Keralite *tantri*s are men, as are the actual, if not always the titular, heads of most Keralite royal families. But beyond their cursory inclusion in the text of the opinion, women are also and more disconcertingly absent from *Mahendran* at a conceptual level. Even though Paripoornan and Marar formally stipulate that one of the questions for consideration is whether 'the denial of entry ... amounts to discrimination', they never actually analyse the Article 25(1) rights of female devotees.[40] Instead, after briskly articulating the protections afforded to *all* individuals under Articles 15 and 25(1), the Paripoornan and Marar immediately observe that religious denominations are granted the freedom to manage their own affairs under Article 26. *Mahendran* also spares no thought for privacy or dignity concerns that may inhere in being excluded from a public place of worship on the basis of a sex-specific bodily function—a silence that is only partly attributable to the state of relevant jurisprudence in 1991.

Scholars of gender in South Asia have long noted how women are often 'neither subjects nor objects but, rather ... the site on which tradition [is] debated and reformulated' even when the traditions in question are ostensibly all about women.[41] The irony, then, is acute: some three decades after *Mahendran* was issued, the Supreme Court seemingly atoned for that opinion's indifference to women—to their rights, their views, and their concerns—by displaying much the same attitude towards devotees who supported Sabarimala's ban. By that time, however, the dispute over women's entry found itself in a world that was as strange as it was familiar. The forum to which it had moved on was an apex court peopled with embattled jurists who were also empowered by decades of new jurisprudence far more attentive to privacy and dignity concerns. And in a way that had been previously unimaginable, the individuals driving the dispute, from *both* sides, were women—only now, instead of being alleged trespassers or fraudulent publicity-seekers, they were lead petitioners, intervenors, and lawyers. They were also, as the next and final chapter shows, activists whose efforts outside the courtroom are simultaneously integral and frequently underemphasized in the story of the battle for Sabarimala.

6
The Protests

The beginning of the end, in the battle for Sabarimala, was marked by a tweet. In November 2015, Ayyappan and his most famous temple arrived, not quite triumphantly, in the social media feeds of thousands of individuals who may have been otherwise uninterested in Indian constitutional law. There they stayed, thanks to the simultaneous start of two very different social movements, led by two very different women, for nearly two years. By the time Ayyappan and Sabarimala ceased being a topic of hashtagged exchanges, the Supreme Court hearings were well underway and the *IYLA* opinion, although perhaps only a dozen people knew this, was within a few weeks of being released.

Few narratives of the *legal* dispute over women's entry seriously explore the roles played by these women, Nikita Azad and Trupti Desai, because, at least originally, neither of them was a party to the formal proceedings in *IYLA*.[1] But as both lawyers and anthropologists well know, formal law is a just one of the things that matter inside a courtroom—and, anyway, as the rest of this chapter demonstrates, the boundaries separating the courtroom from everything else are far more porous than either brick or brief would suggest. Azad and Desai were responding to circumstances shaped by law, spoke in a language that appealed to law, and confronted opponents whose authority was grounded in law, all before either of them participated in any explicitly legal action. In other words, they drew sustained and hitherto unprecedented attention to the *legal* as well as the *ethical* validity of Sabarimala's admissions practices. And, in the process of doing this, both women cast doubt on two propositions that have tended to carry the aura of axiomatic truth in India's legal universe.

The first of these truths, namely, that the Indian Supreme Court floats with unruffled probity above the self-interested and news-driven chaos characterizing Parliament, has admittedly been shaky for some time now. The transformation of the Court's signal progressive achievement—public interest litigation—into a tool for urban moralists and corporate interests, the growing frequency of corruption scandals involving its members, as well as their collective and increasingly petulant refusal to tolerate the least criticism or helpful suggestion has meant that the institution, as a whole, has lost a good deal of its once-considerable sheen. Nor has the Court been helped by the regularity with which recent Indian Chief Justices, not limited to Dipak Misra, have been exposed for personal or professional failures that would have gone virtually unnoticed in one of the country's parliamentarians but that remain, at least for the time being, shocking in a leader of its apex court.

Any discussion of these failings sits poorly with the Court, which has, after several decades of determinedly populist rhetoric (as well as some populist jurisprudence) become used to hearing itself lauded as 'the last resort for the oppressed and the bewildered'.[2] In the service of this image, India's most powerful jurists have begun self-consciously engaging with public discourse to an unprecedented degree and across a remarkable range of venues and media. They now hold press conferences to air their internal grievances, hastily and reluctantly convene Saturday sessions in response to journalistic furore over the bad behaviour of one of their colleagues, and issue contempt citations in response to social media criticisms by respected lawyers.[3] Consequently, and inevitably, the Court's reputation as an institution of sober good governance, one that is more concerned with the well-being of Indian citizens than their elected representatives tend to be, and also one that is better able to ignore the vicissitudes of public opinion—*that* reputation has taken a punishing hit.[4]

Though it has been little remarked, the Court's reaction to Azad and Desai coheres with its ongoing pursuit of public approbation. Chapter 3 noted that, after the *IYLA* writ petition was filed in 2006, the case periodically cropped up for short and inconsequential hearings until it was finally referred to a three-justice bench in 2008.[5] Even then, however, litigation remained stalled. It was not until January 2016, a scant two months after Azad and Desai's efforts had begun (less, if one factor in the weeks-long December holidays) that the Court began hearings in earnest. Anthropologists tend to eschew discussions of causality for the same reason that lawyers and economists are fond of them—they reduce complex social phenomena to one or two manageable nuggets of behaviour more suitable for further analysis—but there are coincidences and then there are coincidences. After almost ten years spent languishing in the convoluted and overburdened innards of India's apex judicial body, the Sabarimala dispute resurfaced with alacrity just weeks after two high-profile campaigns drew attention to the temple and to the problem of women's access to religious institutions more broadly. Within two years of Azad and Desai's involvement, a length of time that is dizzyingly short in the Indian judicial system, the Court delivered its *IYLA* opinion.

A second truth that emerged uncomfortably unsettled from the campaigns waged by Azad, Desai, and their supporters was the idea that the Constitution prohibits caste-based untouchability—or, more exactly, that it *only* prohibits caste-based untouchability. The constitutional abolition of untouchability (Article 17) and the related declaration that the state may open public Hindu religious institutions 'to all classes and sections of Hindus' (Article 25(2)(b)) have overwhelmingly and not-unreasonably been understood to address discrimination on the basis of caste. With few exceptions, the Court's early temple-entry cases, which were also among its most prominent religious freedom cases, concerned institutions that sought to portray themselves as *not* public, *not* Hindu, or *not either* as a way to continue their practices of excluding low caste or *avarna* individuals. Indeed, caste-based discrimination is so widely considered to be the deepest failing of Hindu society as well as the most formidable obstacle to Indian democracy that it is ceaselessly compared to anti-Black racism in the United States, a comparison that is just apt enough to seem miraculously fresh each time it is made.[6]

But—and this is news to no one who has in any way experienced or studied India—practices of untouchability and the ritual demarcations of purity and pollution on which they are based extend well beyond caste and beyond Hinduism itself. Untouchability is frequently observed among non-Hindus and between members of different faiths, not even excepting faiths that are nominally committed to the equality of all persons and to which some Hindus have turned in an effort to escape the strictures of casteism. Syrian Christians in Kerala, for instance, exchange food with Nairs as an expression of caste parity but only give food to *avarna* Hindu castes as well as to Latin Catholics, both of whom Syrian Christians view as their inferiors.[7] Similarly, a 2014–15 survey of Dalit Muslims in Uttar Pradesh asked interviewees about seating arrangements, serving order, plateware selections, and other food-related practices at feasts where both Dalit and non-Dalit Muslims were present, and the results left 'no room for any confusion that the practice of untouchability'—not just caste, but untouchability—is 'confined to Hindus alone'.[8]

If one of Hinduism's worst features has impacted members of other faith communities, Azad and Desai's campaigns made it abundantly clear to anyone still entertaining doubts on the matter that menstruation renders even *Hindu women* both briefly verboten and eternally suspect with respect to their ritual purity. The campaigns did this both explicitly (Azad) and implicitly (Desai), but in both cases the connection to caste was unmistakable. Most significantly, thanks to Azad, who had become one of the intervenor-applications, and also thanks to the Court-appointed *amicus*, the idea that differential treatment on the basis of menstrual pollution was not just embarrassing but could perhaps also be unconstitutional made its way into the Supreme Court hearings. As Chapter 3 noted, the concept and potential unconstitutionality of menstrual untouchability eventually appeared in three of the four *IYLA* opinions and found acceptance in the eyes of the eminently citable and eventual Chief Justice, D. Y. Chandrachud.

All of this thanks, in no small part, to two *social* movements.

6.1 #HappyToBleed

On 20 November 2015, a college student named Nikita Azad posted an open letter online.[9] The website where it appeared, *Youth ki Awaaz* ('Voice of the Youth'), floats creatively and uncommittedly in the space between newspaper, blog, and networking platform as 'a growing community of more than 75000 … where young Indians speak up, spread awareness and take action on issues that matter'. *Youth ki Awaaz*'s founder, Anshul Tewari, a charismatic thirty-something who started the website as a teenager, speaks eloquently of the need for citizen-led journalism and generational change. His website, which sorts articles into categories ranging from 'Campus Watch' and 'Careers' to 'Caste' and 'Disability Rights', has received recognition from the Obama Foundation, the Ashoka Foundation, and the International Telecommunications Union agency of the United Nations. It receives hundreds of submissions per day, according to Tewari, and has an archive of over 60,000 articles. But even within this sizable universe of commentary and exchange, Nikita Azad's letter as well as the nationwide movement it triggered stand apart: until recently, Azad's was one of just four success stories prominently featured on *Youth ki Awaaz*'s 'About' page.[10]

Azad's letter was responding to a speech, given on 13 November, by the then-recently inaugurated president of the Travancore Devaswom Board.[11] By all accounts, that speech should have disappeared quietly into the electronic ether: Prayar Gopalakrishnan was a long-time Congress Party worker, a one-time state legislator, and he was speaking to the press club of his hometown, Kollam. He was, in other words, an experienced political hand making a minor political appearance, and his party—although considered more progressive at the national level—was, in Kerala, the more conservative option and therefore firmly wedded to preserving the status quo regarding Sabarimala's ban. And yet, none of this seems to have helped.

When asked about Sabarimala's ban, Gopalakrishnan gave an answer that blended Hindu ritual with technoscientific fantasy in a way that would have seemed unexceptional had it come from a member of the BJP but was striking coming from a Congress stalwart. For some time now, Hindu nationalist conjurings of a gloriously scientific Indian past, one where sages conducted nuclear tests and demons operated airports, have simultaneously entertained and horrified newsrooms around the world. In 2019, *Caravan* magazine collected a list of the scientific wonders attributed to deities, cows, and the occasional Sanskrit epic protagonist that had been made, with surprising frequency, during the first administration of Prime Minister Modi (2014–19).[12] *Caravan*'s list is long and uncomfortably fascinating; by comparison, Prayar Gopalakrishnan's 2015 musings on the future of women at Sabarimala were more remarkable for the political affiliation of their author than for their imaginative flair:

> A time will come when people will ask if all women should be disallowed from entering the temple throughout the year. These days there are machines that can scan bodies and check for weapons. There will be a day when a machine is invented to scan if it is the 'right time' for a woman to enter the temple. When that machine is invented, we will talk about letting women inside.

Reactions to Gopalakrishnan's statement were plentiful and sounded in all the usual keys of amusement, bemusement, shame, indignation, and sarcasm. Nevertheless, it was Nikita Azad's letter, which nicely blended these standard responses with strains of both Hindu female respectability (*My parents always taught me how to bow in front of idols of numerous gods and goddesses*) and post-millennial critique (*I thank you for giving women an opportunity to get rid of the utopian-liberal discourse of freedom*) that garnered the most attention.

Azad's letter, which begins benignly enough, ends with a phrase—*young, bleeding woman*—whose unvarnished accuracy transformed it into a sensation in its own right as well as a kind of shorthand for the missive it concludes. In between salutation and signature, the *young, bleeding woman* reproaches her *Respected Sir* for perpetuating beliefs that have left her *dumbstruck* and *shattered*. Azad's focus is not so much on Sabarimala itself—*I have no interest in entering the temple, for I refuse to believe in a God that considers his own children impure*—as it is on the idea that menstruation is ritually polluting. Accordingly, although her direct questions and accusations are reserved for Gopalakrishnan alone, Azad tosses out observations about god-men, shopkeepers, upper caste communities, her parents, her brother, and society at large that are cutting in the way that only unintentional or incidental barbs can be. She is simultaneously dutiful and defiant, to excellent effect.

Three days after her letter appeared on *Youth ki Awaaz*, Azad published another statement clarifying her intentions, which she said were to mount a generalized critique of patriarchy and misogyny, and thanking readers for supporting the social media campaign that had materialized in response to her first missive.[13] Although only seventy-two hours had passed, Indian news websites were already awash in social media photographs of women holding up anything they could find—sanitary napkins, sheets of paper, placards, and even a paper lantern—that could be festooned with illustrations of blood drops and female reproductive organs and, above all, with the message #HappyToBleed.[14] Alongside this main campaign also appeared expressions of solidarity that endearingly, if sometimes awkwardly, repurposed marketing taglines (#OwnThoseFiveDays, originated by a prominent maker of feminine hygiene products) and political slogans (#LalSalam, or 'Red Salute', originally a form of greeting between communists).[15] *Youth ki Awaaz* reposted the original letter on the platform *Medium*, headquartered in San Francisco, and Azad started a petition on *Change.org* asking the National Commission for Women, a statutory body that advises the Government of India, to take a public stand on the issue of menstrual discrimination.[16]

Until this point, Azad's campaign had been conducted entirely online and largely on Twitter, which in India is not quite the powerhouse of everyday communication between ordinary people that it was, or claimed to be, in the United States.[17] Notwithstanding rapid internet and mobile phone penetration in India, and notwithstanding even the globally third-place size of India's Twitter population, social media penetration remains relatively low: few rural Indians use their phones for anything except the streaming of audio and video entertainment content and Twitter, in particular, has not really caught on.[18] The tweets of support greeting Nikita Azad's open letter may have signalled more popular, pan-India engagement with the Sabarimala dispute than it had ever before received, but that engagement came from a very particular type of Indian. So too did the inevitable response.

Hinduism and Hindutva have both done very well for themselves in the age of networked connectivity. There are now internet *puja*s and 'Internet Hindus'; the Prime Minister's @narendramodi account continues to fare impressively well among worldwide Twitter rankings (top three among political leaders, top ten overall), and the BJP finds its 'digital assets' so valuable that it has a team of paid workers dedicated to managing them with the help, as of 2017, of around 100,000 volunteers.[19] The war of catchy slogans that has burned consistently, if episodically, between Hindu nationalists and their vaguely progressive opponents has simply moved online, and it has done so without much impacting win-loss ratios that have generally favoured the Hindu nationalists. Thirty years ago, the BJP's rallying cry *Garv se kaho, hum Hindu hain* ('Say it with pride, we are Hindus!') inspired countervailing stickers on Mumbai trains that responded, with touching if minimally impactful determination, *Prem se kaho, hum insaan hain* ('Say it with love, we are human beings!'). Now, @narendramodi defiantly tweets *Main bhi chowkidar* ('I too am a watchman') in response to Rahul Gandhi's assertion that *Chowkidar chor hain* ('The watchman is a thief')—and Modi wins the exchange, if 3.2 million retweets in a single day are anything to go by.[20]

It was therefore unsurprising that Azad's #HappyToBleed campaign should be met with an opposing hashtag, #ReadyToWait. It was also unsurprising that the creators of #ReadyToWait would—like Azad—successfully petition the Supreme Court to be admitted as intervenor-applicants in the *IYLA* litigation. What was less foreseeable, however, was the thoroughness of the pro-ban response: not only was the war of the hashtags hard-fought and not very clearly won, but both sides enjoyed high-profile courtroom triumphs. Azad, represented by the awe-inspiring lawyer-scholar Indira Jaising and supported by the careful argumentation contained in Raju Ramachandran's *amicus* brief, transformed menstrual untouchability and the true scope of Article 17 into issues that three of the five *IYLA* justices felt obliged to consider. Several #ReadyToWait leaders, in turn, incorporated themselves in Chennai as a non-profit organization, People for Dharma, that received widespread recognition for making the inventive if inevitable argument discussed in Chapter 3—namely, that Ayyappan, too, enjoys constitutional rights.

6.2 Chingari

On 20 December 2015—exactly one month after Nikita Azad posted her open letter—a very different woman began a profoundly different campaign that nonetheless also owed much and did much to the dispute over women's entry at Sabarimala. When she began her movement for temple entry, Trupti Desai was in her early thirties, a homemaker, a vocally practicing Hindu, and, five years earlier, she had founded a community group called the Bhumata Brigade ('Mother Earth Brigade'). Until that point, the Brigade's efforts had been eclectic, ranging from protests against the rising price of onions to supporting the movement for a national *lokpal* ('people's ombudsman') bill to heckling and occasionally assaulting men accused of violent crimes against women. After the temple entry campaign concluded, Desai bent the group's attention to the task of making their home state of Maharashtra liquor-free. In the end, however, members of the Brigade have become best known as critics of a very specific type of gender discrimination.

Like the writ petition at the heart of *IYLA*, Desai's interest in temple entry was inspired by a newspaper article. She read that the priests at a temple in Shani Shingnapur, a village some three hours' drive away from her home in Pune, had conducted purification rituals after a woman was known to have entered the temple sanctum. On 20 December 2015, she and the Brigade travelled to the village and attempted to storm their way into the forbidden area. Although the Shani Shingnapur temple is as accessible as Sabarimala is remote—the temple is situated in a village, not a forest, and its central image is in an open plaza because the deity expressed a wish to have no roof above him except the sky—it was, as the Brigade discovered, nonetheless very well guarded. Desai and her co-workers returned to Pune without having achieved their goal of offering prayers in the area reserved for men.

In the final days of 2015 and throughout most of the following year, Desai and the Brigade continued their attempts to enter the Shani Shingnapur temple. They were hardly alone in their focus on women's entry; indeed, much like actresses visiting Sabarimala in the 1980s, Maharashtra in 2016 seems to have been teeming with activists fighting for women's access to religious institutions. On 1 April, for instance, Vidya Bal and Neelima Vartak won a PIL case challenging the exclusion of women at temples like Shani Shingnapur on the grounds that this practice violated the Maharashtra Hindu Place of Worship (Entry Authorisation) Act (1956).[21] In June of the same year, Noorjehan Safia Niaz and Zakia Soman won another PIL case challenging shifts in the admission policies of the Haji Ali *dargah* in Mumbai, which had previously allowed women access on par with men but began excluding them from the inner sanctum in 2011.[22] Press coverage simultaneously noted these victories and the fact that they were largely overshadowed by Desai's more spectacular forays into the same arena.

Bal, Vartak, Niaz, and Soman are women's rights activists in a well-established mode: they are educated, urban professionals for whom the judicial system represents an important ally in the fight for gender parity. In 2007, Niaz and Soman co-founded the Bharatiya Muslim Mahila Andolan ('Indian Muslim Women's Movement') as 'an autonomous, secular, rights-based mass organization led by Muslim women'.[23] The BMMA explicitly frames socio-economic development in the language of rights and constitutional principles. Meanwhile, Bal, who passed away in January 2020, had served for thirty years as the founder and editor-in-chief of multiple feminist publications. Although she was best known for her journalism, few of her obituaries failed to characterize her as a 'vigorous crusader' for an assortment of legal rights—euthanasia, women's public toilets, and women's temple entry among them.[24] And Vartak, who declared that she herself does not believe in 'publicly professing' her beliefs by engaging in temple worship, actually *is* an attorney.[25]

Trupti Desai was decidedly and unapologetically different.[26] To be sure, law was also integral to her Brigade's operations and Desai wore her knowledge of its workings like the proverbial coat of armour. She took her lawyers along to 'agitations' and confidently made declarations that 'in cases like ours'—meaning, in instances where public protests lead to police detentions—'the offence is bailable'.[27] During one of her later visits to Shani Shingnapur, she even wielded a copy of the Bombay High Court order won by Bal and Vartak, albeit to little effect since the temple remained cordoned off by a crowd of local residents and police officers.

And yet, despite this willingness to deploy law in the pursuit of her particular ends, Desai did not address herself *to* the law—to the principles of equality and freedom contained in the Constitution, to the broader language of human rights enshrined in international covenants, or to the courts charged with interpreting the one and considering the other. The equality she sought, and which in her eyes was violated by the practices of temples like Shani Shingnapur and Sabarimala, was divinely rather than legally mandated. 'I refuse to accept', she declared, 'this is what *the god* desired'.[28] More than activists like Bal and Vartak, who sought support in the courts for a right they did not personally want to exercise, more even than Nikita Azad, whose open letter was strewn with not only protestations of cultural compliance but also featured references to democracy and the disavowal of 'a God that considers his own children impure', Desai's understanding of the women's entry issue reflected a kind of politicized *bhakti*. 'I felt the pure joy of being close to God. That force directly empowers you. That's why women must get inside.'[29]

Desai's attitude towards the legal system was not all that set her apart from her more cosmopolitan counterparts. Journalists interviewing her during the height of her temple entry campaign could not unsee that old Indian trope, the clash between tradition and modernity, when they looked at her short hair and cropped coats, her media savvy, and her assertiveness, and then contrasted these with the 'pulp patriotism' of her kitschy cell phone ringtone, her lack of impressive educational or professional credentials, and her spirituality.³⁰ Her entirely conventional personal life (married, with one son) seemed to fit poorly with her decidedly unconventional willingness—and ability—to drive halfway across the state at a moment's notice in order to lead a dozen women in the literal siege of a religious institution. Her strategies and her very self were, equally, unusual in the world of Indian feminism. Small wonder then, that when Vidya Bal was asked about the woman who had tried to bodily implement the victory that she herself had won in court, Bal declared that although she found Desai to be a 'dashing and bold lady', their 'intellectual understanding' of women's issues diverged considerably.³¹

But if Trupti Desai did not fit comfortably in with other progressive activists pursuing women's entry in the mid-2010s, neither did she blend easily with the women who have, over the last several decades, come to constitute a major resource for Hindu nationalist politics. There are, to be sure, more than a few similarities. Desai is female but not feminine: her gender-neutral hair and clothes, along with the relative invisibility of her husband and child, invoke the kind of ascetic renunciation that has worked so well for Hindu nationalist women like Sadhvi Rithambara and Uma Bharati.³² Her loose but loyal network of mostly female followers echoes the 'matronage' systems characterizing women on the Hindu Right, as does her constant physical mobility and omnipresence. Indeed, it is hard to not read, in Vidya Bal's carefully crafted statement, an explicit nod to the female Hindutvavadis whose influence is especially strong in Maharashtra and who are known, even among themselves, as 'dashing ladies'.³³ Most telling is the consistency with which Desai avoids speaking in the secular-democratic idiom that is common to Bal, Vartak, Niaz, and Soman—an idiom that readily lends itself to arguments for gender parity. By her own admission, she was reaching for god, not equality, even if the one sometimes entails the other.

And yet, Desai is no Hindu nationalist. Not only has she determinedly eschewed affiliation with any of the right-leaning organizations littering Maharashtra, she also contrasts starkly with Hindu nationalists in substance, if not in style. Desai seems thoroughly uninterested in the nativist, 'sons-of-the-soil' messaging that is a defining characteristic of Hindu nationalism across India (where it is usually deployed against Muslims) and especially in Maharashtra (where it arguably originated and where it initially targeted non-Marathi speaking populations). Nor does she often appeal to a sense of shared Hindu culture, or to the notion, proffered by Hindu nationalists almost as frequently as the concept of a gloriously scientific past, that true—meaning Vedic—Hinduism is inherently feminist. Her arguments are individualistic, stressing personal agency and devotion, rather than being social or cultural and stressing collective wellbeing. She will not be found marching down the streets of metropolitan India shouting, like the saffronistas of the late twentieth century, about the fiery nature of Hindu womanhood.[34] If this focus on individuality coheres suspiciously well with the criticism, made regularly by former collaborators, that Desai is primarily concerned with her own fame, it also—along with praise bestowed by women leaders from both the left and the right—troubles any effort to categorize her according to India's established identity politics.[35]

Few things better capture the difficulty in typecasting Desai or, indeed, many of the other characters in the women's entry debate, than a late 2016 confrontation involving the Bhumata Brigade. After successfully pressuring the trustees of Shani Shingnapur to allow women within the inner sanctum, Desai and the Brigade moved on to the Mahalakshmi temple in Kolhapur, the Trimbakeshwar temple in Nashik, and the Haji Ali *dargah* in Mumbai before eventually turning to what had emerged as the litmus test of the push for women's access: Sabarimala.[36] In August 2016, Desai announced her intention to take her campaign outside Maharashtra for the first time, arguing that in light of the Bombay High Court order in *Niaz v. Maharashtra*, Sabarimala's administrators ought to revise their admission policies as well.[37] That the Travancore Devaswom Board felt differently was, of course, to be expected. Less foreseeable was the speed with which her disclosure united individuals in Kerala who had thus far done little but disagree with one another over Sabarimala's ban.

Rahul Easwar, the Thazhamon grandson and occasional spokesman, immediately declared that Desai would not be allowed to enter Sabarimala and added for good measure that 'women activists' committed to preserving the temple's traditions would block both Desai and any other 'ultra feminists' she might choose to bring with her.[38] Easwar's pronouncements found unmistakable if inexact echoes in statements made by both current *and* former ministers for Devaswom Affairs.[39] In a particularly striking turn of events, one of these officials addressed vague but unambiguously discouraging public statements to Desai, observing that the government of Kerala would be forced to act if Sabarimala experienced any 'law and order' problems.

That official, G. Sudhakaran, had been the Devaswom Minister during the Jayamala episode; soon after the Desai episode, in the wake of Bindu Ammini and Kanakadurga's 2019 visit to Sabarimala, he would also become the government actor who called Easwar's uncle, Kandararu Rajeevaru, a 'Brahmin monster'.[40] In 2016, Sudhakaran held the influential cabinet portfolio of Public Works. His personal preference for repealing the ban was well known, which made his warnings to Desai and his implicit alignment with Rahul Easwar all the more striking. After alerting Desai to his government's probable reaction to her presence, Sudhakaran went on to add that his party, the CPI(M), had long explored various means of expanding women's access to Sabarimala and added that instead of pursuing a ground campaign like she had previously done, Desai should fight in the courts alongside the State of Kerala. In the face of this unanticipated unity between communist officials and priestly relatives, rumours began to spread that Desai would be driven to carry out her visit in disguise, and police security around the 2016 pilgrimage season was tightened.[41] For most of that December and early into the new year, I awoke each day expecting to read that Desai and her followers had successfully entered the temple premises while I slept.

They had not. By all available accounts, Desai did not attempt a trip to Kerala in 2016; instead, she announced that her next campaign would be to make Maharashtra liquor-free.[42] After the *IYLA* opinion was handed down two years later, she again announced her intention to visit Sabarimala, this time in the exercise of a right rather than in protest of its violation. Once again, however, her intentions went unrealized—this time, though, in a more spectacular fashion. After over twelve hours inside the domestic terminal of Kochi's international airport on 16 November 2018, during which time protestors amassed outside the airport, taxi drivers declined service to the visiting Brigade members, and police officers tried, in vain, to persuade one or the other group to change their minds; Desai and her half-dozen colleagues returned to Pune without exiting the airport building.[43] Rahul Easwar promptly declared victory, as did the usually (but decreasingly) downtrodden Kerala wing of the BJP. Sabarimala itself, the subject of years-long litigation, a Supreme Court opinion, and countless protests—now also the unreachable target of a nascent women's temple entry movement—remained much as it had always been.

6.3 Whose Temples? Whose Entry?

If Azad and the *amicus curia* were largely responsible for ensuring that the analogy between caste and gender made its way into the Supreme Court, Desai made the same connection on the ground in dazzlingly corporeal fashion. Her temple entry agitations hearkened, obliquely but unmistakably, back to a series of early twentieth-century movements that took place—in Maharashtra and Kerala, no less—with the goal of increasing *avarna* individuals' access to Hindu temples. And yet, media coverage of Desai, which was hardly minimal, nonetheless rarely compared or contrasted her doings with these earlier efforts in any explicit fashion, and Desai herself seldom if ever drew the connection. Indeed, the silence emanating from press, politics, and public discourse regarding the four pre-independence temple *satyagraha*s was such that even those of us who consider ourselves moderately well-versed in the histories of nationalist politics and Gandhian methods might be forgiven for hesitantly consulting our primers. Were there really *no* similarities worth noting? No differences worth recalling? There were both, of course, in heaps, as a brief excursion beyond the *courte durée* would have made clear.

The four temple entry agitations of pre-independence India centred on institutions in Vaikom and Guruvayur, in Kerala, as well as in Pune and Nashik, in Maharashtra. They spanned over a decade, from 1924 to 1935, and they drew the attention of eminences like M. K. Gandhi and B.R. Ambedkar despite the considerable scepticism that each leader felt regarding both the methods and the goals of the movements. First came the Vaikom *satyagraha*, which occurred in the northern part of Travancore between 1924 and 1925 and brought together *avarna*, Nair, and Nambudiri leaders in a way that caught national, and nationalist, attention. Workers from Punjab came to open free kitchens to feed the protestors, newspapers outside Kerala covered their peaceful marches and uncontested arrests, and monetary donations flowed to Vaikom from all over India.[44] Following some initial disagreements with the Ezhava leader T. K. Madhavan over the timing of the protest, Gandhi came to accept Madhavan's view that Travancore's high levels of literacy and considerable history of educational and economic reforms made it uniquely and immediately 'ripe for temple entry'.[45] The 40,000-strong readership of his *Young India* newsletter soon began reading Gandhi's regular and admiring descriptions of the *satyagraha*, and later on, the Mahatma himself travelled to Kerala in support of the cause. But despite all this, Vaikom was in fact not a temple *entry* movement: the *satyagrahi*s sought only to open public roads surrounding the temple to Hindus of all castes, and even in this much more moderate ambition, they were just partially successful. In the end, only three of the four roads at issue were made accessible to *avarna*s, while non-Hindus were newly and wholly excluded.

As Vaikom suggested but Guruvayur confirmed, Gandhi's attitude towards temple entry, like so much else, was complex. While was he cautious about the appropriate moment in which to pursue this particular mission, he was definite about who should be in charge of the pursuit: none other than the very caste Hindus whose perpetration of untouchability made them the only ones capable of eradicating its evils. Indeed, Gandhi increasingly came to believe that even non-violent agitation over a particular temple was appropriate only if a majority of caste Hindus connected to the temple had already agreed to expand access. He meant this quite literally: under his influence, Congress members proposed temple entry bills in the Madras Legislature (1932) and the Central Legislature (1933) that conditioned expanded access upon the signed consent of caste Hindus who regularly worshipped at the temples in question. When a former Vaikom *satyagrahi* named K. Kelappan began a fast in protest of Guruvayur's admission policies, Gandhi rebuked him for giving the temple's trustees inadequate opportunity to mend their ways. Kelappan was persuaded to call off his protest in return for a promise, namely, that Gandhi would join him in a second fast if the trustees did not experience a change of heart within three months; a referendum, which polled an estimated 27,000 of 30,000 potential caste Hindu temple-goers and found that over 60% of them were neutral or supportive of expanded access.

The Maharashtrian movements, which occurred between 1929–30 (Pune) and 1930–35 (Nashik), are a study in contrasts. Despite Ambedkar's early involvement, Pune fizzled quickly—within around three months—after the temple's trustees shut its doors and hired guards, and after the Congress Party began calling for an end to the agitation.

Nashik, on the other hand, refused to end: it was a protracted, fitful, and acrimonious effort that owed much of its fame, and perhaps some of its acrimony, to Ambedkar's sustained involvement. Nashik was also more violent than earlier temple entry *satyagraha*s, with caste Hindus physically assaulting *avarna*s as the latter attempted to pull a ceremonial chariot during an annual temple festival. Above all else, and certainly more than any of the other movements, Nashik made clear that British officials and caste Hindus were united in their perception of temple entry as a problem of contested property rights, more akin to a pesky trespass dispute, than as a matter of civil liberties. When a local district magistrate criticized the *satyagrahi*s for being unable to identify which of their legally cognizable rights had been violated, the law the magistrate pointed to was the Indian Penal Code's section on property disputes.[46] When government officials tried to diffuse the situation by temporarily closing the temple, its priest once again relied on property rights by providing caste Hindu worshippers with continued access to the temple through his own home. Finally, in 1934, bitter and disillusioned by the orthodoxy's ability to win official support, Ambedkar disassociated himself from the Nashik agitation in order to focus on less spiritual forms of uplift.

6.4 Temple Entry, Then and Now

It is hard, these days, to write *of* Gandhi and Ambedkar without being obliged to write at length *about* them; so strong is the gravitational pull surrounding the Mahatma and the Babasaheb in an India that, out of either pride or sorrow, has grown fonder than ever of its past. It is equally hard to write persuasively about four temple entry movements that, between them, decisively opened no temples. Vaikom, of course, was concerned only with roads; Guruvayur ebbed in anticipation of legislative action; Pune was called off in less time than it takes to recite the Three Refuges; Nashik flared and subsided for five years without ultimate fruition. Nevertheless, like the social movements of 2015–16, and particularly like the agitations led by Trupti Desai, these early twentieth-century efforts generated unprecedented national awareness of a struggle whose successful conclusion is habitually portrayed as a triumph of the courts and the courts alone.

The dismantling of caste barriers to entry at Hindu temples, though it is usually attributed to Supreme Court opinions like *Venkataramana Devaru* and the *Satsang case*, was not simply the product of judicial fiat. To be sure, both *Devaru* (1957) and the *Satsang case* (1966) were powerful decisions that signalled judicial commitment to a creative and progressive interpretation of the Indian Constitution, and they rightly rank among the Court's most famous opinions. The *Devaru* Court decided that, properly understood and contrary to the interpretations of the temple's own priests, the Sanskrit texts governing ritual practice at a south Indian temple allowed *avarna*s a limited right of entry into the temple. The Court's exegetical strategy was nothing if not original. It began with a declaration that the Sanskrit texts in question viewed public temple worship as benefiting all Hindus, followed this with an observation that the temple's exclusionary practices were anomalous because they suggested *avarna*s could benefit from worship in which they could not participate, and finally corrected the anomaly by redefining the 'exclusion' faced by *avarna*s to mean 'insignificant participation'.[47] *Avarna*s' right of entry, the *Devaru* Court held, were no less and no greater than that of the caste Hindus who frequented the temple but were forbidden from its inner sanctum.

The *Satsang* opinion went broader still. It began with the 'historical and etymological genesis of the word "Hindu"',[48] went on to suggest that Hindus were most accurately viewed as a 'geographic' community, and concluded with a now-popular riff on the *Rig Veda*: '[t]ruth is one, but wise men describe it differently.' This, not coincidentally, is the kind of comfortably progressive Hinduism that would emerge in Chief Justice Misra's plurality opinion, complete with a thinly paraphrased articulation of the same *Rig Veda* line.[49] Although the *Satsang* Court performed the practical and politically inescapable work of categorizing the appellant religious community as Hindu and, consequently, of making their temples subject to constitutional and statutory provisions mandating temple entry for *avarna*s, it did so with a kind of rhetorical aplomb—and a brevity—that is now rarely matched.

Through these and other opinions issued over the course of some twenty years, the Supreme Court made great strides in working out the mechanics and logistics of opening temples to Hindus of all castes. But despite their prominence in the Court's Fundamental Rights jurisprudence, and by extension their centrality to the Court's global reputation as a formidable driver of sociopolitical transformation, caste-based temple entry decisions were incremental, not heroic, interventions. Like *IYLA*, they too came at the end of concerted public activism that was not limited to the four *satyagraha*s discussed here. They too arrived in the wake of statutes passed by the governments of British, princely, and independent India—over a dozen statutes before 1950—and in response to a Constitution that was painstakingly constructed with transformational ends very much in mind. (It is less clear whether they too met with the kind of vehement resistance that characterized *IYLA*'s reception; somewhere in the quantitative social sciences, there is a doctoral dissertation waiting to be written on the measurable consequences of cases like *Devaru*, complete with percentages, surveys, and Likert scales.) What is indisputable is that the Court's successful undertakings with respect to one type of temple entry during the twentieth century rested on popular, statutory, and constitutional antecedents every bit as much as the decision that is widely considered to be its great failure with respect to another type of temple entry, over fifty years later.

Not only this. In the referendum of caste Hindu opinion that was imposed on Kelappan's Guruvayur efforts, in the violence and subterfuge characterizing caste Hindu resistance in Nashik, in Prayar Gopalakrishnan's wishful musings, and in the crowd that greeted Trupti Desai at Kochi International Airport, in all of this run whispers of the belief that access is to be given rather than owed. *Let them come when we are ready.* In the determination and occasional ridicule that greeted each of these moments runs the rejection of that idea. *We will come when we are ready.* None of this is exceptional. That any community seeking to police its own boundaries should grant itself constabulary power is, of course, mundane in the extreme; in-groups are in-groups by virtue of designating certain others as out-groups. But in India, at least since 26 January 1950, communities themselves are not the only ones wrestling with the question of whether liberties are to be graciously granted or simply acknowledged: this puzzle is deeply encoded into the Indian Constitution itself as between citizens, who are sometimes sovereign, and the state, which is sometimes subservient. The Supreme Court's efforts to negotiate this balance in 2018 simultaneously led it to chase its own footsteps and to venture into new and nameless territory.

Conclusion

In the end, the dispute over women's entry went back, more or less, to its beginnings. After *Mahendran* determined the contours of the ban and after the Jayamala episode broadcast them to the rest of the country, after Bhakti Pasrija and her colleagues filed a petition, after protests, a judicial decision, and some more protests—after all of this, the legality of Sabarimala's admissions policies returned to the matter of 'what is essentially religious, [and] essential to religion'.[1] Even in a country known for long-lived litigation and even in the context of a religious tradition that is shot through with themes of cyclicality, the afterlife of the Sabarimala dispute has been remarkably long. It has now stretched to encompass the tenures of six chief justices, and has involved at least two dozen other Supreme Court jurists as well as several dozen attorneys. If we acknowledge all of the petitioners and respondents and intervenors who, thanks to this unusual temple's unusual policies, have found themselves inspired or obliged to have their say before a court of some kind, the cast list is many times longer. If we include those who participated in *namajapam*s and human chains, it is epic.

In the long and still-expanding roll call of cases that make up the battle for Sabarimala, the name *Kantaru Rajeevaru v. Indian Young Lawyers Association* is just one more entry. Nevertheless, it represents at least two distinct and differently important moments. During the first of these moments, a five-justice bench mostly comprising the same judges who had issued *IYLA* determined whether the Court should reconsider that earlier decision. Chief Justice Gogoi, writing for himself, Justice Khanwilkar, and Justice Malhotra, chose, in a way that is second nature to lawyers but often infuriating to everyone else, to make no choice at all.[2] By keeping the review petitions 'pending', the Gogoi-led majority in *Kantaru Rajeevaru* suggested that one of three things *might* be true about the Sabarimala litigation. Perhaps the *IYLA* Court had made a mistake so obtrusive that, like an arithmetic error on a graded exam, it could be gleaned from the written record alone. Perhaps the pro-ban petitioners had mustered some new, important, and previously unavailable evidence. Or, finally, perhaps there was some 'other sufficient reason' to undo what had already been judicially done. Chief Justice Gogoi's three-page opinion did not specify which of these grounds for review had been satisfied nor which of the petitioners had provided satisfaction, but the dissent—Justices Nariman and Chandrachud—expended over ten times that page count to explain why none of these justifications were possible.

Instead of explaining its outcome, the three pages of Chief Justice Gogoi's *Kantaru Rajeevaru* opinion were devoted to supporting an altogether separate proposition: namely, that, along with their re-evaluation of the Sabarimala dispute, the members of some future Supreme Court bench ought to decide other, parallel, issues for the sake of building an improved jurisprudence of religious freedom. Just as *Mahendran* transformed a dispute over violations of temple protocol into a re-examination of Sabarimala's entry policies, the *Kantaru Rajeevaru* majority parlayed a dispute over Sabarimala's entry policies into a re-examination of the Essential Practices Doctrine writ large. This suggestion became known as the 'reference' question, in contrast to the simpler matter of 'review'. Besides Sabarimala, the foundation stones for this jurisprudential revisitation were to come from three writ petitions then circulating in the Supreme Court: one regarding the right of Muslim women to enter mosques and shrines, a second regarding the right of Parsi (Zoroastrian) women to enter fire temples, and a third regarding a type of female genital mutilation that some members of the Shi'a Ismaili community of Dawoodi Bohras consider essential. Religion, gender, and law: the other tricolour.[3]

Although the reference question was specifically linked to all three of these disputes as well as to women's entry at Sabarimala, the *Kantaru Rajeevaru* majority framed its efforts at doctrinal spring cleaning in terms that far exceeded any one of them. Like so many of its predecessors, the Court sought nothing less than the establishment of clear and stable solutions to the perpetually vexing problems of religious life in India. What constitutes a 'section of Hindus'?[4] Does Article 26 protect the essential practices of a religious denomination?[5] Who is an acceptable PIL petitioner in religious freedom cases?[6] Answers to these questions (and to four others) would, the Gogoi majority declared, lead the

Court towards an 'authoritative enunciation' of religious freedom in contemporary India.[7] It was time, according to the majority, 'that this Court should evolve a judicial policy befitting to its plenary powers', and that task required 'a larger Bench of not less than seven Judges'.[8]

Seven is a magical number here, as it often is elsewhere. In India's bench-based system of judicial operations, the biggest small bench usually has three members, while the smallest big bench—the kind of bench needed to hear a case 'involving a substantial question of law as to the interpretation' of the Constitution—consists of five judges.[9] A five-judge bench is an acknowledgement of significance by a Court that, all too often, finds itself caught up in the emphatically mundane. It is also a *bid* for significance, inasmuch as the Constitution itself offers no explicit guidance regarding the identification of matters that are substantial enough to warrant five or more justices. When the Chief Justice assembles a five-judge bench, he is at the very least telegraphing his own, and perhaps not only his own, estimation of the matter's importance. A *seven*-judge bench, then, is something rather special. It is more than the five-judge workhorse of constitutional analysis at India's apex court: it is a statement that the matter under consideration is extraordinary.

Seven is also a magical number because, back in 1954, that is how many justices sat on the bench that issued *Shirur Mutt*, the opinion that lies at the core of the Sabarimala dispute and is omnipresent in Indian religious freedom jurisprudence. As chapter three observed, the doctrine that *Shirur Mutt* created has attracted no small amount of criticism, and that criticism is not wholly undeserved. In 2019, *Shirur Mutt*'s vulnerability became all too clear when the Chief Justice made his ominous declaration that 'apparent' conflicts between the nearly seventy-year-old decision and subsequent case law required 'consideration by a larger Bench' of 'not less than seven Judges'.[10]

Newspapers and blogs immediately began rehashing the Essential Practices Doctrine, if not in anticipation of its immediate demise—after all, coequal benches cannot directly overrule one another—then in the wholly justified expectation of its imminent and rapid decline. Even if they could not eliminate the doctrine or its perpetually overlooked fraternal twin, the Denominational Test, the seven jurists that Chief Justice Gogoi seemed to be recommending to the next occupant of his office could nonetheless engage in some profoundly influential reanalysis. They could, via the 'reference question', reimagine religion-state relations in ways that would strengthen individual autonomy or that would empower community identity or, at least, that would de-emphasize judicial responsibility for balancing the one against the other. Any one of these shifts would trickle down into the mundane administrative aspects of Indian religious life (and the less mundane aspects of Indian political life) far beyond Sabarimala or Ayyappan devotees or Kerala or even Hinduism itself. A re-evaluation of *Shirur Mutt* would, quite simply, be epochal. But just as the full ramifications of a seven-judge bench began to make themselves fully felt, the new occupant of Ranjan Gogoi's office, the forty-seventh Chief Justice of India, appointed *eight* of his colleagues to sit alongside him for next phase of what was still, but only marginally, the Sabarimala dispute.

'Ordinarily', noted one news columnist, 'a reference from a five-judge bench lies before a seven-judge bench'.[11] That *nine* justices were called to hear the reference question in *Kantaru Rajeevaru* was thus a strong signal as well as a rare occurrence. In the seven decades between the moment, in 1950, when India's Constitution came into force and the creation, in 2020, of that nine-judge bench, only fifteen other cases had been deemed to merit an equal degree of judicial attention.[12] Some of those cases explicitly delineated the contours of democratic governance in India, including how Supreme Court jurists are to be appointed and how state governments may be dissolved.[13] Others introduced new substantive rights (like privacy) or new concepts to modify existing rights (like the economically 'creamy layer' of disadvantaged castes, who were deemed ineligible for caste-based reservations).[14] A re-evaluation of the Essential Practices Doctrine would indeed be weighty enough to warrant inclusion within this rarefied circle, and the new Chief Justice of India, Sharad Arvind Bobde, seemed determined to find a place for it there along with all the other issues bundled into the reference question. 'The Chief Justice', the news columnist went on to say, 'in his wisdom and under his authority ... apparently wants all the issues to be settled for times to come'.[15]

Chief Justice Bobde and his eight colleagues—none of whom had sat on the 2018 or 2019 Sabarimala benches—issued two orders in comparatively quick succession; for the duration of 2020, these orders constituted the entirety of Supreme Court efforts respecting both the Sabarimala review and the reference question it had inspired. They also represented the second stage of the proceedings in *Kantaru Rajeevaru*.

In February, the nine-judge panel brusquely announced that it was within the Court's rights to 'refer questions of law to a larger bench in a review petition'.[16] The panel's two-sentence interim order was followed by seven questions for consideration, none of which were unique to a dispute over women's entry, whether at Sabarimala or elsewhere.[17] In issuing any order at all, the justices were responding, after a manner, to the criticisms of several senior attorneys who are individually famous and collectively rarely in agreement, but who, during those three days of hearings in early February, converged on the point that the Court was proceeding in violation of its own rules. 'It will be outside your jurisdiction to do that', declared one lawyer, not without courage.[18] Another argued that the reference and review could not proceed simultaneously; a third pointed out the lack of error in *IYLA*; a fourth noted the lack of error in *Shirur Mutt*.[19] What was there to review in these circumstances, the attorneys wondered? What was there to be referenced?

In May, they found out. Chief Justice Bobde's panel issued an explanatory order with one overarching and increasingly familiar theme:

... the Constitution of India empowers the Supreme Court ... [20]

... there are no restrictions on the power of this Court ... [21]

... there is no fetter in the exercise of the jurisdiction of this Court ... [22]

... there is no fetter on the exercise of discretion of this Court ... [23]

... it is for this Court to consider whether any matter falls within its jurisdiction ... [24]

... the inherent power of this Court ... shall not be limited by the Rules ... [25]

And, inevitably:

This Court has acted well within its power in making the reference.[26]

There were other arguments, too, of course. The nine justices, who in a striking show of unanimity agreed to the entirety of the order, also gestured towards comma placement, the meaning of the word 'proceeding', the non-necessity of facts in a matter of pure law, and the unique qualities of PIL petitions.[27] Their order, like the decision issued by Ranjan Gogoi's five-judge bench, is easy to poke fun at. It argues that PIL petitions, precisely because they bear upon issues of weighty constitutional import, are neither civil nor criminal proceedings and are therefore exempt from the strict rules governing review petitions for civil and criminal matters. It uses the Court's own prior statements as proof that there exists a question of pure law requiring reference to a larger bench. And it insists, with a repetitiveness and petulance that is at times difficult to stomach, that—in the absence of express limitations in either the courtroom rules (that it writes) or the laws (that it interprets)—there are 'no restrictions on the power of this Court'.[28]

Commentary on the May order, like on the November opinion that preceded it, ranged from confused to critical. And yet, the many iterations of *Kantaru Rajeevaru* are not *entirely* without 'legal reasoning or thought', notwithstanding the declaration of one especially frustrated lawyer.[29] For instance, it is indeed hard to find, in the rules governing Supreme Court proceedings, any explicit indication as to whether PILs take on the attributes of civil cases during the review process (and it is hard to argue that they more closely resemble criminal matters). Even if PILs *are* most appropriately civil-ized for the purposes of identifying the procedural rules that apply to them, there is no gainsaying the panel's assertion that 'the rules of procedure do not *strictly* apply' to public interest cases—that was, after all, PIL's chief attraction.[30] Malleability and informality are virtues until they are not.

The authors of *Kantaru Rajeevaru* also fare better—or their opponents fare worse—when the May order is juxtaposed against earlier stages of the Sabarimala litigation. For instance, Justices Nariman and Chandrachud, who objected so strongly to reviewing *IYLA* in the absence of new information or apparent error, had been far less vexed, when they were presented with *IYLA*, by the prospect of reviewing *Mahendran* under similar circumstances and after considerably greater delay. In 2018, Justice Chandrachud took just a few perfunctory steps towards justifying the Supreme Court's revisitation of Sabarimala's ban. The Kerala High

Court's approach had been 'incorrect', he maintained, because it assumed that a religious community enjoyed 'complete autonomy' in identifying its own essential practices.[31] The High Court also misinterpreted the material placed before it, which actually demonstrated that 'that the practice of excluding women from the Sabarimala temple was not uniform' and therefore could not, legally, be considered essential.[32] Justice Chandrachud's 2018 reading of the *Mahendran* material was decidedly strategic and moderately questionable, but—more to the purpose—it never led him to seriously analyse the appropriate basis for review or reference.[33] Instead, and not unlike his colleagues behind the February 2020 *Kantaru Rajeevaru* interim order, his consideration of whether or not the dispute over women's entry could be referred to a more powerful bench was limited to two sentences and a set of broad questions.[34] Justice Nariman did even less than this in *IYLA*—and Justice Malhotra, for her part, objected in *IYLA* to what she would later authorize in *Kantaru Rajeevaru*.[35]

Developments in the nine-justice hearings seemed poised to ebb and flow over the course of 2020. Somehow, despite massive protests against the *Citizenship Amendment Act* during the early weeks of the year, the violence surrounding President Trump's first visit to India in February, and the onset of the coronavirus pandemic in March that triggered the same-day imposition of a harsh nationwide lockdown, Sabarimala and the reference question kept surfacing in the news for the first half of 2020. As it happened, however, the May order would be the Supreme Court's last significant action for quite some time.

Within Kerala, Sabarimala continued to generate news and concern for reasons having nothing to do with the women's entry dispute. In March 2020, the Travancore Devaswom Board urged devotees to stay away as Kerala's coronavirus infection rates climbed steadily. In April, for the first time that anyone could remember, Sabarimala observed Vishu without allowing any devotees to be in attendance. By May, the TDB was beginning to panic about its drastically reduced income, which was around ₹2 billion (roughly US$27 million) lower than usual and was severely impeding the board's ability to support hundreds of poorer temples around Kerala; half of that loss was attributed to Sabarimala's closure alone. (In another, roughly contemporaneous demonstration of Sabarimala's regional influence, the Government of Kerala decided to replicate the 'virtual queue' technology developed for the temple for use in state-operated liquor stores.) So painful were the fiscal consequences of Sabarimala's shutdown that, by early June, the TDB was making hopeful noises about reopening under restricted conditions for that month's customary five-day *puja*, as well as for some special festival activities. Nevertheless, just a few days later, the *tantri* and the state government agreed to cancel those plans.

August 2020 brought a rush of developments: the state decided to forge ahead with the pilgrimage season that was set to begin in less than three months, TDB temples *other* than Sabarimala reopened to devotees, and Sabarimala was granted permission to reopen for monthly *pujas* in October. But more than any of these things, August was marked by an announcement that is still hard for me to fully accept despite years of familiarity with the financial dynamics of temple management in Kerala: Sabarimala was out of money and needed to draw down, or at least monetize, its assets.

Near the end of August, news broke that the TDB would approach both the Reserve Bank of India and the Modi administration with proposals to allow the Board to monetize Sabarimala's massive gold reserves. The bars, coins, ornaments, and other gold items donated by Sabarimala's millions of pilgrims would either serve as collateral for a loan with the Reserve Bank or as the basis for a deposit with the central government's Gold Monetisation Scheme, which is operated by designated providers and offers guaranteed interest.[36] Monetizing gold is not, by itself, an unusual route for temple systems or boards—the Tirupati temple in Andhra Pradesh, the richest Hindu institution in the world—has participated in the Gold Monetisation Scheme since 2017, just two years after the Modi government introduced the system.[37] But unlike Tirupati, which began putting its gold reserves to work long before the pandemic, the TDB was raiding its larders in response to a crisis and it was doing so despite ostensibly receiving a cash infusion from the Government of Kerala.[38]

Matters did not improve after August. The annual search for new *melsanthi*s to officiate at both Sabarimala and the nearby Malikapurathamma shrine received remarkably low applicant numbers, and the entire process was delayed by the logistical challenges of conducting background checks on out-of-state candidates during a pandemic.[39] Temple officials were heartened by the announcement that 250 pilgrims would be allowed to visit daily during the off season, although those pilgrims had to book slots in the temple's virtual queue, carry certificates of good health, and follow COVID protocols during their trek up the hillside.[40] During the *mandalam-makaravilakku* season of 2020–21, that allotment was set to rise to a maximum of between 1000 and 5000 depending on the day. And yet, within the first week of the season, which began on 16 November 2020, it became clear that actual numbers would be even lower because many aspiring pilgrims—at least 50 a day and sometimes up to 40% of those who had registered—simply failed to appear.[41] Just 9,000 people visited Sabarimala during those initial seven days, compared to the roughly 300,000 who would normally have climbed its hills, bought snacks and memorabilia from its stalls, and added donations to its coffers.[42] Because of that shortfall, the TDB lost yet another source of income as the vendors who normally rent those stalls, some 160 of them in total, showed a marked disinclination to throw good money after non-existent customers by signing leases.[43]

Despite these bleak and pandemic-driven developments, neither Sabarimala nor the women's entry disputes are likely to recede into the background. Culturally, economically, and politically, the temple is—more than most banks in Kerala—simply too big to fail. Even the Kerala High Court, so long concerned with bringing order and restraint to Sabarimala's management, urged the TDB to show flexibility when restricting operations and introducing safety protocols during the long-awaited 2020–21 season.[44] Like houseboats, coconuts, and communist governance, Sabarimala has, for both better and for worse, become a part of the image Kerala projects to the rest of India and around the world and so, in some form or another, it persists.

The unsettled status of the women's entry dispute also persists. There was every reason to expect that Chief Justice Bobde would move the *Kantaru Rajeevaru* petitions forward in some way before his retirement, but that did not happen. After a tenure that was overwhelmed by the coronavirus pandemic, Bobde's retirement in April 2021 coincided with a terrifying rise in India's infections and fatalities that consumed national resources and attention.[45] His successor, N. V. Ramana, held the chief justiceship until August 2022, and was followed (for some seventy-four days) by U. U. Lalit, which made it plausible—but not, in the end, possible—for two more leaders of the Supreme Court to leave their marks via the dispute.[46] As of this writing, the chief justiceship is in the hands of none other than D.Y. Chandrachud, who has around twenty months more to provide some closure regarding temple and doctrine alike. Perhaps he will: Indian chief justices are by now addicted to grand finales, which renders the Sabarimala litigation—to say nothing of the broader essential practices analysis it has triggered—jurisprudentially and politically irresistible.

Why is this so? Why have the peculiar entry policies of a peculiar temple in a still more peculiar (and not particularly influential) state garnered so much attention? Why have they inspired and enraged so many very different people—and sometimes the same people at different moments? These are all versions of the question I set out to ask as a doctoral student intrigued by the persistence of temple-entry disputes in twenty-first-century India. To answer them, let me momentarily try to stop being either an anthropologist or a lawyer, both of whom are professionally habituated to speaking for or through others and instead speak only on behalf of myself. *My* self is at once dominant caste and uncomfortably irreligious, more foreign than my India-born cousins and more Indian than my foreign-born friends, trained in American law but fascinated by India's approach to all things legal, and—lest I forget—it is a self that, for all practical purposes, is still unable to visit the temple at the heart of this book.

To my very particular and yet hardly unique eyes, the Sabarimala dispute, from before *Mahendran* to after *Kantaru Rajeevaru*, exemplifies the multiplicity that is most entrancing about India, even if seeing that multiplicity sometimes requires us to squint at the kaleidoscopic whole in order to avoid seeing the sharply glinting parts. It is a multiplicity not only of 'religious beliefs', which is a tiresome and generic phrase best relegated to glossy promotional materials, but of the most specific, unlooked-for, quotidian, and theological kind. *What are god's*—this *god's, this* iteration *of this god's—preferences? Do they vary from place to place or moment to moment? And what if you and I cannot agree?*

It is also a multiplicity of *ism*s, of feminisms, liberalisms, casteisms, Hinduisms, and yes, even secularisms, as well as a multiplicity of paths to societal transformation. For instance, while the battle for Sabarimala features the usual assemblage of powerful men—men who make laws, men who interpret and enforce them, men who speak for deities, and the men who speak for *those* men and, of course, the male deity born of two male deities whose ostensible preferences stand at the centre of it all—there are also women aplenty, and they are more than mere foils for their masculine counterparts. There are the women who have asserted, at various times with varying kinds of religious conviction, their right to be present in Sabarimala; the women who have objected; and the women who have represented all of those women in court, in the press, and before the public, howsoever defined. Then there are the male judges and justices who proclaimed women's right of entry and the female justice who argued against it; the man who facilitated the only successful entrance of women in the prohibited age range and the women who have coordinated across geographic and temporal boundaries to demand that people like them wait to visit Sabarimala.

Multiplicity produces microcosmic appeal, and the Sabarimala dispute is no exception. It distils India's considerable best and worst into a discrete set of issues that, moreover, happen to unfold against a charmingly idiosyncratic background. Untouchability, misogyny, and patriarchy all sit alongside enviable indices of gender equality, religious practices that subvert divisions of caste and faith, and transformational legal frameworks that have been lauded around the world. All of this complexity can be, to put it mildly, delightful.

But as much as the battle for Sabarimala continues to fascinate for these reasons, something else better explains its vitality and longevity. The events that comprise this dispute—events that, as I have suggested, extend farther back than 2018 or even 2006—are an object lesson in the multiplicity of *legal* possibilities that has long characterized, and with any luck will continue to characterize, Indian nationhood. Sabarimala, in other words, matters because it showcases India's legal duality in addition to the cultural, religious, and political multiplicity that also characterize the country. The back and forth inspired by constitutional guarantees of religious freedom and religious reform, between citizens-as-sovereigns and citizens sharing sovereignty, between Jayamala and the courts, between *Mahendran* and *IYLA* and the various *Kantaru* judgements, between social movements to open Sabarimala and social movements to keep access unchanged—all of this messy, complicated movement is integral to the never-ending project of imagining India. Under the best of circumstances, distinct ways of imagining citizen-state relations in India can exist in a kind of perpetually dynamic equilibrium. And yet, as the Sabarimala dispute makes all too clear, in dangerous moments and lesser hands, the existence of mutually conflicting imaginaries allows for partial analysis and perpetual chaos.

More concretely, the battle for Sabarimala has become a battle for the Essential Practices Doctrine. In the absence of easy or even moderately challenging solutions to the problem of India's galloping saffronization, the Essential Practices Doctrine, in its original iteration, offered an imperfect but innovative guideline for courts adjudicating religious freedom disputes. The Doctrine's earlier emphasis on identifying what is essentially religious (as opposed to what is religiously essential) and its explicit, now largely ignored, directive to prioritize religious precepts over judicial preferences provided guardrails that were, in retrospect, badly needed. Revitalizing that earlier understanding of the Doctrine will not singlehandedly resolve the battle for Sabarimala nor will it render more manageable any comparable disputes that may come before Indian courts—there is, as I have tried to show, far too much plaguing the courts themselves, and there is also, which I have not dared to describe, even more driving the authoritarian and Hindu nationalist shifts in Indian politics. But the genius of the Doctrine never lay in its ability to falsely simplify that which is exceedingly complex. The Doctrine's true contribution, like that of the Constitution that inspired it, lies in its reflection of a commitment: the commitment to grapple sincerely, constantly, and generously with conflicting visions of the political good in the interests of pursuing an India for all Indians.

Acknowledgements

Although the convention is to thank relatives last, it has been one of the great good fortunes of my life that the people I love most are not only my family, but my friends and colleagues as well. My mother, Mallika, and my husband, John, made this project possible and kept this project interesting. They edited proposals, supported fieldwork, mobilized contacts, located or safely stored documents, kept vigil with me at consulates and visa processing centres, debated analytic concepts and prose stylings, read and reread drafts. John's awe-inspiring scholarly breadth and moderately controlled bibliophilia, combined with his rootedness in a field and a time-place that complement my own, have effectively transformed our home into an on-demand library and workshop that I am privileged to enjoy. Amma's willingness to reach outside her own disciplinary background into the unfamiliar and interdisciplinary waters that I occupy has inspired every stage of this book—which I wrote, quite literally, with her in mind—as has her ability to luxuriate in language, in its sounds and rhythms and communicative nuances; whether parsing the lyrics of a Kannadasan song or debating the turn of phrase in a scholarly paper, talking language with Amma remains one of my favourite things to do. She and John are my first and favourite intellectual companions, for all projects.

This book emerged from the dissertation I completed at the University of Chicago and bears, I hope, at least some traces of the people who advised me there. John Kelly provided an early anchor in the Department of Anthropology and an entrée into the study of South Asia, while Justin Richland guided the final stages of this project with an eye towards my deepening commitment to interdisciplinary scholarship. William Mazzarella, who oversaw my master's thesis and co-chaired my dissertation committee, pushed me to think with a theoretical intensity I found exhilarating while never allowing me to lose sight of the geographic and temporal context in which I worked. None of this would have produced an actual dissertation if it were not also for Anne Chi'en, who managed the Department and all of us in it with an efficiency that was as delightful as it is legendary.

Above all, John Comaroff co-chaired the dissertation that led to this book and continues to be an inspiration and a support long after we have both left Haskell Hall. I have never asked him for help that was not promptly and generously given, and I have never received advice that was not equal parts astute and warm. Even as I have wandered further afield from John, institutionally and intellectually, I return regularly to ask for his thoughts on professional matters that are, of course, always personal matters, too. I hope someday to do all this and to be all this for someone else.

The fieldwork behind this project was conducted in 2009 and 2010–11 with the help of a summer stipend from the University of Chicago and an International Dissertation Research Fellowship from the Social Science Research Council. What made that time productive, however, were the interlocutors who generously shared their time and thoughts with me, and the family and friends who made fieldwork bearable during a period of uncommon personal hardship. Foremost in the first category is Krishnakumar Mangot, whose advisory position in the Kerala High Court opened the logistical doors and provided the substantive knowledge without which my dissertation could not have been completed. But many others stepped in as interlocutors whom I repeatedly relied on, and who readily shared information and made introductions: Mr Vijayaraghavan (former counsel to the Travancore Devaswom Board), Mr Unnikrishnan (then counsel to the Cochin Devaswom Board), Mr Balakrishnan K. (professor at the National University of Advanced Legal Studies), Mr Unni Nampoothiry (Secretary of the Yogakshemasabha), Mr Rahul Easwar (the grandson of Sabarimala's then-*tantri*), Mrs Bhakti Pasrija Sethi (attorney), and Mr Rajasekharan Pillai (attorney). Others—Justice K. S. Paripoornan, Kandararu Maheswararu, G. Sudhakaran, Rama Varma Raja, and Ambalapuzha Rama Varma, among them—provided key insights.

Meanwhile, my cousins Rashmi *chechi* and Pradeep *chettan*, and Sridevi *chechi* and Prakash *chettan*, made introductions, arranged housing, ensured that I ate daily and that, at least occasionally, I also did things for fun. Two of my aunts, Nandu *mema* in Chennai and Ammu *valiamma* in Palakkad, provided getaways that were desperately needed *when* they were most needed and thereby made it possible for me to remain in the field. And Aprajita Anand—to me always the wildly creative girl with enormous braids who I met on the first day of college—Apra not only came to visit me in Kochi, bringing her boundless enthusiasm and some of my old self

ACKNOWLEDGEMENTS 163

along with her, but she also donated her magnificent artistic talents so that this book could have an outside that reflected something of its inside.

The years since I returned from the field have been filled with too many conferences, workshops, articles, reviewers, and fruitful conversations to exhaustively name here. Tom Ginsburg, whom I met the summer before I began law school, has been a source of constant encouragement despite sharing neither my disciplinary nor geographic nor theoretical predilections; Tim Lubin received a 'cold email' from a college senior writing her undergraduate thesis and thereafter continued to show interest and provide support across an expanse of time that is now simultaneously gratifying and sobering; Herman Tull, after patiently enduring my awkward undergraduate forays into Sanskrit, has long since become more friend than teacher and has most recently added 'manuscript reader' to my reasons for being grateful to him.

The American Council of Learned Societies (through its Religion, Journalism, and International Affairs Fellowship) and the Indo-German research collaboration ICAS: MP (through its Senior Fellowship) made it possible for me to spend a year writing this book. In truth, though, they did much more: their support gave me the luxury of staying safely at home during a world-altering pandemic, of enjoying intellectual community despite being at home, and of building relationships beyond my house, my institution, my field, and even beyond my country. During the writing process, Erica Nicholson provided excellent help with indexing and formatting, while Saloni Jaiswal ably collected and catalogued many of the media and legal materials I relied on. Eric Feldman, Mark Massoud, Jothie Rajah, and Kim Scheppele kept me in good cheer during the unexpectedly challenging process of bringing this book to print.

Finally, Leo Coleman, Arvind Elangovan, Madhav Khosla, and Adnan Zulfiqar have all been insightful interlocutors of this manuscript or some of the works that preceded it, but I am even more grateful to have counted them as friends and fellow travellers. And, although I found them long after the fieldwork for this project was finished, a circle of (admittedly no longer very) junior legal anthropologists became extremely influential for me as I wrote; Matthew, Matt, Riaz, Jeff, Anya, and Anna: it continues to be a privilege and a great pleasure to think with you.

APPENDIX A

A Note on Interdisciplinary Interventions

For a book that claims to sit at the intersection of anthropology and law, the preceding pages contained remarkably little explicit engagement with the literatures of either discipline, and none at all in the main text. I took this approach, which lacks neither risks nor critics, for several reasons.

Most of all, I wanted this book to be readable. This is not thinly disguised condescension towards the technical know-how of non-academic audiences; it is thinly disguised dissatisfaction with the structural and stylistic conventions of academic book-writing. I particularly wanted to avoid the artfully packaged (but inevitably identifiable) literature review and the curated sprinkle of key terms from key predecessors that are now, equally, inescapable elements of monographs in the humanities, social sciences, and law. To be sure, these practices have goals that are worthy: demonstrating intellectual mastery and acknowledging intellectual obligation. They also have goals that are less palatable, like paying professional obeisance and branding a manuscript for marketing and prize-winning purposes. To some degree, all of these objectives likely inform any given decision to cite or quote above the line, and I do not mean to belittle authors whose job security hinges on their willingness to heed such imperatives. But to my mind, as well as to my eye and ear, the end result is often unpleasant prose. One of the many luxuries of being trained in a field that values books but housed in a field that values articles is the freedom to choose among practices of writing as well as practices of argumentation and proof, all the while remaining secure in the knowledge that one's institutional superiors will at worst be indifferent and one's readers, regardless of discipline, may well be displeased. In the exercise of that freedom, this book uses endnotes to attribute analysis or information that directly contributes to the story it tells, but it avoids in-line references, parenthetical or otherwise, that might better fulfil any of the other purposes of scholarly citation.

I also wanted this book to be about the Sabarimala dispute rather than about any of the scholarly subfields that might be interested in it. For that reason, the main text incorporates insights from a broad range of disciplines without emphasizing either the individual academics behind them (they are cited in endnotes) or the disciplinary trajectories out of which these insights emerged. In other words, I do not dive into competing scholarly perspectives on this or that topic, and I do not explain methodological or theoretical transformations within any of the disciplines I draw on. Indeed, barring two disciplines—anthropology and law—I do not much talk about disciplinary histories and transformations at all, and even then I relegate the discussion to this appendix. This too is a luxury born of interstitial existence: when there are multiple disciplinary lineages one might reasonably be expected to acknowledge, it is sometimes preferable, and it is at least *feasible*, to recognize few or none. The very existence of this appendix suggests that it may be too difficult to wholly excise metacommentaries about how one's material reflects and resists traditions in the disciplines one is speaking from within. But, by the same token, those commentaries need not intrude into the story one is trying to tell.

Finally, I omitted explicit discussions of disciplinary concerns from the main text out of a desire to follow the grade school maxim about showing, telling, and the superiority of one over the other. One of the ways in which this book deviates from ordinary anthropological practice is in its attention to law as lawyers might understand it rather than as anthropologists choose to interpret it.[1] This distinction between inside and outside knowledge is an old one within anthropology, perhaps among the oldest, and in at least one of its most well-known incarnations it was specifically articulated with respect to law.[2] Whatever its formulation, I have always found the usefulness of the dichotomy to lie in the importance it accords to *both* its constituent parts, and its recognition that *all* knowledge is partial, particular, and yet worthwhile. Curiously enough, however, the more anthropologists have become convinced of the need for reflexivity and the impossibility of thinking in ways that are truly outside our own conceptual horizons, the less interested we seem to be in questioning the treatment accorded to categories, like law, that we earlier stigmatized as too culturally particular and too analytically thin. But since this is a more than minimally involved argument to make, I have chosen to make it here, after the fact, rather than earlier on in the main text, on the theory that explanations do better when they follow examples rather than when they compete with them.

*　*　*

This account of the Sabarimala dispute has depended on the once deeply entwined, now increasingly estranged disciplines of anthropology and law. Some of anthropology's nineteenth-century forebearers, the dead white men of introductory classes and hallway art, were lawyers who brought their curiosity to bear on societies other than their own: Maine, Bachofen, McLellan, and Morgan, for instance.[3] They were followed, several decades later, by a series of scholars—no less white or male, but rather more anthropological than lawyerly in their training and orientation—who were also interested in the content and structure of legal rules around the world: Barton, Malinowski, Schapera, and Hoebel, among many others.[4] More anthropological studies that also attended to what we would now characterize as formal law appeared in the 1950s and 1960s, including two works responsible for precipitating a years-long debate between Max Gluckman and Paul Bohannan on the feasibility of intercultural translation.[5] All of this is to say, as I have said elsewhere: anthropology and law were once far more intertwined than recent scholarship in either discipline would suggest.[6]

A lifetime has passed since the height of the Gluckman-Bohannan debate. Those intervening years have been filled with studies that were formative for more than just my generation of legal anthropologists, and whose exclusion makes this brief history feel strangely, profoundly, truncated.[7] Nevertheless, I will pause the disciplinary retrospective here because this book is responsive *and* resistant to a trajectory taken by legal anthropology that is more or less traceable to that mid-century disagreement—a trajectory that places law at the periphery, rather than at the centre, of a field that is ostensibly concerned with it.

The Gluckman-Bohannan debate, as many sociocultural anthropologists will still be able to tell you, centred on the proper goals and mechanics of intercultural translation. Gluckman advocated for the use, where appropriate, of Western legal terms and concepts that could help explain law as the ethnographer found it in other societies. Bohannan thought, for the most part, that this practice was *never* appropriate because it treated the ethnographer's own 'folk' system for navigating everyday action as if it were an 'analytic' system for conducting scholarly analysis. This broad disagreement crystallized over a single issue, namely, Gluckman's assertion that a concept—the 'average reasonable man'—was an adjudicative aid used in much the same way by the Lozi of Northern Rhodesia as by the Common Law judges familiar to his largely Anglo-American audience. Bohannan argued that this approach 'forced the Lozi folk concepts into a Western model'.[8] He himself scrupulously refused to use the language of Western law to explain practices among his Tiv interlocutors, just as he avoided translating important vernacular terms for fear of imbuing them with meanings they did not have but that were inescapable in English. Because the disagreement animating the debate—on whether and how to translate native terms and concepts—applied to far more than the anthropological study of law, it influenced far more than the anthropological study of law. It was, in fact, a moment where the sub-discipline spoke to the discipline at large, and even to areas of doctrinal legal analysis like international and comparative law theory.

Although Laura Nader tried, through a series of edited volumes and journal issues, to mediate between the positions espoused by Gluckman and Bohannan, her compromise approach never really took.[9] Bohannan's critiques of explicit cultural comparison and his scepticism regarding the possibility of translational accuracy proved extraordinarily influential, no doubt because they both reflected and reinforced trends that were developing within the discipline writ large.[10] Late-twentieth-century anthropology was marked by escalating calls for researchers to view elite actors and their own home societies as suitable sites for ethnographic exploration, as well as for anthropologists to be more aware of their role in co-producing ethnographic insights. All of this more comfortably cohered with Bohannan's (rather than Gluckman's) approach to comparison and translation. From the 1970s onwards, consequently, anthropologists increasingly moved away from using terms and concepts considered internal to law as it was practiced in the researcher's home society. Instead, they deployed language that was specifically anthropological to study things that were variously legal, but that were not, to any great degree, about the content of formal law itself. The rise of political anthropology as a cognate sub-discipline seems to have completed this transformation, so that the anthropology of law is now more aptly called something like anthropology of politico-regulatory forms.

Just as anthropology has been moving away from law, so too has academic law (speaking only for its elite Anglo-American instantiations) been moving away from anthropology. Notwithstanding promising early moments in the nineteenth century, tantalizing windows of opportunity during the early twentieth-century heyday of legal realism, and periodic crossover successes as when Clifford Geertz was invited (in 1981) to give the Storrs Lectures at Yale Law School, legal scholarship has generally accorded little importance to the kind of granular, highly contextual insight that anthropology is capable of offering. This downward trend has been particularly noticeable since the rise, beginning in the 1970s, of the law and economics movement within the American legal academy and the corresponding prominence of generalizable, numerical, model-oriented information—what Sally Merry has, in a not-unrelated context, called 'the seductions of quantification'.[11]

So low, in fact, is anthropology's appeal to mainstream legal scholars that when I was admitted to law school at the University of Chicago—not coincidentally a stronghold of law and economics scholarship—and met briefly with a faculty member there while deciding whether to matriculate; I was told that my PhD from the same university would not only be useless to me in my search for a faculty position at a law school, but that precisely because it was in anthropology it might very well *hurt* my chances. Chicago, I should note, is to academic anthropology, what Yale is to academic law: there is simply no gainsaying its dominance.[12] Put differently, while the idea that a doctorate from Chicago's anthropology department constituted a demerit on the law teaching market was certainly a snub, it was a snub directed at my discipline rather than my pedigree. Of course, since I had by that point already spent six years at Chicago (even if not in the economics department), my reaction to this rather daunting assessment was to conduct a financial cost-benefit analysis that indicated I should attend law school and attend *Chicago*—regardless.

It is, in other words, undeniably the case that neither anthropologists nor lawyers want much to do with the core of each other's interests or methods anymore. Suggesting that they should break with this trend, or even that they *could* do so, flies in the face of several decades of developments in both disciplines and is not something to be attempted in passing. I attempt it here, however, because I continue to be perplexed by the degree to which anthropology and law can borrow from—or *raid*, to use more ethnographically familiar language—one another and yet return from the excursion almost empty-handed.[13] Whether that is because they never venture beyond the front doorway, as with law, or because they studiously avoid heirlooms hanging on the walls, as with anthropology, the effort seems to yield impressively little of value to either the subject or the object of the raid.

* * *

I say that this account of the Sabarimala dispute depends on anthropology and law not merely because I studied temple governance in Kerala ethnographically, although I did, nor because I analysed Indian case law and statutes on religious freedom, although I did this too. Nor is this an interdisciplinary exercise simply because its objectives—constructive critique regarding the substance of legal rules and the unsettling of assumptions about the human condition—are among the primary objectives of each field. The disciplinary concerns of anthropology and law have driven my engagement with the battle for Sabarimala in equal measure because, together, they have given me a way of thinking about law-in-society that neither discipline could offer by itself. In the process of writing this book, and over a series of multi-year exchanges with other legal anthropologists, I have begun referring to the confluence of these perspectives as a 'cultivated attentiveness' to law, and I have started calling the product of that attentiveness, in many cases (including this one) a kind of 'constitutional ethnography'. Neither of these terms are my own, but both have proven so useful to think with that I borrow them with gratitude.[14]

Cultivated attentiveness is what distinguishes the anthropological endeavour. It is what makes anthropology 'surprising, insightful, novel, useful, meaningful', and it has this effect because the anthropologist 'is capable of *attending* to things that her interlocutors might attend to differently (ignore, naturalize, fetishize, valorize, take for granted, etc.)'.[15] This kind of attentiveness may be inextricably associated with the fieldwork activities that most conventionally facilitate it and with the theoretical language that helps express it, but it is not dependent on or limited to particular modes of research or writing. Like the story I have told here, cultivated attentiveness is anthropological without necessarily being ethnographic. Importantly, if self-evidently, attentiveness can be *cultivated*—it is not 'some sort of extraordinary sensibility, an almost preternatural capacity to think, feel, and perceive like a native'.[16] Equally evident is that some people will be better at cultivating certain kinds of attentiveness, while others will be more successful in their efforts at cultivating *every* kind of attentiveness. And perhaps inevitably, now that I have said all this, there are different ways of being attentive. 'One can learn to slow down, listen deeply, listen further, converse, elicit, observe nuance, piece things together, interpret, map, connect dots, situate, historicize, contextualize, improvise.'[17]

Cultivating attentiveness *to law* thus demands that the anthropologist consider both what her interlocutors might overlook with respect to things legal and what they are often all too concerned with. In this book, it has meant attending to the logic of law *not only* through its aesthetics, institutions, material forms, performative practices, or any of the other avenues that anthropologists have tended to take for at least two to three decades and that, by and large, emphasize things that are conceptually or literally adjacent to what the rest of the world might recognize as law.[18] Instead, it has *also* entailed unblinking engagement with the content of law: with judicial opinions, statutory texts, and constitutional provisions. Attentiveness to law need not always involve reading it, but neither can it exist unproblematically without doing so. The stuff of law, those statutes and judicial opinions and constitutions that are often deemed too theoretically impoverished to merit engagement by serious anthropologists, are in truth potential points of valuable insight—far more so than they are now perceived to be.

In much the same way, this book presents an interpretive approach to law that is neither prescriptive nor descriptive after the schema of most contemporary American legal scholarship, although it has at times been one or the other. Waiting for the fix at the end of a piece of scholarship has always struck me as rather like hurrying through a *thali* meal for the bit of betel nut one chews at the end; at any rate, one of the goals of this book has been to show why—in India, regarding Sabarimala—there were always multiple, highly differentiated nuts to choose from. For this reason, and to the chagrin of at least some colleagues and readers, I cannot say that *IYLA* was (or was not) rightly decided because both outcomes have ample constitutional foundation.

Relatedly, the battle over Sabarimala shows, once again, that the task of description is not as uncomplicated as law folk might want to believe. The history of Sabarimala's ban, the nature of Ayyappan's celibacy, the very terminology with which courts should describe the community of Ayyappan worshippers—all of these are matters of description that, by virtue of also being matters of classification, became self-evidently important and terribly complex. But outside of the litigation war story, the courtroom commentary, or the informal exchanges between judges and former clerks—all devices that often unproblematically scaffold legal analysis done by lawyers—description is deemed methodologically suspect and analytically uninteresting when it is undertaken, far more systematically, by anthropologists. This should not be so.

Interpretation is, however, a markedly dangerous word among anthropologists, for whom the idea of an 'interpretive approach' most readily evokes the conceptual predilections and prose stylings of Clifford Geertz. More than fifteen years after he died, Geertz remains the 'ambassador from anthropology' for most of the English-language academic world, but his work, like an overly successful film or too-famous painting, is the kind of oeuvre that no sophisticated commentator can admit to enjoying overmuch.[19] *Interpretation* is not exactly baggage-free among law folk, either, inasmuch as it calls to mind the plethora of theories about how judges should interpret legal texts as well as the paucity of understanding about how they actually do so.[20] Despite these risks, which are more fundamental on the legal side of things and more polemical on the anthropologists', I want to suggest that an interpretive approach facilitated by the kind of cultivated attentiveness to law I have described here, an approach that is neither coy about its prescriptive implications nor imaginatively hobbled by them, is precisely what is missing in contemporary legal scholarship. Put differently, law's long-standing fixation on the 'ought' of collective existence, like its much more recent fascination with the 'is', generally proceeds without extensive thought as to how the two are connected. Interpretation—at once selection, contextualization, comparison, and conclusion—provides that link.

Instead of either accompanying anthropologists away from things that are self-consciously legal or following lawyers from the library into the living rooms of legal luminaries, this book uses the methods and sources of both to arrive at something more truly hybrid: a 'constitutional ethnography' of the women's entry dispute.[21] Others, drawing on slightly different ancestors and addressing slightly broader audiences, have done similarly; what I am suggesting here with respect to 'law and anthropology' is akin to what the New Legal Realism (NLR) movement has long been advocating with respect to 'law and social science'.[22] Indeed, although I was only introduced to NLR towards the tail end of this project, I have been struck by the congruence between my own work and that of the NLR community. Both this book and the work produced by NLR scholars are concerned with translating graciously and effectively between law as a discipline and law as the focal point of *other* disciplines.[23] Our questions, too, are broadly similar (although one is perhaps less likely to find, in NLR works, the kind of detailed analysis of case law contained in Chapter 3): What are the logics underpinning a system of constitutional law? How do they manifest on the ground and in the books—and are these different modes of instantiation even meaningfully distinct from one another? Who undertakes the work of reaffirming and refreshing constitutional principles, and how, and when?

Answering these questions in the idiom of constitutional ethnography is not as onerous a task as it may appear to be on first glance. Anthropologists need not 'take on the technicalities'[24] of law—they can simply cease politely ignoring them. Lawyers need not conduct years-long field studies since they may, instead, commit to the kind of cultivated attentiveness that, far more than hurriedly scribbled notebooks or hours of interviews, is the true marker of anthropological analysis. And no one need limit themselves to the world of constitutions simply because I have chosen to do so.

There are distinct advantages to anthropologically engaging with formal law and with the disputes to which it gives rise. Formal laws—constitutions perhaps more so than most—are like concretized bits of culture, floating in and out of self-consciously legal venues and demanding that we follow their unpredictable journeys off the written page in order to reveal their (often carefully hidden) assumptions. No judicial opinion and no statute could, by itself, have demonstrated the twin impulses of citizen sovereignty and shared sovereignty that emerged over the course of the women's entry dispute: that insight was the product of observations and conversations I had conducted as part of my fieldwork on secular governance and temple administration long before the *IYLA* writ petition rose to national prominence. Conversely, no anthropological focus on the ethnographic present or on the more evanescent forms of lawness now in vogue would have captured how profoundly the dispute over women's entry has shaped and been shaped by technical law—by the Essential Practices Doctrine, by public interest litigation, by *suo motu* intervention and the contours of Supreme Court review. We might surely choose other ways to talk about Sabarimala's ban that do not involve conceptualizing it as one dispute ranging over many cases and many events, but I have yet to be persuaded by any of them.

Because it is a constitutional ethnography, this book will have had too much law for anthropologists, too much society for lawyers, too few archives for historians, and so on. This, as economists enjoy saying, is a feature rather than a bug. Pleasing any one constituency overmuch is dangerous to truly hybrid endeavours. Moreover, constitutions are not only documents or cases or histories or litigants; they are, as this book has shown, all of these things, simultaneously and serially. Any study that claims to engage with constitutions as both law and social artefact must need be eclectic, expansive, and incomplete.

APPENDIX B

Legal Materials

Constitution of India

Article 14

The State shall not deny to any person equality before the law or the equal protection of the laws within the territory of India.

Article 15 (redacted)

(1) The State shall not discriminate against any citizen on grounds only of religion, race, caste, sex, place of birth or any of them.
(2) No citizen shall, on grounds only of religion, race, caste, sex, place of birth or any of them, be subject to any disability, liability, restriction or condition with regard to—
  (a) access to shops, public restaurants, hotels and places of public entertainment; or
  (b) the use of wells, tanks, bathing ghats, roads and places of public resort maintained wholly or partly out of State funds or dedicated to the use of the general public.
(3) Nothing in this article shall prevent the State from making any special provision for women and children.
(4) Nothing in this article or in clause (2) of article 29 shall prevent the State from making any special provision for the advancement of any socially and educationally backward classes of citizens or for the Scheduled Castes and the Scheduled Tribes.
(5) Nothing in this article or in sub-clause (g) of clause (1) of article 19 shall prevent the State from making any special provision, by law, for the advancement of any socially and educationally backward classes of citizens or for the Scheduled Castes or the Scheduled Tribes

(6) Nothing in this article or sub-clause (g) of clause (1) of article 19 or clause (2) of article 29 shall prevent the State from making,—
   (a) any special provision for the advancement of any economically weaker sections of citizens other than the classes mentioned in clauses (4) and (5); and
   (b) any special provision for the advancement of any economically weaker sections of citizens other than the classes mentioned in clauses (4) and (5) in so far as such special provisions relate to their admission to educational institutions . . .

Article 25

(1) Subject to public order, morality and health and to the other provisions of this Part, all persons are equally entitled to freedom of conscience and the right freely to profess, practise and propagate religion.
(2) Nothing in this article shall affect the operation of any existing law or prevent the State from making any law—
   (a) regulating or restricting any economic, financial, political or other secular activity which may be associated with religious practice;
   (b) providing for social welfare and reform or the throwing open of Hindu religious institutions of a public character to all classes and sections of Hindus.

Explanation I.—The wearing and carrying of kirpans shall be deemed to be included in the profession of the Sikh religion.

Explanation II.—In sub-clause (b) of clause (2), the reference to Hindus shall be construed as including a reference to persons professing the Sikh, Jaina or Buddhist religion, and the reference to Hindu religious institutions shall be construed accordingly.

Article 26

Subject to public order, morality and health, every religious denomination or any section thereof shall have the right—

   (a) to establish and maintain institutions for religious and charitable purposes;

(b) to manage its own affairs in matters of religion;
(c) to own and acquire movable and immovable property; and
(d) to administer such property in accordance with law.

Article 17

'Untouchability' is abolished and its practice in any form is forbidden. The enforcement of any disability arising out of 'Untouchability' shall be an offence punishable in accordance with law.

Statutory Law

The Kerala Hindu Places of Public Worship (Authorisation of Entry) Act, 1965

Section 3

Places of public worship to be open to all sections and classes of Hindus.— Notwithstanding anything to the contrary contained in any other law for the time being in force or any custom or usage or any instrument having effect by virtue of any such law or any decree or order of court, every place of public worship which is open to Hindus generally or to any section or class thereof, shall be open to all sections and classes of Hindus; and no Hindu of whatsoever section or class shall, in any manner, be prevented, obstructed or discouraged from entering such place of public worship, or from worshipping or offering prayers thereat, or performing, any religious service therein, in the like manner and to the like extent as any other Hindu of whatsoever section or class may so enter, worship, pray or perform:

Provided that in the case of a place of public worship which is a temple founded for the benefit of any religious denomination or section thereof, the provisions of this section shall be subject to the right of that religious denomination or section, as the case may be, to manage its own affairs in matters of religion.

Section 4

Power to make regulations for the maintenance of order and decorum and the due performance of rites and ceremonies in places of public worship.—

(1) The trustee or any other person in charge of any place of public worship shall have power, subject to the control of the competent authority and any rules which may be made by that authority, to make regulations for the maintenance of order and decorum in the place of public worship and the due observance of the religious rites and ceremonies performed therein:

Provided that no regulation made under this sub-section shall discriminate in any manner whatsoever, against any Hindu on the ground that he belongs to a particular section or class.

(2) The competent authority referred to in sub-section (I) shall be,—
  (i) in relation to a place of public worship situated in any area to which Part I of the Travancore-Cochin Hindu Religious Institutions Act, 1950 (Travancore-Cochin Act XV of 1950), extends, the Travancore Devaswom Board;
  (ii) in relation to a place of public worship situated in any area to which Part 11 of the said Act extends, the Cochin Devaswom Board; and
  (iii) in relation to a place of public worship situated in any other area in the State of Kerala, the Government.

The Kerala Hindu Places of Public Worship (Authorisation of Entry) Rules, 1965

Rule 3[1]

The classes of persons mentioned here under shall not be entitled to offer worship in any place of public worship or bath in or use the water of any sacred tank, well, spring or water course appurtenant to a place of public worship whether situate within or outside precincts thereof, or any sacred place including a hill or hill lock, or a road, street or pathways which is requisite for obtaining access to the place of public worship:

   …

   (b) Women at such time during which they are not by custom and usage allowed to enter a place of public worship.

Case Law

Indian Young Lawyers Association v. State of Kerala, 2018 SCC Online SC 1690 ('*IYLA*')

IYLA was issued in 2018 by the Indian Supreme Court. A group of lawyers practising at the Supreme Court read news reports of purification rituals that were conducted at Sabarimala after the actress Jayamala confessed to having entered the temple nearly twenty years earlier, while she was in the prohibited age range. The lawyers filed a public interest petition arguing that Sabarimala's admissions policy was unconstitutional because it discriminated against some Ayyappan devotees on the basis of their sex in violation of Articles 14 (equality), 15 (non-discrimination), and 25 (freedom of religion). Hearings for this petition began in earnest in 2016; at that time, the petitioners were joined by a young activist, Nikita Azad, and they were also opposed by several individuals, devotional associations, and Sabarimala's chief priest. In 2018, a five-judge bench of the Supreme Court headed by then-Chief Justice Dipak Misra determined that Sabarimala's ban was indeed unconstitutional. *IYLA* was immediately met with both widespread approval and intense criticism.

S. Mahendran v. The Secretary, Travancore Devaswom Board, AIR 1993 Ker 42

Mahendran was issued in 1991 by the Kerala High Court. A concerned devotee notified the High Court that women in the prohibited age range appeared to be visiting Sabarimala in violation of the temple's customary practices. The judge to whom the complaint was addressed, K. S. Paripoornan, had a long-standing interest in reforming temple governance in Kerala and converted the complaint into a public interest litigation petition so that the High Court could consider it. Rather than rule strictly on the issue of any specific violation or violator, the High Court examined the constitutionality of Sabarimala's admissions policy writ large. Ultimately, the High Court held that the ban on women was an essential practice that merited constitutional protection *and* that the ban should be understood to apply year-round.

Kantaru Rajeevaru v. IYLA, 2020 Supreme Court Cases 1, (14 November 2019)

Kantaru Rajeevaru was issued by a five-judge bench of the Supreme Court around fourteen months after *IYLA*. Four of the five judges had also sat on the bench that decided *IYLA*; the fifth was the new Chief Justice, Ranjan Gogoi, who had ascended to his office in the period between the two decisions. *Kantaru Rajeevaru* was issued in response to several dozen petitions asking the Supreme Court to 'review' its *IYLA* opinion and countervailing arguments that maintained the Court had no appropriate basis for review. In the end, *Kantaru Rajeevaru* did not explicitly determine whether it would be appropriate for the Court to hear review petitions on the Sabarimala litigation. The decision did, however, call for a broader question regarding Essential Practices Doctrine and its application to various disputes at the intersection of religion and gender to be 'referred' to a larger bench.

Commissioner, Hindu Religious Endowments v. Sri Lakshmindra Thirtha Swamiar of Sri Shirur Mutt, AIR 1954 SC 282 ('Shirur Mutt')

Shirur Mutt was issued by the Indian Supreme Court in 1954 in response to a new temple governance system established by the Madras Hindu Religious and Charitable Endowments Act, 1951. Under some circumstances, the Act allowed a statutory body to appoint managers for religious institutions even if those institutions already had religiously appointed leaders. One leader who was thus displaced argued that the Act and the system it created violated his constitutional rights and the rights of the religious community he led. Although the Supreme Court ultimately disagreed and upheld the statutory scheme, *Shirur Mutt* became famous for creating a test and a doctrine that both became influential in religious freedom cases. The first, the Denominational Test, stipulates that in order for a community to qualify as a 'religious denomination or section thereof' that is eligible for Article 26 protections, the community must have a name, a faith, and an organization in common. Even more famous is the Essential Practices Doctrine, which stipulates that 'what constitutes the essential part of a religion is primarily to be ascertained with reference to the doctrines of that religion itself'. Both the Denominational Test and the Essential Practices Doctrine would prove influential during the Sabarimala litigation.

Acharya Jagadishwarananda Avadhuta v. Commissioner of Police, Calcutta, AIR 1984 SC 51 ('Ananda Marga I')

The Ananda Marga litigation spans at least two decades but at its core is a dispute over the public performance of a ritual dance involving a human skull, a small knife, and a *trishul* (trident). While the Commissioner of Police of Calcutta argued that the dance violated a section of the Criminal Procedure Code outlawing public assemblies involving weapons, the community argued that the dance was an essential practice of their faith. In *Ananda Marga* I (decided in 1983), the Supreme Court found that the community did constitute a separate religious denomination that was entitled to Article 26 rights. However, the Court held that the dance was not an essential practice of Ananda Marga faith. Subsequently, the community's leader revised its central text to stipulate that the dance *was* an essential aspect of that religion, and the litigation continued. In a later *Ananda Marga* decision (released in 2004), the Supreme Court ruled that changes to religious beliefs that are made in response to litigation could not satisfy the Essential Practices Doctrine.

Notes

Preface

1. This version of the Ayyappan story, told in my own words, combines elements from narratives I've heard and read over the years in contexts that are both professional and personal. Like any mythological narrative, it is partial and particular—there are other Ayyappan stories and, indeed, other Ayyappans requiring stories. I chose to tell Ayyappan's story at the beginning of this book because, although it rarely becomes a point of direct contention, it is everywhere in the background of the dispute. Likewise, I chose to tell *this* version of the story because it is the one I encounter most often and because it speaks to the celibate character of the deity.
2. Readers should note that I use the terms 'lawyer' and 'attorney' interchangeably even though, in the United States, a distinction is sometimes made such that *lawyer* designates anyone who is a law school graduate, while *attorney* designates law school graduates who are licensed to practice law.

Introduction

1. The chief priest's public justification for the purification ritual was that one of the astrologer's assistants had been within the period of ritual pollution that follows a close relative's death, and consequently, the assistant should not have participated in the *devaprasnam*. *Hindu* (July 13, 2006).
2. Indian Young Lawyers Association v. State of Kerala, 2018 SCC Online SC 1690 (henceforth '*IYLA*'). Readers should note that all citations to the Supreme Court's 2018 opinion are to the paragraph numbering used in the SCC Online version of that opinion. Citations to other materials, especially briefs, generally use page numbers instead of paragraph numbers.
3. On 'dynamic equilibrium,' see Das Acevedo (2016a, 558).
4. In Malayalam, *ambalam* and *kshethram* are both commonly used to mean a Hindu temple, although *kshethram* tends to have a more expansive meaning that extends to the lands, bathing tanks, and other holy spaces associated with the temple (Warrier, Bhattathiry, and Warrier 2009, 79, 368).
5. In Indian usage, Mangot's position would be commonly understood as that of an *amicus* or 'friend of the court,' and indeed, he was sometimes referred to as such in writing or conversation. However, he first introduced himself to me, and most often referred to himself, as the assistant to the *devaswom* ombudsman, and so that is what I have called him here.

6. Mazzarella (2003, 33) describes his 'most immediately stimulating' informants as 'the "insider-outsiders," those who were the most ambivalently or ironically positioned in relation to their work.'
7. Moodie (2019) (on Kalighat); Nanda (2011) (on the 'State–Temple–Corporate Complex' facilitated by globalization); Das Acevedo (2016c) (on the Padmanabhaswamy temple). Academic engagements with the Ayodhya dispute are, to put it mildly, numerous.
8. In this way, the book contrasts with many exciting recent works at the intersection of anthropology and law, including Cabatingan (2018), Kahn (2019), Lemons (2019).
9. Scheppele (2004).
10. In keeping with this approach to nomenclature, I have also usually (but not invariably) referred to jurists using colloquial titling conventions rather than official ones. For instance, the Supreme Court of India's website identifies a 'Chief Justice' and various 'Judges,' but in conversation and public commentary, all of the Court's members are usually referred to as *justices* (chief or otherwise). Compare *Chief Justice & Judges*, SUPREME COURT OF INDIA, https://main.sci.gov.in/chief-justice-judges (accessed April 12, 2022) with Kakkar (2022) (using 'justice'). Meanwhile, members of the Kerala High Court are often colloquially referred to as both judges (more often in speech) and justices (more often in writing) and consequently I use both terms here. See, e.g., *Present Judges*, HIGH COURT OF KERALA, https://hckerala.gov.in/judges.php (accessed April 12, 2022) and Haneef (2022) (using 'justice').
11. *Pace* Lubet (2018). For more on evidentiary concerns in the ethnographic study of law, see the Appendix A.
12. Leach (2020 [1954], 1) put it best: 'This book ... is also intended to provide a contribution to anthropological theory. It is not intended as an ethnographic description. Most of the ethnographic facts to which I refer have been previously recorded in print. Any originality is not therefore to be found in the facts with which I deal, but in the interpretation of the facts.' As I discuss in Appendix A, that makes this a work of anthropology more than ethnography, albeit one that grows out of ethnographic fieldwork.
13. As Appendix A makes clear, I have found it increasingly useful to think of anthropology as predicated on *cultivated attentiveness*. This handy term comes from Kaushik Sunder Rajan's syllabus for a graduate methods course at the University of Chicago, and it is worth quoting Sunder Rajan in full:

> 'the fundamental *problem* of fieldwork is <u>not</u> technical ... how to interview or transcribe or code, how to do surveys, how to do participant observation, how to get access, what questions to ask and so on .... Instead, the fundamental problem of fieldwork involves the *cultivation of attentiveness* .... What makes good ethnography work ... is the fact that the ethnographer is capable of *attending* to things that her interlocutors might attend to differently' (Sunder Rajan 2015, emphasis in original).

14. Raj and Schultz (October 18, 2018).

15. *Scroll* (September 28, 2018).
16. *Indian Express* (September 29, 2018).
17. Bhaskar (September 30, 2018).
18. Gettleman, Kumar, and Schultz (September 27, 2018).
19. S. Mahendran v. The Secretary, Travancore Devaswom Board, AIR 1993 Ker 42.
20. Kantaru Rajeevaru v. IYLA, Review Petition, page 7 (Question 1).
21. On Sabarimala directly, see Das Acevedo (2016a, 2016b, 2018, 2020). On temple governance and religion-state relations more generally, see Das Acevedo (2013a, 2013b, 2016c). The title for this book comes, with permission, from Das Acevedo (2019).

Chapter 1

1. The *Kerala Mahatmyam* ('In Praise of Kerala' or 'The Greatness of Kerala') is an apocryphal Sanskrit text that, among other things, describes the creation of Kerala by the mythological character Parasurama. Like other *mahatmyams*—a genre of Sanskrit texts extolling the greatness or glory of a particular subject (for instance, the *Devi Mahatmyam* describes the majesty of the goddess)—the *Kerala Mahatmyam* does not easily fit into contemporary notions of 'history' and is usually classified as a religious text.
2. This is based on 2011 census figures which put the percentage of each community within Kerala's overall population at 18.38 (Christian), 26.56 (Muslim), and 54.73 (Hindu) (Government of India 2011).
3. Katz (2000, 12–13) and Frykenberg (2008, 92–93) discuss origin traditions and timelines among Keralite Jews and Christians.
4. For more on Hindutva strategies in Kerala, see Arafath (2021).
5. For statistics on the rebellion's casualties and a quick note about my great-grandfather, M. P. Narayana Menon, see Hardgrave (1977, 82, 91).
6. For instance, even though 'Kerala has been unusual among Indian states in that overtly communal politics has continued to be a prominent, and accepted, feature of the local scene', it is a 'pragmatic politics of communal rivalry and accommodation' (Chiriyankandath 1993, 663–65).
7. On the human costs of Partition, see Talbot and Singh (2009). For a critique of the notion that Kerala is uniquely predisposed to communal harmony, see Menon (2010).
8. Chatterji (2017) (quoting CPI(M) Member of Parliament M. B. Rajesh).
9. Throughout this book, I have tended to use *avarna*, whereas others would likely use *Dalit. Avarna*, which is a Malayalam-Sanskrit word literally meaning 'without color' but more accurately understood as 'without caste' or 'of low caste', is a designation that is relatively common in the context of Kerala but less so elsewhere in India (Warrier, Bhattathiry and Warrier 2009, 93). The contrasting term is *savarna* (lit. 'of the same color [caste]'), which is loosely used to indicate 'upper caste' status, although, in Kerala, this includes dominant castes like Nairs and

Menons who are usually understood to be in the lowest category of the fourfold *varna* system (Warrier, Bhattathiry and Warrier 2009, 1149).
10. Dempsey (1998, 55). Susan Bayly (1984, 185) has long noted the social importance of Keralite Christian participation in Hindu temple practices: 'The real proof of the Syrians' standing in the precolonial Keralan kingdoms was the fact that members of leading Syrian lineages held the standing of donors—honoured patrons and sponsors—at Hindu shrines and temple festivals in localities all over southern Kerala.'
11. De Varthema (1863, 151).
12. A host of nineteenth-century theorists, many of whom are considered proto-anthropologists, believed that matrilineal descent preceded patrilineal descent in part because physical paternity was assumed to be indeterminable among 'primitive' peoples. Bachofen (2006 [1861]), Morgan (1877), and Engels (1902 [1844]) are just a few examples of this perspective.
13. Fuller (175, 284, 295–98, 300–303).
14. Saradamoni (1994, 501) quoting V. Nagam Aiya.
15. Saradamoni (1994, 501).
16. This estimate is based on the Sample Registration System (SRS) data for 2014–18, which states that the life expectancy at birth for women across India is 70.7, while in Kerala it is 77.9 (Government of India 2020b, 6).
17. This is based on the SRS maternal mortality rates (MMR) for 2016–18, which showed that the all-India MMR was 113, while Kerala's was 43 (Yadavar 2020).
18. In 2018 Kerala had a 'crude birth rate' of 13.9 (births per 1000 persons) and the average Keralite woman could expect to have 1.7 children over the course of her lifetime (the 'total fertility rate') (Government of India 2020a, 225). By comparison, the crude birth rates for the United States, United Kingdom, and India were, respectively, 11.6, 11, and 20, while the total fertility rates for the same countries were 1.73, 1.68, and 2.2 (Government of India 2020a, 222; World Bank 2018b–2018e).
19. World Bank (2018a) (showing the global female literacy rate as being 82.72% in 2018) and Government of India (2020c) (showing Kerala's female literacy rate as being 94.1% in 2018).
20. Arunima (2003, xv) describes this tension (as well as her own 'ambivalence regarding matriliny') better than I can: 'Matriliny has always been a central part of my life. I grew up with stories of strong grandmothers …. It was all mysterious and atmospheric, but ultimately entirely foreign …. Moreover, it began to dawn on me that being a matrilineal Nayar was a memory that only a small section of the erstwhile elite could afford.'
21. In discussing the queens of Attingal—a small, semi-independent territory within Travancore whose royal house was inextricably tied to that of Travancore's—Pillai (2015, 61) exclaims that '[i]t is quite amazing that while the rest of the world was one where sexual freedoms were permitted only to men, a phenomenon where women had it equal could be found on this sliver of India's west coast'.

22. Of course, not long after this sentence was written, the CPI(M) bucked four decades of precedent to win two state elections in a row—and the leader of Kerala's BJP unit lost *both* the seats he contested (John 2 May 2021).
23. The Kerala Stay of Eviction Proceedings Act, 1957 (Act I of 1957) and the Kerala Agrarian Relations Bill, 1957 (Bill No. 51 of 1957) (henceforth 'KARB').
24. The '25 acres' figure is derived from the original version of the KARB that was passed in 1959; see KARB Ch. 3 § 61(b), p.32. Later iterations of the Act, including a version that was passed in 1969, featured different ceilings (Radhakrishnan 1981, A-130).
25. Note that the downfall of the state government was preceded and largely engineered by a coalition of opposition parties, most especially the Congress, in cooperation with the Nair Service Society, and various Christian communities. This resistance movement is commonly known as the *Vimochana Saranam* ('liberation struggle') (Tharamangalam 1981, 45–46). Daniel Patrick Moynihan comments on the financial support given by the Central Intelligence Agency to the Congress Party (and once, to Indira Gandhi personally) 'in the face of a prospective Communist victory in a state election, once in Kerala and once in West Bengal' (Moynihan and Weaver 1978, 41).
26. For an account that nicely blends approval with critique, and that puts the Campaign into conversation with Partha Chatterjee's idea of political society, see Mannathukkaren (2010).
27. On the PPP, see Franke and Chasin (1997), Vijayan (2004), and Franke (2008).
28. Although the lower caste obligation to go bare-breasted is well documented, as are resistance efforts like the several decades-long nineteenth-century Channar Revolt, there is less analysis regarding the Nair obligation to go bare-breasted before Nambudiris. Still, this practice is regularly mentioned: see, for example, Nair and Devi (2010) and Kent (2004, 216).
29. Osella and Osella (2000, 220–23). Similarly, see Tharamangalam (1981, 57–58), describing the sartorial and speech restrictions applicable to *avarna* labourers in southern Kerala, although not specifically with reference to Nair audiences.
30. Osella and Osella (2000, 222).
31. Until well into the twenty-first century, a few of Kerala's most prestigious temples admitted men wearing shirts or women wearing the ubiquitous and hardly titillating (but suspiciously Islamic-feeling) *salwar-kameez*; my own first awkward attempts at draping a sari occurred in the guest bedrooms and hotels that I inhabited during my collegiate temple tour rather than during the weddings or dance recitals more common among my second-generation peers.
32. Louise Ouwerkerk, an instructor at the Maharaja's Women's College in Trivandrum and a figure in Travancore's public life between 1929 and 1939, noted that 'Christians, Muslims, cows, goats and dogs could use these roads, but not the untouchables' (Ouwerkerk 1994, 57).
33. Subrahmanian (2019) and Vijayan (2004).
34. Anitha et al. (2008).

35. Devika (2010, 275).
36. Menon (2020, 41) (regarding women in the labour force), Chacko (2003, 57) (regarding the prevalence of domestic violence and the rise of dowry deaths), and Mukhopadhyay (2007, 24–26) (regarding sex-selective abortions). See also Jeffrey (1992). Notwithstanding the fact that matrilineal succession to *joint* property was abolished by the Kerala Joint Hindu Family System (Abolition) Act, 1975, 'the loose ends of matriliny still crop up regularly in civil litigation' (Jeffrey 2004–2005, 653). In 2001, Menski declared that 'Marumakkathayam law in Kerala is still alive … [although] it is now restricted to rules concerning succession to individual property' (Menski 2001, 324). Meanwhile, Jeffrey observes that, at least as of 2002, the Kerala High Court held that 'the law of 1976 abolished matrilineal practice governing the property of individuals and joint-families but not … for property held under old tenurial forms' (Jeffrey 2004–2005, 653).
37. Jeffrey (1992) and Mukhopadhyay (2007).
38. As of June 2019, Kerala had the third highest unemployment rate of all major states (8.4%) and a lower worker population ratio (employed individuals per 1,000 persons) than its southern-state neighbours (Government of India 2020d, A-70, A-74).
39. Dasgupta (2017, 252) (noting that although agriculture contributed barely 14% of Kerala's domestic product and grew at merely 0.5% between 1997 and 2008, it provided employment for around 33% of the population as of 2009–10).
40. Kurien (191) (discussing 'Gulf pockets') and Percot and Rajan (using nurses as a case study in the high percentage of Keralite migrants in the Middle East). Note that Kerala has, for some time now, ceded its earlier position as the largest supplier of migrant Indian labour to the Middle East and elsewhere (Wadhawan 2018, 3) (showing that between 2011 and 2017, Uttar Pradesh and Bihar sent the most migrant labourers). Nonetheless, Gulf migration remains culturally significant in Kerala, including in the way 'oil's hidden affective presence … is fathomable in Kerala's cultural and literary productions' (Menon 2020).
41. *FirstPost* (2019) (describing how, during the 2019 Sabarimala riots, a 64-year-old female cancer patient collapsed at the railway station in Thiruvananthapuram and died following what her relatives alleged was a delay in accessing ambulance service) and *The New Indian Express* (2020) (describing how, in 2020, a 60-year-old man with a heart condition died after the state-run bus operator went on a flash strike and brought Trivandrum to a standstill for several hours).
42. Compare Halliburton (1998, 2341) (drawing on National Crime Records Bureau data to say that 'Kerala has the highest suicide rate in India'—and by a substantial margin of three times the national average and 50 per cent more than the second highest state) with Government of India (2020e, 195) (showing that Kerala was #6 as of 2019).

43. Although Kant was one of the driving forces behind the campaign, the actual phrase 'God's Own Country' came from Walter Mendez of Mudra Communications (Madhukar 2013).
44. Continuing fascination with Kerala as a land of multiple sacralities is evident, for example, in Khan (2009, back cover), where the author embarks on a quest 'to discover "sacred" Kerala', encountering on her way 'an array of picturesque characters and many a fascinating shrine'.
45. Menon (1983 [1878], 171).
46. See, for instance, Kooiman (1992, 597), who states that '[t]here is wide-spread agreement that this ceremony was first and foremost a political manoeuvre. Religion was marshalled behind the throne and the state's integrity was protected by making any future rebellion against the government sacrilege against Sri Padmanabha' (internal citations omitted).

    A widespread perception is that only the ruling king and queen of Travancore hold the title *Padmanabhadasa* ('servant of Padmanabha', feminine: *Padmanabhasevini*), and that Anizham Thirunal received the title as a result of his donation of the kingdom. See, e.g., Government of India (n.d., stating that 'In December 1749, he took the major step of dedicating his kingdom to Sri Padmanabha and assumed the title of Padmanabha Dasa'), Kooiman (2005, 158) (describing Ayilyam Thirunal's approval of the phrase 'Padmanabha dasa' on a coat of arms on that grounds that it was well known as the first of his long list of titles as ruler), and Das Acevedo (2013a, 42–43). However, the Travancore royals have indicated that they believe all members of the royal family bear the title and that they did so well before Anizham Thirunal's donation. See Marthanda Varma, at ¶5, n. 7 and Uthradom Tirunal (2010, 30) ('All the male members of the family were made Padmanabhadasas on their first birthday. Records show that such ceremonies took place even before Anizham Tirunal Marthanda Varma dedicated the State of Travancore through Tiruppadidanam.').
47. Interview with Ramavarma, Raja of Pandalam, 25 July 2011.
48. Bayi (1815, 1823).
49. Appadurai (1977).
50. Appadurai (1977, 50) (internal citations omitted).
51. Moolam Thirunal (1922).
52. Moolam Thirunal (1922). Menon (1964, 19) discusses the deliberations that led to this decision. Within the committee assigned to deliberate on the feasibility of creating a Devaswom Department, all but one member argued that 'the State was sovereign proprietor of the Devaswoms and therefore was accountable to none'. The lone dissenting member stated that the state stood in the role of a trustee-manager, not a proprietor, and that since the trustee had merged the trust properties with its own, it was obliged to meet the expenses of maintaining the trust property even if this required it to draw on its own funds.
53. Aiyer (1998, 653) notes that in 1912–13, well before the creation of the Devaswom Department, 'the Hindu subjects of His Highness considered that the

Government was utilising, for their own purposes, the funds derived from the properties of the Devaswoms' while 'the impression was entertained by the non-Hindu subjects that the expenditure incurred on Devaswoms ... was wholly met out of the funds derived from the general tax-payer'.

54. Chithira Thirunal (1936).
55. Almost all the statutes I am aware of were enacted between 1947 and 1950, with the exception of the Bombay Hindu Temple Worship (Removal of Disabilities) Act, 1938, and the Madras Temple Entry Authorization and Indemnity Act (1939) (Das Acevedo Work in progress).
56. Protection of Civil Rights Act, 1955, § 3. Note that this Act was formerly known as the Untouchability (Offenses) Act. See Galanter (1964).
57. Idicheria (1942) (proposing 'a beautifully painted, life-size model in wood, of the Temple Entry, illustrating Hindus of all nationalities, belonging to all the various castes, their faces bright with enthusiasm, walking on for worship into the age long and time honoured temple, the gates of which now swing welcome to all'.) and Aiyer (1943) (objecting to accusations of segregated worship and ritual purification and to claims that Travancore's temple entry proclamation was the direct result of Gandhi, M. K's efforts).
58. One legislator debating the introduction of a similar policy for the British-controlled region of Malabar exclaimed that, 'everybody acquainted with that proclamation knows, and in fact, all of us know, that the order was issued because the Maharaja possesses autocratic powers' (Extracts 1938, 17). Another added 'An autocratic mandate! When such autocratic States are unfit to come into the Federation with democratic British Provinces, I would very much like to know whether a mandatory order passed by the Sovereign of Travancore can be taken as a proper example for introducing this reform here' (Ibid at 28).
59. Literature exploring or partially addressing the relationship between temples and sovereign authority in Tamil country is too plentiful to exhaustively capture here, particularly when considering time periods from the precolonial to the postcolonial. A few prominent works include the following: Appadurai (2008 [1981]), Appadurai and Breckenridge (1976), Breckenridge (1977), Dirks (1996), Fuller (1984), Good (2004), Presler (1987), Price (2008 [1996]), Mudaliar (1976), and Stein (1977).

Burton Stein's works on the Tirupati temple in Andhra Pradesh (1958) and (1960) are classics. See also Kumari (1998) on the management of Hindu religious institutions in Andhra Pradesh. For a broader analysis of the relationship between sovereignty and devotion in the Kingdom of Mysore (present-day Karnataka) see Simmons (2020, ch.5).

Despite a not-insignificant literature on Keralite religious practices (Caldwell 1999; Tarabout 1986; Kurup 1973)—many of which specifically include temples within their scope of analysis (Vaidyanathan 1982; Pillai 1986; Osella and Osella 2003; Bhalla 2006)—research speaking to temple regulation has, on the whole, been a patchwork of descriptive works and hagiographies. In the first category

are two monumental studies of individual temples by P. R. G. Mathur (2009, 2019), as well as two studies of temples in Kodungallur, in central Kerala, by Induchudan (1969, 1971); government-sponsored surveys of Keralite temples by Jayashankar (1999, funded by the Census), as well as Sarkar (1978, funded by the Archaeological Survey of India); and Srinivasan (1971), Padmanabhan (1977), and Moorthy (1991), which variously explore what is often called 'temple culture'.
60. On colonial transformations of the law of trusts as they apply to religious endowments and temple deities, see Birla (2009).
61. Until recently, the Pathur Nataraja dispute was the most internationally well-known dispute featuring a deity as litigant. See, e.g., Davis (2010) and (1999). The image had been seized at the British Museum, where it was sent for restoration after a London dealer sold it to a Canadian firm; the Government of India was heavily involved in directing and bankrolling litigation in British courts that sought the image's return to India. A key—and by far, the most sensational—aspect of the Government's case was that the claim of the deity Nataraja to his own bronze image was superior to the claim of the Canadian firm over the same image. See Bumper Development Corp. (1991) (rejecting the Canadian firm's appeal from the Queen's Bench decision).
62. The Pathur Nataraja case has arguably been somewhat overshadowed by the Ayodhya dispute, in which 'Bhagwan Sri Ram Virajman' (the deity Ram) figured as the lead plaintiff in one of the suits that were consolidated for hearing by the Supreme Court. More remarkably still, the same suit also featured a second plaintiff: 'Asthan Shri Ram Janam Bhumi' (the land alleged to be Ram's literal birthplace). In a unanimous decision widely believed to have been authored by Justice Chandrachud, D. Y., the Court sustained the claims of the deity but declined to recognize the personhood of the land and ultimately granted control over the land to Hindus via a government-established trust (M. Siddiq v. Mahant Suresh Das 2020; Mahapatra 2019).
63. Frykenberg (2000, 5–8). The deity that appeared on Fort St. George's currency was Tirupati Venkateswara. The statute was the Madras Endowments and Escheats Regulation of 1817 (Regulation VII of 1817).
64. Among the five contemporary south Indian states—Andhra Pradesh, Karnataka, Kerala, Tamil Nadu, and Telangana—only Karnataka, which was part of the princely state of Mysore, lay outside the boundaries of the Madras Presidency.

Regarding commonalities between statutes: to take just one example, the 1817 Act, its 2013 Tamilian iteration, and the Travancore-Cochin Act all empower the state to approve or appoint trustees for individual temples under certain conditions. Regulation VII of 1817, at ¶¶10–13, Tamil Nadu Hindu Religious and Charitable Endowments Act (1959) (as amended 2013) ¶2 (inserting a new sub-section titled '*Qualifications of trustees*'), and Travancore-Cochin Hindu Religious Institutions Act (1950) (as amended 2007) ¶41.
65. Frykenberg (2000, 7)

66. To be sure, the trajectories and current statuses of these administrative infrastructures vary across south India. The Andhra Pradesh Endowment Department unveiled a new, centralized Temple Management System in 2021, while in 2022, the Chief Minister of Karnataka announced his government's intention to devolve power back to the 34,000 temples currently administered by the state (*Times Now* 2021; *Economic Times* 2022).
67. Moodie (2019) (on Kalighat) and Mishra (2006) (on Jagannath).
68. Both acts have undergone several amendments, one of the more recent and notable of which was an amendment to the 1951 Act that was passed in 2008 and that created the Malabar Devaswom Board.
69. What else besides a fascinating act of constitutional translation is one to see in, for instance, the Madras Hindu Religious and Charitable Endowments (Amendment) Act, 2017, which stipulates that administrative jurisdictions under the Malabar Devaswom Board shall each be headed by an Area Committee consisting of 'one member from the Scheduled Castes or Scheduled Tribe Communities; one woman member; one philosopher of Hindu Religion or performer of temple art or a person who has authored works on Hindu literature; and four other members'? Act 9 of 2017, at ¶2.
70. Jacobsohn (2009) and Bhatia (2019).
71. See, e.g., Bhagwati (2005).
72. Constitution of India, Part IV: Directive Principles of State Policy, art. 44.
73. Constitution of India, Part IV: Directive Principles of State Policy, art. 51(A)(e) and (h).
74. The nearly 150-year-long history of rationalist activism in India has an especially strong South Indian element. One of the first Indians to self-identify as a rationalist was the Keralite activist Mookencheril Cherian Joseph (1887–1981), popularly known as *Yukthivadi*, while the Indian Rationalist Association held its first convention in Madras in 1949 (Quack 2011, 92–94). ('Rationalist' is the translation commonly given for *yukthivadi* by the associations themselves—see Das Acevedo (2013a, 2016a) for a discussion of Keralite rationalist groups in connection with a different dispute over Sabarimala—and I have decided to retain the term.)
75. Constitution of India, Part III: Fundamental Rights, art. 25: 'Subject to public order, morality and health and to the other provisions of this Part, all persons are equally entitled to freedom of conscience and the right freely to profess, practice and propagate religion.'
76. Ananda Marga I.
77. Mohd Hanif Qureshi.
78. Wahi (2016, 962–63) argues that 'The fundamental right to property in India has come full circle …. Importantly, however, the trajectory of the right to property in the Constitution … demonstrates the Indian State's continual attempts to reshape property relations in society to achieve its goals of economic development and social redistribution.' The Constitution (86th Amendment) Act, 2002,

created Article 21(a), which requires the state to provide free and compulsory education for all children between six and fourteen years of age.
79. Elkins, Ginsburg, and Melton (2009, 151) (arguing that 'According to the predictions of our epidemiological model, India's framers have built a document to last generations' and offering several reasons explaining this robustness).
80. Austin (1999 [1966], 50).
81. De (2018, 10).
82. Dhavan (2001, 311) (describing the 'three salient principles' of the Constitution's secular design as being 'religious freedom', 'celebratory neutrality', and 'regulatory and reformative justice').
83. Jacobsohn (2010, 216).
84. Constitution of India, Part III: Fundamental Rights, art. 26, which reads as follows:

> Subject to public order, morality and health, every religious denomination or any section thereof shall have the right—
> (a) to establish and maintain institutions for religious and charitable purposes;
> (b) to manage its own affairs in matters of religion;
> (c) to own and acquire movable and immovable property; and
> (d) to administer such property in accordance with law.

85. As Chapter 3 argues, though, the doctrine has shifted considerably away from this original purpose.
86. Shirur Mutt, ¶20.
87. See generally Parashar (1992) on the unifying and modernizing impulses animating legislative reforms of Hindu law.
88. Agnes (2016, 908).
89. The relevant statutory language is available in the notes to Chapter 3.
90. This phrase, of course, comes from Sunil Khilnani, who argued that 'the presumption that a single shared sense of India—a unifying idea and concept—can at once define the facts that need recounting and provide the collective subject for the Indian story has lost all credibility' (Khilnani 1997, 2).
91. See Kaviraj (2000), in note 282.

Chapter 2

1. On the general importance of name-invocations, Jackson (1994, 42) observes that 'in a wide range of Hindu traditions and circumstances the holy name was believed to have an inherent extraordinary potency, bringing one in touch with the being or reality name'. Similarly, Beck (1995, 188–89) states that ' "taking the name" (nāma-japa) is an essential step in professing one's Bhakti, since most sects hold God and his name are somehow identical'.
2. Lamb (2002, 116).

3. Warrier, Bhattathiry and Warrier (2009, 118–19).
4. Devika (2019a).
5. Devika (2019b).
6. The quoted phrase is the tagline for one of the People for Dharma's designated focus areas, 'Value system' http://peoplefordharma.org (accessed 27 February 2021).
7. Mehra (2017 at 2:17) (in which George describes herself as an Internet Hindu).
8. Sethi (2002) argues that Hindu nationalist women are able to move between identities as 'nurturing mothers and obedient wives' and 'avenging angels in moments of crisis'. For more on the complicated empowerment of women in Hindu nationalism, see the special issue on 'Women and Religious Nationalism in India', the *Bulletin of Concerned Asian Scholars*, including Sarkar (1993), Bacchetta (1993), and Basu (1993), as well as Hansen (1994).
9. Gopinathan (23 October 2018).
10. *OnManorama* (24 December 2018).
11. Both the Kerala Muslim Jamaath Council and the government telecommunications entity BSNL cited the damage that she had caused to Hindu religious sentiments as grounds for their severance of all relations with Fathima. Fathima was fired from her job after she attempted to visit Sabarimala and posted several social media messages on the issue. She was evicted from her BSNL employee residential quarters a few months later after being charged with posing 'seminude in front of her minor children, allowing them to paint on her bare body and sharing the video on social media' as part of what she claimed was an effort to critique societal taboos on nudity and sex (*Hindustan Times* 21 October 2018; *New Indian Express* 30 June 2020; *News Minute* 28 July 2020).
12. *News Minute* (31 December 2018) (noting that over 176 other sociopolitical organizations participated in the protest).
13. Koshy (3 October 2018); Babu (20 November 2018).
14. *News Minute* (31 December 2018).
15. Ameerudheen (2 January 2019); Ashraf (3 January 2019).
16. Schultz (18 January 2019).
17. Meethal (3 January 2019).
18. Devasia (9 February 2019).
19. *India Today* (3 January 2019).
20. *News Minute* (3 January 2019).
21. *Outlook* (21 January 2019).
22. Koshy (5 February 2019).
23. See, e.g., Binu v. State of Kerala (protest march and pelting stones at a state-operated bus), Ravi v. State of Kerala (participating in an unlawful assembly and pelting stones at a state-operated bus), Sree Prasad v. State of Kerala (attacking the police), and Vipin v. State of Kerala (pelting stones at a state-operated bus and using 'criminal force' against the police). In February 2021, the Pinarayi Vijayan administration decided to withdraw all cases against individuals who participated in the Sabarimala protests, as well as in protests against the central government's

Citizenship Amendment Act. Estimates of the number of affected cases ranged from the merely sizable (*Kerala Kaumudi* (24 February 2021): 2,300 cases) to the truly mind-boggling (Philip (25 February 2021): 17,000 cases involving 68,000 people).
24. K. Sivadasan v. State of Kerala.
25. Sivan v. State of Kerala. The provision for anticipatory bail can be found in the *Criminal Procedure Code, 1973* §438, although the Code itself does not use that term.
26. On the rise of the 'good governance' Court, see Robinson (2009a).
27. Law Commission of India (1969, 320–21: ¶39.9). I have characterized anticipatory bail as a judicial creation because Commission itself notes that courts had already been considering the permissibility of anticipatory bail at the time it was crafting its report; consequently, the Commission frames its own discussion of the topic as a suggestion for universal acceptance of an existing practice. *Id.* Still, there is no question that anticipatory bail became a widespread phenomenon after it received the imprimatur of the Law Commission. The Supreme Court, in Gurbaksh Singh Sibbia, broadly accepted the Article 21 impulses behind anticipatory bail. Gurbaksh Singh Sibbia, at 576: ¶10, 586: ¶26. (Chandrachud, CJ). In 2017, the Law Commission cautioned that 'the Cr.PC does not form a part of Article 21 of the Constitution of India' and suggested 'making the anticipatory bail operational for a limited time' (2017, 48: ¶6.5 and 53: ¶6.12). However, in 2020, the Supreme Court seemed to reject this proposal in Sushila Aggarwal, saying that 'the normal rule should not be to limit the order [of anticipatory bail] in relation to a period of time' (Sushila Aggarwal, at 47: ¶7.6 (M. R. Shah, J.)).
28. The Law Commission noted in its 2017 report that there has been 'rampant misuse' of the anticipatory bail provision (2017, 47: ¶6.3). Others have criticized the kind of analysis that anticipatory bail demands of courts. Sekhri (2019) notes that anticipatory bail creates jurisdictional 'muddle', while Bhattacharya (2016) argues that anticipatory bail requires courts to issue opinions 'based on presumption'. More broadly still, Mustafa (2020) argues that Indian bail jurisprudence is problematic in terms of the length, content, and conditions of bail decisions.

Although bail is primarily a High Court and Sessions Court concern, Robinson notes that criminal matters (which include bail appeals) have always constituted one of the largest categories within the Court's docket—and, moreover, that despite its chronic backlog the Court likely prioritizes these cases (2009b; 2013a, 596). Indeed, to deal with this problem the Court recently began hearing appeals on regular and anticipatory bail matters in offences with a maximum jail sentence of seven years using hitherto unprecedented single-judge benches (*Times of India* 13 May 2020).
29. Sreekumar v. State of Kerala (concerning an offence under §67 of the Information Technology Act of 2000). The case, for which I only have a 6-page opinion to guide me, seems to concern a dispute between a 'lady de facto complainant' and

a petitioner (the accused seeking anticipatory bail) over strong words and social media postings on the topic of women's entry. To my understanding, the husbands of both complainant and petitioner had participated in a televised debate on *IYLA*, after which the petitioner posted messages on the complainant's Facebook page that described the complainant's husband in 'highly abusive and unparliamentary and unprintable words' (Sreekumar, at ¶5). The complainant, an Assistant Professor of Law (and, along with her husband, a CPI(M) activist), argued that the petitioner intended to insult her womanhood, caused her mental distress, and raised lascivious interest in the hearts of visitors to her Facebook page. Id, at ¶2.

30. Dasgupta (1 January 2019).
31. Kumari (16 October 2018).
32. Interview with Bhakti Pasrija, Delhi, 14 September 2011.
33. Phone interview with Bhakti Pasrija Sethi, 27 April 2020.
34. *Week* (30 October 2018).
35. *FirstPost* (20 November 2018).
36. Mathew (4 January 2019).
37. NIMBY (not-in-my-back-yard) is the term commonly used in the United States to describe homeowners who oppose publicly beneficial land use projects, like nuclear power plants, waste management facilities, or homeless shelters—all good things that, according to the NIMBY, are in need of being done but are better done elsewhere. NIMBYs are widely portrayed as selfish and even as irrational, since they often also stand to benefit from the proposed development along with the rest of their communities. At the same time, others have argued that even when the expected outcome of the development is clearly beneficial to the NIMBY, it is possible to understand their reluctance to cooperate as a rational response to unknown fluctuations in the value of a primary asset (Fischel 2001).
38. Ashraf (10 January 2019).
39. Ashraf (10 January 2019).
40. Singh (2020 [1930]).
41. Daniyal (11 February 2018).
42. Chanda-Vaz (18 February 2018); Kumar (11 March 2018).
43. Ilaiah Shepherd (24 March 2018).
44. Tharoor (10 November 2018).
45. Tharoor (10 November 2018).
46. *India Today* (24 May 2019); Kochukudy (27 May 2019).
47. *NDTV* (26 May 2019).
48. Kochukudy (27 May 2019).
49. *Economic Times* (24 May 2019).
50. Varma (25 October 2019).
51. *Times of India* (28 November 2018).
52. *OnManorama* (21 June 2019); Nair (27 June 2019); Anand (30 May 2020).
53. Kesavananda Bharati v. State of Kerala.

NOTES   197

54. Austin (2008 [1996], 164).
55. Constitution of India, Part III: Fundamental Rights, art. 32; Constitution of India, Part VI: The States, art. 226.
56. Baxi (2000, 157); Baxi (1985, 107). *See also* Balakrishnan (2008, 2) (stating that PIL 'has come to be recognized as a characteristic feature of the higher judiciary in India').
57. Anand (2003, 383).
58. George (2005).
59. Vandenhole (2002, 155).
60. Galanter (2014, 74).
61. Carlisle v. United States held that a federal district court could not grant, *sua sponte*, a judgement notwithstanding the verdict to remedy the late filing of that motion by the petitioner. In Trest v. Whitley, the United States Court of Appeals for the Fifth Circuit moved *sua sponte* to reject a habeas corpus claim because of procedural default, citing an obligation to do so. The Supreme Court ruled that this was not obligatory, but declined to rule whether it was permitted (Trest v. Cain).
62. Galanter (2014, 77).
63. The first significant use of 'constitutional morality' in recent years is likely in Dipak Misra's opinion for a five-justice bench in *Manoj Narula* (2014). But the Court did use the phrase earlier—for instance, in *S. P. Gupta* (1981) (also known as the 'First Judges' Case').
64. Mehta (2010).
65. Lemons (2019, 35).
66. In the *Supreme Court Advocates-on-Record Association v. Union of India* (2016), a five-justice bench invalidated the 99th Amendment to the Indian Constitution and the National Judicial Appointments Commission Act (2014). The decision, which became known as the 'NJAC case', ensured that the Court did not lose virtually unchecked formal authority over appointments to the higher judiciary.
67. Barring death, impeachment, or retirement, the individuals destined to occupy the Chief Justice's seat after the current Chief Justice, D. Y. Chandrachud, are: Sanjiv Khanna, B.R. Gavai, Surya Kant, and Vikram Nath. In 2027, B.V. Nagarathna should become the first female Chief Justice of India. (Kashyap 18 May 2022; Constitution of India, Part V: The Union, art. 124).
68. Sengupta (2019, 37).
69. Ganz (17 May 2017) notes that the factors to break ties are, in order: (1) time of swearing-in, (2) years of High Court service, and (3) bench over bar appointments.
70. Chhibber (29 May 2020) and Saluja (17 July 2020). Indeed, Nagarathna *was* elevated and is scheduled to become India's first female Chief Justice (Bose 2021).
71. This chronology triangulates being various sources, including *Business-Standard* (6 May 2019), Saheli et al. (2019), Complainant (2019), and Yamunan and Chakravarty (9 May 2019).

72. Das Acevedo (2021a).
73. Lalwani (7 May 2019) notes that '55 protestors—52 women, three men' were detained.
74. Yamunan (2 October 2018).
75. Bagriya (12 January 2019).
76. Mandhani (2 November 2019).

Chapter 3

1. Pillai and Sekhar (24 July 2018) offer this description of Subramanian Swamy v. Union of India.
2. For more on the 'polyvocal' nature of the Supreme Court, see Robinson (2013b, 184).
3. Robinson (2009b, 2013a).
4. The justices assigned to hear the Sabarimala dispute in January 2018 were Chief Justice Dipak Misra, Justice A. K. Sikri, Justice A. M. Khanwilkar, Justice D. Y. Chandrachud, and Justice Ashok Bhushan (*Economic Times* 15 January 2018).
5. On the shifts in PIL jurisprudence, see Thiruvengadam (2013) and Gauri (2009).
6. Patel (2019) and Transparency International (2018).
7. Briefs submitted by the Nair Service Society, People for Dharma, and the Raja of Pandalam are cited below and appear in the bibliography, which also includes citational information for the brief filed on behalf of Nikita Azad. Briefs for Usha Nandini and the All India Democratic Women's Association do not appear in the bibliography: the one because the copy I have been able to obtain lacks an identification number comparable to the other briefs, and the other because I have not been able to acquire a copy of the brief itself.
8. Jain (21 February 2017).
9. Shirur Mutt, at ¶20.
10. For a different approach to religious freedom jurisprudence that is critical of the Essential Practices Doctrine, see Neo (2018), which argues for a deferential two-step enquiry.
11. Shirur Mutt, at ¶15.
12. Constitution of India, Part III: Fundamental Rights, 26(a) (religious and charitable organizations), 26(b) (internal affairs), art. 26(c) and 26(d) (property rights).
13. Shirur Mutt, at ¶15. For an example of the reliance on Shirur Mutt that is itself an influential decision, see S. P. Mittal v. Union of India, at ¶21.
14. IYLA, at ¶95 (Misra, CJ).
15. IYLA, at ¶96 (Misra, CJ).
16. IYLA, at ¶122–23 (Misra, CJ).
17. Kerala (Authorisation of Entry) Act (emphasis added), discussed in Mahendran, at ¶26.
18. Kerala (Authorisation of Entry) Act.

NOTES 199

19. Brief for Nair Service Society, at ¶1; Brief for People for Dharma, at ¶7–9. In contrast, the Raja of Pandalam implied that fertile women were dangerously appealing to *male pilgrims* and that menstruation made it impossible for fertile women to observe the forty-one-day penance. Brief for Raja of Pandalam, at ¶9.
20. IYLA, at ¶144.iii and x–xii (Misra, CJ). The Chief Justice also briefly considers whether the right to religious freedom protected by Article 25(1) can be enforced against the Travancore Devaswom Board, but I have not analyzed that discussion here.
21. AIR 1993 Ker 42.
22. IYLA, at ¶171 (Nariman, J.).
23. IYLA, at ¶169–70 (Nariman, J.).
24. Shastri Yagnapurushdasji, at ¶26.
25. Sri Venkataramana Devaru, at ¶17.
26. Consider, for instance, Seshammal v. State of Tamil Nadu (discussed in Fuller (1988)).
27. Mallampalli (2010, 1045–1046) notes that '[a]s As the colonial state gained greater access to "empirical" data concerning Indian society, the courts became less willing to listen to what litigants had to say about their own customs' and felt emboldened to dispense with 'pandits and maulvis, whose role in interpreting Hindu and Muslim law for the courts ended in 1864'.
28. After Shirur Mutt (1954) and Venkataramana Devaru (1957), a series of cases in the 1960s developed the Court's greater role in marking the boundaries of religion. In Durgah Committee (1961), the Court declared its obligation to not only distinguish between religion and non-religion, but between true religion and mere superstition; this task would, of course, require the Court to disregard, or at least discount, the views of the religious community in question as to the true content of their own faith. Govindlalji v. State of Rajasthan (1963) continued this trend, which culminated in the Satsang case (1966), when the Court essayed its first major post-independence definition of Hinduism. The 'overarching, all-embracing' version it constructed in that case (and in contrast to the views of the religious community in question) 'has become hegemonic' in Indian jurisprudence (Sen 2010, 14–19).

    Two cases from the 1980s further demonstrated the Court's pre-eminence in defining religion for the purposes of constitutional protection: in the space of a single year, the Court decided that Aurobindo's followers *were not* a religious denomination according to Article 26, while Ananda Margis *were*. S. P. Mittal (1983), Ananda Marga I (1984). A series of temple administration cases authored in the 1990s by Justice K. Ramaswamy upheld an even broader understanding of what the Constitution protects—'dharma rather than conventional religion'—in the course of advancing state oversight of major Hindu shrines. See Sen (2010, 61–64), discussing Ramaswamy's opinion in A. S. Narayana Deekshitulu (1995).
29. IYLA, at ¶174 (Nariman, J.).

30. IYLA, at ¶175 (Nariman, J.).
31. IYLA, at ¶175 (Nariman, J.).
32. IYLA, at ¶176 (Nariman, J.).
33. IYLA, at ¶176–77 (Nariman, J.).
34. Although D.Y. Chandrachud is the Chief Justice of India at the time of this book's final editing and production, I will continue to refer to him as a Justice of the Supreme Court when discussing events predating his elevation.
35. Puttaswamy v. Union of India.
36. Romila Thapar v. Union of India (Chandrachud, J., dissenting).
37. Joseph Shine v. Union of India.
38. Ministry of Defense v. Babita Puniya (Indian Army) and Union of India v. Annie Nagaraja (Indian Navy).
39. Deepak, not surprisingly, has become something of a darling among the Hindu Right and consequently a figure of note among their critics. A report discussing the Hindu Right's response to a 2021 virtual conference called Dismantling Global Hindutva noted that one of Deepak's tweets was among the most retweeted critiques of the event (Ahmed, Devulapalli, and Saldarriaga 2022).
40. Ainge Roy (16 March 2017).
41. Fleming (forthcoming) conducts a sustained exploration of Anglo-Hindu case law and Dharmashastra precepts on temple ownership.
42. Doctor (11 August 2018) suggests that in the years following the landmark 1925 case Pramatha Nath Mullick, there was 'an explosion of cases where deities went to court'. This may be somewhat overstating the matter, but it is certainly true that divine litigants are not unfamiliar in the landscape of Indian jurisprudence.
43. IYLA, at ¶166.8, FN 45 (Nariman, J.) and IYLA, at ¶310 (Malhotra, J.).
44. IYLA, at ¶247–56 (Chandrachud, J.) and Bhatia (2016, 367–70).
45. ¶303.2 (Malhotra, J.).
46. ¶303.4 (Malhotra, J.).
47. ¶303.7 (Malhotra, J.).
48. The case that developed *after* PIL's emergence is Bijoe Emmanuel.
49. Vakil (2022) makes a much more nuanced version of this core argument.
50. IYLA, at ¶308.9 (denominational status), ¶309.13 (essential practices), and ¶311.6 (Rule 3(b)) (Malhotra, J.).
51. IYLA, at ¶305 (Article 15) and ¶310 (Article 17) (Malhotra, J.).
52. IYLA, at ¶304 (discussing religion and rationality) and ¶309.9 (discussing Hindu deities) (Malhotra, J.).
53. IYLA, at ¶304.2 (Malhotra, J.). For instance, Justice Malhotra's assertion seems to fly in the face of the well-known line from an earlier Supreme Court opinion that the courts must identify 'practices [which] though religious may have sprung from merely superstitious beliefs and may in that sense be extraneous and unessential accretions to religion itself', Durgah Committee, at ¶34.
54. IYLA, at ¶95 (Misra, CJ); IYLA v. State of Kerala, Writ Petition by Indian Young Lawyers Association, at 52–54 ('Grounds—G'); IYLA v. State of Kerala, Brief of

Intervenor-Applicant No. 30 of 2016 (People for Dharma), at 15–16; IYLA v. State of Kerala, Brief of Respondent No. 6 (Nair Service Society) at 2–3.
55. IYLA, at ¶309.9 (Malhotra, J.).
56. On the individuality of Hindu temple deities, see Appadurai and Breckenridge (1976, 190), who write: 'Still further evidence of the presence of the deity as a person is his or her eligibility for marriage ... capacity of having sexual relations, desire to take holidays, and willingness to engage in conquest, quarrels or other playful acts.'
57. This point is quite obviously inspired by Winnifred Fallers Sullivan's argument regarding the 'impossibility of religious freedom'. Sullivan concludes her book by observing that 'what is sought by the plaintiffs' in religious freedom cases 'is not the right of "religion" to reproduce itself but the right of the individual, every individual, to life outside the state—the right to live as a self on which many given, as well as chosen, demands are made. Such a right may not be best realized through laws guaranteeing religious freedom but by laws guaranteeing equality' (2005, 159).
58. IYLA, at ¶209 (Chandrachud, J.). *Venkataramana Devaru* is frequently identified as the first time the Court shifted its focus from what is 'essentially religious' to what is 'essential to religion'. See also Dhavan and Nariman (2000, 259 n. 19).
59. IYLA, at ¶216 (Chandrachud, J.).
60. Parthasarathy (2020, 135), for instance, declares that the Doctrine has been 'transformed into an absurdity'.
61. IYLA, at ¶¶225, 227–229 (Chandrachud, J.).

Chapter 4

1. *Times of India* (5 July 2006a).
2. *Hindu* (17 June 2006).
3. Tarabout (2015, 60).
4. *Hindu* (18 June 2006); *Hindu* (20 June 2006).
5. Nijeesh (7 December 2016).
6. Roopesh (2017, 12–13).
7. 'Thazhamon Madom', Travancore Devaswom Board, https://sabarimala.tdb.org.in/node/129.
8. *The New Indian Express* (4 May 2011).
9. *Times of India* (5 July 2006b).
10. *Indo-Asian News Service* (20 July 2006).
11. On the Sudha Chandran case, see *OnManorama* (29 September 2018).
12. Writ Petition by Indian Young Lawyers Association, at 7; Brief for the *Amicus Curiae*, at ¶6; IYLA, at ¶144(iii) (Misra, CJ).
13. Chatterjee (1989).
14. Osella and Osella (2003). See also chapter seven of Daniel (1984), containing an account of the author's pilgrimage to Sabarimala.

15. In the early 2000s, Osella and Osella (2003, 731) estimated that between 6 and 10 million devotees visited Sabarimala during the annual pilgrimage season. Almost twenty years later, Joseph et al. (2020) estimate that this number has expanded to around 25 million. The truth is likely somewhere in between. In 2018, then-President of the TDB, A. Padmakumar, estimated that a little over 3 million people had visited Sabarimala during the pilgrimage season—although it is worth noting that his announcement did not account for the extremely high crowds that gather at the temple towards the climax of the season, in early January. *The Hindu* (26 December 2018). Padmakumar's estimate was based on a TDB analysis stating that a maximum of 92 pilgrims could ascend the 18 steps to the temple sanctum in one hour—which, to put it mildly, seems low. By comparison, and also in 2018, the Kerala State Police, who are involved in the administration of the annual season, estimated that '[f]or proper crowd control, at least 75 pilgrims should pass through the steps *every minute*' (Kanth 12 October 2018, emphasis added).
16. First-hand ethnographic accounts of the pilgrimage are overwhelmingly written by or based on the experiences of male scholars. See, for instance, Osella and Osella (2003), in which Filippo Osella participated in the pilgrimage; Daniel (1984), Clothey (1978), Younger (2002)—and also Wilson (2016), a study of the pilgrimage by a female scholar who did not personally participate in it (2016, 122). The only first-hand account by a woman I have located is Sekar (1992).
17. On the range of *prasadam* offerings, see Fuller (2004 [1992], 74–75).
18. Daniel (1984, 247).
19. Osella and Osella (2003, 746).
20. Osella and Osella (2003, 747). See also Wilson (2016, 120), arguing that the pilgrimage provides 'the chance to prove one's manhood in the company of other South Indian men ... [and that] in the process of bonding with other men, pilgrims often exploit opportunities to network, to pool information, and to form business alliances'.
21. Osella and Osella (2003, 746).
22. On avatars in Hinduism, see Coleman (2018), stating that 'the avatāra concept was originally a Brahmanical device by which indigenous deities were assimilated into the orthodox pantheon and subordinated to Brahmanical gods who supported a highly ritualized religiosity within a hierarchical social order'.
23. The popular Indian comic publisher Amar Chitra Katha issued a special issue on Vishnu's avatars in which Buddha is featured as the ninth avatar. Chandrakant (2008 [1978]). P. V. Kane (1941, 720–24) discusses various articulations of Vishnu's avatars, some but not all of which include Buddha; in particular, Kane notes a seventh-century south Indian inscription listing Buddha as an avatar and concludes that 'at least before or about the 10th century A.D. Buddha had come to be looked upon as an avatāra of Visnu throughout India' (1941, 723). Meanwhile, Miller (1997, 22) notes Jayadeva's inclusion of the Buddha as one of ten manifestations of Jagadisa (Krishna) in the *Gītagovinda*.

24. Holt (2004) (examining how Vishnu was incorporated within Sinhala Buddhist culture).
25. See, e.g., Sreenivasan (2003, 185). ('In all likelihood, Sabarimala was the locale of Buddhist Vihara, nurturing both human and animal needs, situated in the trade route to the West from Tamil nadu across the mountain barrier.')
26. *Kochi Post* (1 September 2013) notes that, in the course of a television reality show he participated in, Easwar 'mentions he has done a short term course in philosophy from LSE'. Meanwhile, Ittyipe and Kochukudy (24 October 2018) note that Easwar's claim to be an alumnus of the LSE and IIM(A) is based on 'his attendance of summer programmes and short-term courses'.
27. Easwar (14 July 2020) (a Twitter post in which Easwar writes: 'Waheguru Ji Ka Khalsa / Waheguru Ji Ki Fateh / Insha Allah, may our unity win / Jai Hind'), Haneef (30 November 2018) (noting that Easwar opposed the BJP's demand that non-Hindus be barred from Sabarimala), and Varma (27 October 2017) (regarding the Hadiya case).
28. Easwar (6 September 2018) notes that he 'lean[s] to the Hindu Right' and believes that homosexuality is a 'deviation' rather than a 'variation'. He also argues that the notion 'that women are barred from entering the Sabarimala shrine is farcical and untrue' because 'lakhs of women [outside the prohibited age range] come to Sabarimala every year' (Easwar 15 January 2016).
29. Easwar (14 July 2020). Easwar's website, formerly located at www.rahuleaswar.com, no longer appears to be functional. However, a screenshot taken on 15 July 2020 (on file with author) states that 'Rahul Easwar is known as a right of centre voice in national and Kerala Media'.
30. *Free Press Journal* (17 May 2020).
31. Interview with C. Rajagopal, Superintendent of Police, Kottayam, Kerala, 19 July 2011.
32. See the discussion of Justice Malhotra's opinion in Chapter 3. For examples of this line of reasoning during the litigation, see IYLA, at ¶309.9 (Malhotra, J.); Brief for Intervenor-Applicant No. 30, People for Dharma (24 July 2018), at ¶8–9; Brief for Respondent No. 6, Nair Service Society (1 August 2018), at ¶¶2(i)–6, 12, 24.
33. Easwar (15 January 2016).
34. Easwar (15 January 2016).
35. Nor is Easwar alone in holding this view. See, e.g., Jenett (2005, 55) and Sreedhar Mini (2016, 63), whose opening line is 'This article takes as its object of study the Attukal Bhagwati temple of Kerala in South India, renowned as the "Sabarimala of women"'.
36. Bajpai (2011, 48, 77) states that during the drafting of the Constitution, limited multicultural and assimilationist/integrationist perspectives won the day and that this was responsive to general nationalist sentiment that 'the strengthening of attachment to minority groups took place at the *cost* of loyalty to the nation'. Conversely, Kaviraj (2000, 154) argues that 'Indian nationalism … retained its confidence in the idea that identity and patriotism were necessarily a complex

and multilayered affair and that there was no way of being an Indian without first being a Tamil or Maratha or Bengali. Indian nationalism was therefore a second-order identity, but not something insubstantial, fraudulent or artificial.'

37. Interview with G. Sudhakaran, former Minister for Devaswom Affairs, Trivandrum, Kerala, 18 July 2011 and Telephone interview with H. M. Ramachandra (Jayamala's husband), 30 June 2011.
38. This phrase was inspired by a newspaper article title 'Kannada actor does a Jaimala'. *Indian Express* (4 July 2006).
39. *Hindu* (3 August 2006).
40. *Zee News India* (24 July 2006).
41. *Kerala Kaumudi* (18 June 2019).
42. *Hindu* (10 June 2007).
43. Jayamala v. State Of Kerala, at ¶2.
44. See Jayamala v. State Of Kerala, at ¶2 (noting that the FIR was filed on 14 June 2007).
45. Debroy (2001) and Bhattacharya (2014). §20 of the *Factories Act* begins: 'In every factory there shall be provided a sufficient number of spittoons in convenient places and they shall be maintained in a clean and hygienic condition.'
46. Protests over the Sethusamudram Shipping Canal Project have been ongoing for over twenty years, fueled by concerns that the canal would destroy a rock and sand bridge between India and Sri Lanka that is believed to have been built by the Hindu deity Rama. Manoj (29 December 2020). The Shri Ram Sena, Bajrang Dal, and other Hindu nationalist organizations have harassed unmarried couples found celebrating Valentine's Day; for instance, in 2009, the leader of the Sena announced that his group would follow such couples with video cameras and force them to get married (Shetty 2009). See also Laine (2012) (discussing his own experiences), Adcock (2016) (discussing the Doniger and Ramanujan controversies), and Viswanath (2016) (discussing the Murugan controversy).
47. Das Acevedo (2016a).
48. *Hindu* (15 June 2011).
49. *Times of India* (14 October 2011).

Chapter 5

1. During an interview, Paripoornan stated that under English Common Law (and consequently under Indian law), the courts operate as guardians for a 'minor, lunatic, married woman, and deity'. Even to my then-non-legally trained ears, his statement seemed obviously meant as a play on the well-known dictum by the eighteenth-century English jurist Sir William Blackstone, namely, that lunatics, idiots, women, and slaves were 'perpetual minors' who lacked the ability to make contracts or incur liability (Blackstone 1979, 411–47).

2. Interview with K. S. Paripoornan, Retired Justice of the Supreme Court of India, Kochi, Kerala, 23 February 2011.
3. Interview with K. S. Paripoornan, Retired Justice of the Supreme Court of India, Kochi, Kerala, 23 February 2011.
4. Interview with K. S. Paripoornan, Retired Justice of the Supreme Court of India, Kochi, Kerala, 23 February 2011.
5. Rajiv et al. (4 September 2012).
6. Interview with Vijayaraghavan, former standing counsel for the Travancore Devaswom Board, Kochi, Kerala, 18 January 2011.
7. Rajiv et al. (4 September 2012).
8. Interview with K. S. Paripoornan, Retired Justice of the Supreme Court of India, Kochi, Kerala, 23 February 2011.
9. Haneef (3 February 2016).
10. Ibid.
11. Paripoornan Commission Report, at 1.
12. Conversation with Krishnakumar Mangot, Assistant to the Devaswom Ombudsman, Kerala High Court, Kochi, Kerala, 24 February 2011 and Conversation with Krishnakumar Mangot, Assistant to the Devaswom Ombudsman, Kerala High Court, Kochi, Kerala, 3 March 2011.
13. Mahendran, ¶2.
14. Bhuwania (2017, 39–41).
15. Id.
16. Chaturgun Turha, at ¶2 (regarding a right of easement involving household water draining which 'used to flow towards north … from time immemorial'); A. S. Yanglung, at ¶8 (on whether the village of Pushing Chingthak has been in existence 'since time immemorial'); and B. K. Hemanth Kumar, at 8 (on whether the public—and, curiously, the Government of India—have used land involved in a property dispute 'since time immemorial').
17. There are a seemingly limitless number of opinions and orders related to the Ananda Marga litigation, most of which have the same name. Here I am only referencing the Supreme Court opinion issued in 2004.
18. Ananda Marga II, at ¶11.
19. Mahendran, at ¶7.
20. Id.
21. Interview with Ambalapuzha Rama Varma, retired professor, Kottayam, Kerala, 19 July 2011.
22. IYLA, at ¶262 (noting that 'The use of the term "includes" in Section 2(c) indicates that the scope of the words "sections or class" cannot be confined only to "division", "sub-division", "caste", "sub-caste", "sect" or "denomination" … every section or class of Hindus is comprehended within the expression').
23. Mahendran, at ¶¶6–7.
24. See generally Davis (2007, 319) (discussing two perspectives regarding the effect of colonialism on Hindu legal traditions and citing prominent works in this body

of scholarship, and arguing for the view that there was 'significant rupture and disjunction').
25. Doniger (2014, 509–11). Doniger's argument is in fact much more nuanced than the fraction of it I gesture to here: 'both written and oral texts have both fluid and fixed forms ... it makes far more sense to mark the distinction between fluid texts (whether written or oral and fixed tests (again whether written or oral) than to go on making adjustments to our basically misleading distinction between oral and written texts'.
26. Doniger (2014, 510).
27. The writ petition submitted by People for Dharma mustered what textual support it could. It quoted Sabarimala's *sthalapuranam* ('place history') to establish Ayyappan's celibate nature and cited (among others) the *Apastamba Dharmasutra* and Sridhara's commentary on the *Bhagavata Purana* for the proposition that *brahmachari*s are forbidden from 'thinking about, speaking about, playing with, looking at, personally talking with, wishing for sex with, trying for sex with, engaging in sex with women'. Brief for Intervenor-Applicant No. 30, People for Dharma, at ¶8–9. But these are arguments that are middling at best. A *sthalapuranam* is by definition hyperlocal and idiosyncratic rather than abstract and widely applicable, as colonially inspired valuations would dictate, while, conversely, the prescriptions for human bachelors contained in the *Apastamba* and Sridhara's commentary operate at some remove from the customary practices that might be applicable to a particular deity.
28. There is, for instance, an indirect reference to Ayyappan (as Sastha) in the *Brahmanda purana* (Doniger 2014, 323–33).
29. Mahendran, at ¶¶30–32 (noting both the *tantri*'s opinion and the complaint of the Ayyappa Seva Sangham regarding violations of the custom).
30. Sullivan (2005).
31. By contrast, Sullivan argues that plaintiffs in religious freedom cases are seeking 'the right of the individual, every individual, to life outside the state' and that '[s]uch a right may not be best realized through laws guaranteeing religious freedom but by laws guaranteeing equality' (Sullivan 2005, 159).
32. Article 25(1) reads: 'Subject to public order, morality and health and to the other provisions of this Part, all persons are equally entitled to freedom of conscience and the right freely to profess, practise and propagate religion.' Article 26, by contrast, begins by saying that 'Subject to public order, morality and health, every religious denomination or any section thereof shall have the right' (Constitution of India, Part III: Fundamental Rights, 25(1) and 26).
33. Devika (2006, 48) and Sasikumar (2020, 83–84).
34. IYLA, at ¶144iii–iv (Misra, CJ) and IYLA, at ¶296(6) (Chandrachud, J.).
35. The next few paragraphs borrow heavily from Das Acevedo (2020).
36. IYLA, at ¶96 (Misra, CJ) ('Therefore, the devotees of Lord Ayyappa are just Hindus and do not constitute a separate religious denomination.').

37. Named references occur at Mahendran, ¶¶2, 3, 9, and 43. Indirect references ('2nd respondent' or 'all respondents') occur at Mahendran, ¶¶9, 11, and 43.
38. Direct references by name or otherwise occur at Mahendran, ¶¶13, 26; an indirect reference ('the counsel appearing for the two intervenors') appears at ¶11.
39. The High Court notes that of nine potential witnesses, one was 'given up' and another, who was wrongly served, was also 'given up' (Mahendran, ¶3). Of the remaining seven, only four are identifiable: the *tantri*, or chief priest, of Sabarimala; the *tantri* of another Keralite temple; the head of the erstwhile royal Pandalam family, which is closely connected to Sabarimala; and the head of a devotional association, the Ayyappa Seva Sangham.
40. Mahendran, ¶12.
41. Mani (1998, 79).

Chapter 6

1. See, e.g., Menon (2020), which condenses a narrative of Keralite history, Ayyappan, Sabarimala, the pilgrimage, and the litigation into twenty pages but does not mention either Nikita Azad or Trupti Desai.
2. State of Rajasthan, at 70. Cited in Baxi (1985, 107).
3. Deshpande (19 August 2020) discusses the contempt hearings against noted lawyer and activist Prashant Bhushan that were initiated by the Supreme Court in response to two tweets Bhushan published critiquing the Court. This was, moreover, by no means Bhushan's first contempt citation for critiquing the Supreme Court; in the past, he has been held in contempt for suggesting that former chief justices were corrupt (Das Acevedo 2021a, 240).
4. Robinson (2009a).
5. *Scroll* (19 July 2018).
6. See, for instance, Garner (31 July 2020), calling Isabel Wilkerson's new book analogizing race in America to caste in India an 'instant American classic'.
7. On the casteism ingrained in Keralite food-sharing practices, see generally Thomas (2022).
8. Trivedi et al. (2016, 36). Note that I have used the term 'Dalit' here, unlike in the rest of this work, because that is the term used in the study itself.
9. Azad (2015a).
10. *Youth Ki Awaaz*, https://www.youthkiawaaz.com/about/ (showing a photo of Azad and with the caption 'My letter on YKA went viral. What began with one account, became a national campaign, with hundreds of people participating.'— Nikita Azad).
11. *News Minute* (15 November 2015).
12. Solomon (26 June 2019).
13. Azad (2015b).

14. Echavez (23 November 2015).
15. Narayan (24 November 2015) (#LalSalam), Sanjana (10 April 2016) (#OwnThoseFiveDays).
16. The reposted letter on *Medium* is available here: https://www.change.org/p/national-commission-for-women-happy-to-bleed-an-initiative-to-break-menstrual-taboos-and-myths. Azad's *Change.org* petition is available here: https://www.change.org/p/national-commission-for-women-happy-to-bleed-an-initiative-to-break-menstrual-taboos-and-myths.
17. This paragraph was written before Elon Musk's 2022 acquisition of Twitter and the arguably negative impact on Twitter's influence within the United States that followed this change in ownership.
18. India Cellular and Electronics Association (July 2020), at 23; *CNBC* (30 March 2022). Kumar (2019, 240) discusses 'the role that print and television news media have played in generating an image of Twitter as being for "high-class" people', while Udupa (2015, 436) notes that many of her interlocutors in Mumbai believed that 'Facebook is timepass; Twitter is for serious people.'
19. See Udupa (2015) and Mohan (2015) on 'Internet Hindus', and Sundaram (3 October 2018) on online *puja*. Rodrigues and Niemann (2019, 362) note that as of 2019 Narendra Modi was the third most popular political leader on Twitter, while Pal et al. (2017) offer some explanation for that popularity via an analysis of Modi's use of sarcasm. Note that as of March, 2023, Modi's overall rankings appear to have improved to the top ten, see TweetBinder (2023) and Dixon (2023), but the year's rankings are still incomplete. Udupa (2015) discusses 'the media practices of Hindu activists in the internet age' and in particular (2018, 456) the BJP's 'IT cell'.
20. Dutt (29 May 2019).
21. *Deccan Herald* (1 April 2016).
22. Noorjehan Safia Niaz, at ¶11 (noting that 'women were permitted entry in the sanctum sanctorum right upto 2011–2012').
23. 'About', *Bharatiya Muslim Mahila Andolan*, https://bmmaindia.wordpress.com/about/.
24. *Outlook* (30 January 2020) (noting that 'Bal was a vigorous crusader for euthanasia, violence against women, female empowerment, fought legal battles for entry to women in temples or places of worship in India, providing public toilets for women in Pune and across Maharashtra.').
25. Murthy (17 April 2016).
26. Since the first drafting of this chapter, Desai has largely moved away from social activism into reality television, and consequently, I refer to her activist efforts in the past tense. However, she is still the leader of the Bhumata Brigade and is periodically mentioned in the news media in connection with the organization.
27. More (29 January 2016).
28. Ghadyaipatil (12 April 2016) (emphasis added).
29. Anand (29 April 2016).

30. Ghadyaipatil (12 April 2016) describes the ringtone on Desai's phone as 'is one of those typical pulp patriotism songs which scream at you on 15 August and 26 January every year'.
31. Anand (29 April 2016).
32. On women on the Hindu Right, see the essays in Sarkar and Butalia (1995).
33. Bedi (2016) (on 'dashing ladies') and Sen (2007).
34. Basu et al. (1993, 86) discuss, and Mazumdar (1995, 1) opens with the now-infamous Hindu nationalist slogan: *Hum Bharat ki nari hain, phool nahin chingari hain* ('We are the women of India, we are sparks of fire not flowers').
35. More (17 November 2018).
36. *Deccan Herald* (28 August 2016).
37. *Deccan Herald* (28 August 2016).
38. Varier (1 December 2016).
39. *OnManorama* (9 December 2016) and *First Post* (26 December 2016). This corrects a mischaracterization in my article, Das Acevedo (2018, 570–71), which described Sudhakaran as the then-current Minister for Devaswom Affairs. Although Sudhakaran had indeed held that portfolio in the CPI(M)'s previous administration, in 2016 he was the Minister for Public Works and Registration.
40. See Chapter 2, note 135.
41. *AsiaNet* (20 January 2017).
42. *New Indian Express* (30 January 2017).
43. *Deccan Chronicle* (17 November 2018).
44. Banerjee (2014, 537) and Raimon (2006, 40–60).
45. Jeffrey (1976, 14).
46. Rao (2009, 102) (discussing §147 of the I.P.C., on 'disputed property'). On the Nashik *satyagraha* generally, see Thakur (2008).
47. Sri Venkataramana Devaru, at ¶22.
48. Shastri Yagnapurushdasji, at ¶27.
49. IYLA, at ¶4 (Misra, CJ). ('All religions are simply different paths to reach the Universal One.')

Conclusion

1. Kantaru Rajeevaru, at ¶2.
2. Sengupta (20 November 2019), discussing the Sabarimala review petitions, observes that:

> It is often said that the Supreme Court is final but not infallible. But increasingly, both litigants and judges themselves appear to be veering around to the view that the Supreme Court is neither final nor infallible. It is one thing for a dissatisfied litigant who feels hard done by to ask for a review of a judgment. It is, however, an entirely different matter when the court itself appears to encourage such a practice. By neither accepting nor dismissing

the review petition filed in the Sabarimala dispute, the Supreme Court seems to have done just that.

3. The 'Tricolour' is a common shorthand for the Indian flag, which features (from top to bottom) equal-width bands of saffron, white, and green as background for a centred, navy blue wheel.
4. Kantaru Rajeevaru, at ¶5.5.
5. Kantaru Rajeevaru, at ¶5.6.
6. Kantaru Rajeevaru, at ¶5.7.
7. Kantaru Rajeevaru, at ¶4.
8. Kantaru Rajeevaru, at ¶4.
9. Robinson et al. (2011).
10. Kantaru Rajeevaru, at ¶7, ¶4.
11. Anand (13 January 2020).
12. Mandhani (16 January 2020).
13. The three 'judges' cases' regarding appointments to the higher judiciary were joined, in 2015 by the 'NJAC' case, which held that the National Judicial Appointments Commission Act, 2014, was unconstitutional. See Sengupta (2019) and Das Acevedo (2021a). The 1994 case S. R. Bommai concerned the application of Article 356 of the Constitution, which allows the central government to dismiss an elected state government and impose 'President's Rule'.
14. In 2017, the Supreme Court held, in the course of affirming the central government's national identification scheme ('Aadhaar'), that the Indian Constitution does indeed support a right to privacy (Puttaswamy, at ¶652). The Indra Sawhney judgement, sometimes called the 'Mandal verdict' after the Mandal Commission Report that was its original if not proximate cause, held (among other things) that the 'creamy layer'—those members of a disadvantaged caste who are socio-economically privileged—should be excluded from educational and professional reservations (Indra Sawhney, at ¶859(3)(d); Jeevan Reddy, J.).
15. Anand (13 January 2020).
16. Kantaru ('February order').
17. Kantaru ('February order').
18. Bhardwaj (5 February 2020) (quoting Fali S. Nariman). Admittedly, Nariman— a long-standing Senior Advocate at the Supreme Court, a former Additional Solicitor General, former President of the Bar Association of India, and the father of then-sitting Supreme Court Justice Rohinton Nariman—is well situated to make this kind of statement. Still, as the experiences of other similarly privileged attorneys like Prashant Bhushan indicate, critiquing or resisting the Indian Supreme Court is an increasingly risky exercise regardless of one's personal and professional standing. Mustafa (16 August 2020).
19. Abhishek Sankritik, reporting for the *Supreme Court Observer*, provided notes from the review/referral hearings. On Day 1, Indira Jaising stated that 'in order to issue a referral, the Court must opine that the 5-judge Bench Sabarimala judgment is wrong. Alternatively, she observed that the referral may have been made

by observing that the 7-judge Bench decision in *Shirur Mutt* was wrongly decided' (Sankritik 13 January 2020). On Day 3, Rajeev Dhavan argued that after 'a judgment has already been given … and a review against it is pending, a reference, in the nature of an appeal, is not permissible'. Similarly, and also on Day 3, Rakesh Dwivedi 'pointed out that a reference from a review cannot be made unless there was an apparent error in the judgment which was being reviewed' (Sankritik 3 February 2020). Note that Sankritik's transcripts are no longer accessible online, including to me.
20. Kantaru ('May order'), at ¶11.
21. Kantaru ('May order'), at ¶12.
22. Kantaru ('May order'), at ¶12.
23. Kantaru ('May order'), at ¶22.
24. Kantaru ('May order'), at ¶22.
25. Kantaru ('May order'), at ¶25.
26. Kantaru ('May order'), at ¶23.
27. Kantaru ('May order'), at ¶15–17 (comma), ¶21 (proceeding), ¶27 (non-necessity of facts), and ¶12–14 (PILs).
28. Kantaru ('May order'), at ¶12.
29. Nivedhitha K. (21 November 2019).
30. Kantaru ('May order'), at ¶9 (emphasis added).
31. IYLA, at ¶229.
32. IYLA, at ¶228.
33. To be sure, the *IYLA* decision resulted from neither a review petition, because it was not asking the Supreme Court to reconsider its own prior ruling, nor from an appeal, because it was not asking the Court to overturn Mahendran. Justice Chandrachud argues that the High Court itself noted that 'even when old customs prevailed, women were allowed to visit the Temple' and he draws from Mahendran to support this contention (IYLA, at ¶228–29). However, many of the examples relayed by Justice Chandrachud are taken from a section of Mahendran where the High Court appears to be paraphrasing for the record the contents of counter-affidavits filed by Chandrika, the Travancore Devaswom Board, and the State of Kerala. Readers will recall from Chapter 5 that all three were respondents who argued that the ban had never been absolute, and so it is to be expected that their affidavits would frame matters accordingly. That the High Court was speaking for the respondents rather than for itself becomes clearer later on in Mahendran: 'The Devaswom Board and the 2nd respondent Smt. Chandrika … have a contention that the restriction of entry is only during the Mandalam, Maharavilakku and Vishu days.' A little further on, it becomes apparent that the High Court was doubtful of the respondents' perspectives, and that consequently that it is difficult to say, as Justice Chandrachud does, that the High Court viewed women aged ten to fifty as being *allowed* to visit Sabarimala: 'Neither the Thanthri nor any of the other witnesses have spoken about the practice of permitting women during other days either for conducting the first rice-feeding ceremony of their children

or to offer worship at the temple. The restriction imposed has been in vogue for a continuously long period ...' (Mahendran, at ¶43).

Justice Chandrachud also paraphrases the testimony of a (pro-ban) devotional association in support of his argument that the High Court knew women were 'allowed' to visit Sabarimala. His description of that testimony, while in no way inaccurate, is also an object lesson in masterful lawyering. The relevant section of Mahendran reads: 'The Secretary of the Ayyappa Seva Sangham ... had [seen] young women in Sabarimala only during the past 10 to 15 years. The Sangham had orally complained to the authorities about this but to no avail ... The witness stated that the sanctity and purity of the surroundings are evaded on account of this' (Mahendran, at ¶32). In IYLA, Justice Chandrachud summarizes and situates that testimony as follows: 'Of importance are some of the observations of the Kerala High Court in *Mahendran*[.] The High Court noted that even when old customs prevailed, women were allowed to visit the Temple ... The Secretary of the Ayyappa Seva Sangham had deposed that young women were seen in Sabarimala during the previous ten to fifteen years ...' (IYLA, at ¶228).

34. IYLA, at ¶205.
35. Justice Nariman discusses Mahendran at ¶167 of IYLA without touching the issue of the review/reference. Justice Malhotra does so at ¶309.8 of IYLA, saying that '[t]he findings contained in the Judgment of the Kerala High Court deciding a Writ Petition under Article 226 were findings *in rem*, and the principle of *res judicata* would apply'.
36. Malhan (3 August 2020).
37. Swamy (28 August 2020).
38. Swamy (28 August 2020).
39. Raghunath (11 August 2020).
40. *New Indian Express* (16 October 2020).
41. Raghunath (22 November 2020).
42. *Mathrubhumi* (23 November 2020).
43. *Kerala Kaumudi* (9 November 2020).
44. *The New Indian Express* (21 October 2020).
45. Rajagopal (23 April 2021).
46. *Free Press Journal* (23 April 2021).

Appendix A

1. Years of conversation suggest that I am part of a generation of legal anthropologists, many of whom are credentialed in both law and anthropology, interested in critiquing this aspect of our sub-discipline. See, e.g., Tejani (2013, 140) and Kahn (2019, 140).
2. Bohannan (1989 [1957], 5). Bohannan later revised his understanding of a folk system as follows: 'a folk system is what an ethnographer thinks and says that

allows him to interact successfully with the people he is studying' (Bohannan 1997 [1969], 406).
3. Goodale (2017, 9–11) describes these four as 'proto-anthropologists', while Nader (1965, 3) adds Redfield to the discussion.
4. Malinowski (1985 [1926]), Schapera (1938), Llewellyn and Hoebel (1941), and Barton (1949).
5. Gluckman (1967 [1955]) and Bohannan (1989 [1957]). See also Gluckman (1997 [1969]) and Bohannan (1997 [1969]), from Laura Nader's edited volume. Other studies published during this period that are still likely to make appearances in contemporary scholarship include Fallers (1969) (whose research was conducted in the 1950s but only written up much later), Gulliver (1963), Nadel (1956), and Pospisil (1958) (whose 1970s exchange with Michael Lowy is likely more familiar to contemporary anthropologists of law than his earlier work).
6. Das Acevedo (2023).
7. This is far too gaping a hole for me to fill in here, but some of the works I have in mind include, in alphabetical order, Comaroff and Roberts (1981), Conley and O'Barr (2005 [1988]), Geertz (2003 [1983]), Greenhouse (1986), Merry (1990), Mertz (2007), Moore (1983 [1978]), Nader (1990), Riles (2005), and Rosen (1998 [1989]).
8. Nader (1965, 11), describing the dispute and characterizing Bohannan's objections to Gluckman.
9. See, e.g., Nader (1965, 11), stating that 'The answer probably lies solely neither with Gluckman nor Bohannan, for how an ethnographer goes about laying bare or describing his society is intimately related to what use he believes can be made of such a description.' Nader makes a similar argument in *Law in Culture and Society*, the edited volume produced out of the Wenner Gren conferences she hosted in the 1960s (Nader 1997 [1969]).
10. On the greater prominence of Bohannan's perspective, see Donovan (2008, 112) and Conley and O'Barr (1993, 50–51).
11. Merry (2016).
12. I make almost verbatim observations in the introductions to two special issues on legal anthropology: Das Acevedo (2022, 2023).
13. Geertz (2003 [1983], 170); see also Kahn (2022).
14. See Sunder Rajan (2015, 1) on 'cultivated attentiveness', and Scheppele (2004) on 'constitutional ethnography'. I have discussed cultivated attentiveness in Das Acevedo (2021b, 2022, 2023).
15. Sunder Rajan (2015, 1).
16. Geertz (1975, 47).
17. Sunder Rajan (2015, 1).
18. Elsewhere, I've called this scholarly tendency a 'prepositional attitude' towards the study of law (Das Acevedo 2023).

19. This title, reportedly bestowed on Geertz by Renato Rosaldo, appears with attribution in Sewell (1997, 35).
20. Bernstein (2017, 569) begins to fill this gap, by showing 'how judicial opinions select text to interpret and how they situate that text within contexts they create'.
21. Scheppele (2004).
22. For a recent and wide-ranging introduction to NLR, see the essays in Talesh, Mertz, and Klug (2021).
23. Erlanger et al. (2005, 336): 'Our goal is to create translations of social science that will be useful even to legal academics and lawyers who do not wish to perform empirical research themselves, while also encouraging translations of legal issues that will help social scientists gain a more sophisticated understanding of how law is understood "from the inside" by those with legal training.' See also Talesh, Mertz, and Klug (2021, 7): '[O]ur version of new Legal Realism is pluralistic' and that 'NLR continues a longstanding attempt to help law professors view law "in action" as well as "in books" ... [a]t the same time, it seeks to educate social scientists about the "internal" legal view.'
24. Riles (2005).

Appendix B

1. This excerpt is reproduced from *IYLA* at ¶136.

Bibliography

News Media

Unattributed news articles

AsiaNet. 2017. 'Rumours of Trupti Desai's presence near Sabarimala leaves police in jitters'. Jan. 20.

Business-Standard. 2019. 'Chronology of events in sexual harassment allegations against CJI'. May 6.

CNBC. 2022. 'Twitter India is hiring, to focus on country-specific products: Report'. Mar. 30.

Deccan Chronicle. 2018. 'Sabarimala: Women's rights activist Trupti Desai sent back from Kochi airport'. Nov. 17.

Deccan Herald. 2016. 'Trupti Desai offers prayers at Haji Ali Dargah'. Aug. 28.

Deccan Herald. 2016. 'Fundamental right of women to enter temples in Maharashtra: Bombay High Court'. Apr. 1.

Economic Times. 2021. 'Andhra Pradesh govt launches temple management system to check irregularities at places of worship'. Mar. 16.

Economic Times. 2019. 'All but one Left Front candidates lose security deposit in West Bengal'. May 24.

Economic Times. 2018. 'CJI sets up 5-judge constitution bench to hear major issues'. Jan. 15.

FirstPost. 2019. 'Sabarimala protests: Hartal and violence in various parts of Kerala; BJP worker dies after being stabbed in Thrissur'. Jan. 3.

FirstPost. 2018. 'Ramesh Chennithala and other Opposition leaders heading to Sabarimala shrine to protest prohibitory orders briefly blocked by police'. Nov. 20.

First Post. 2016. 'Sabarimala temple row: Activist Trupti Desai won't be allowed inside, says Kerala govt'. Dec. 26.

Free Press Journal. 2021. 'Who is Justice NV Ramana? All you need to know about the next Chief Justice of India'. Apr. 23.

Hindu. 2018. '32 lakh pilgrims visited Sabarimala: TDB chief'. Dec. 26.

Hindu. 2011. 'Jayamala case: Court issues notice to accused'. Jun. 15.

Hindu. 2007. 'Publish report on Jaimala issue: NSS'. Jun. 10.

Hindu. 2006. 'Tantri case: Woman, two others held'. Aug. 3.

Hindu. 2006. 'Purification rituals in Sabarimala on Sunday: Tantri'. Jul. 13.

Hindu. 2006. 'Atonement rituals to be completed in two years'. Jun. 20.

Hindu. 2006. "Devaprasnam' moots free food for devotees'. Jun. 18.

Hindu. 2006. "Devaprasnam' at Sabarimala reveals flaws in temple affairs'. Jun. 17.

Hindustan Times. 2018. 'Activist Rehana Fathima, family expelled by Muslim council over Sabarimala row'. Oct. 21.

Indian Express. 2018. 'Opening the gates'. Sep. 29.

Indian Express. 2006. 'Kannada actor does a Jaimala'. Jul. 4.
India Today. 2019. 'Election results 2019: Shashi Tharoor wins from Thiruvananthapuram for third consecutive time'. May 24.
India Today. 2019. 'Bombs hurled as Kerala burns over Sabarimala | As it happened'. Jan. 3.
Indo-Asian News Service. 2006. 'Sabarimala controversy reaches Kerala High Court'. Jul. 20.
Kerala Kaumudi. 2021. 'NSS welcomes govt's decision of withdrawing cases over Sabarimala'. Feb. 24.
Kerala Kaumudi. 2020. 'Only three auctioned out of 160 stalls in Sabarimala, devaswom board reeling under financial stress, loss mounts to Rs 350 crore'. Nov. 9.
Kerala Kaumudi. 2019. 'Kandararu Mohanararu agrees to pay compensation of Rs 30 lakh to his mother'. Jun. 18.
Kochi Post. 2013. 'Rahul Easwar wins Malayalee house but why?' Sep. 1.
Mathrubhumi. 2020. '9000 pilgrims visit Sabarimala in 1st week'. Nov. 23.
NDTV. 2019. '52 Congress Lawmakers come from 18 states, Union Territories'. May 26.
New Indian Express. 2020. 'Covid norms 'yes', but don't hamper pilgrimage: Kerala HC'. Oct. 21.
New Indian Express. 2020. '250 devotees to be allowed Sabarimala darshan daily, Covid negative, fitness certificates mandatory'. Oct. 16.
New Indian Express. 2020. 'BSNL directs former employee-activist Rehana Fathima to vacate quarters'. Jun. 30.
New Indian Express. 2020. 'The culture of strikes in Kerala must end'. Mar. 6.
New Indian Express. 2018. 'Sabarimala case: Supreme Court appoints woman judge'. Jul. 7.
New Indian Express. 2017. 'Now, activist Trupti Desai to fight for liquor-free Maharashtra'. Jan. 30.
New Indian Express. 2011. 'A. D. Krishnanasan passes away'. May 4.
News Minute. 2020. "Video with kids was to normalise female body': Rehana goes to SC for bail'. Jul. 28.
News Minute. 2019. 'Ayyappa devotee Chandran died of skull injuries, says preliminary autopsy report'. Jan. 3.
News Minute. 2018. 'Kerala gears up for massive Women's Wall event: All you need to know'. Dec. 31.
News Minute. 2015. 'Let machine to scan purity come, will think about women entering Sabarimala: Devaswom chief'. Nov. 15.
OnManorama. 2019. 'Premachandran presents Sabarimala bill in Lok Sabha'. Jun. 21.
OnManorama. 2018. 'The birth of Manithi and its Kerala connection'. Dec. 24.
OnManorama. 2018. 'Sabarimala cinema shoot involving actresses forced rigid curbs on women'. Sep. 29.
OnManorama. 2016. 'Minister Sudhakaran cautions Trupti Desai against Sabarimala entry'. Dec. 9.
Outlook. 2020. 'Noted activist Vidya Bal dies'. Jan. 30.
Outlook. 2019. 'Purification rites: Sabarimala tantri gets more time to give explanation'. Jan. 21.

Scroll. 2018. 'SC allows women entry to Sabarimala temple, says exclusionary practices violate right to worship'. Sep. 28.

Scroll. 2018. 'Sabarimala hearing: Kerala government says it supports entry of women into the temple'. Jul. 19.

TimesNow. 2022. 'Karnataka to do away with government control over temples, says CM Bommai in budget speech'. Mar. 4.

Times of India. 2020. 'In a first, three single-judge benches of SC hear 20 cases each'. May 13.

Times of India. 2018. 'Kerala Speaker denies permission for a bill on Sabarimala'. Nov. 28.

Times of India. 2011. 'Controversy over Sabarimala Temple entry returns to spotlight'. Oct. 14.

Times of India. 2006b. "Vigilance Squad' to grill Jaimala'. Jul. 5.

Times of India. 2006a. 'Another actress fuels temple row'. Jul. 5.

TweetBinder. 2023. 'Most followed accounts on Twitter – 2023'. Mar. 6.

Week. 2018. 'Sabarimala: Rahul Gandhi contradicts Congress stand, favours women entry'. Oct. 30.

Zee News India. 2006. 'Sabarimala priest removed for making 'false complaint''. Jul. 24.

Attributed news articles

Ahmed, Manan, Sriharsha Devulapalli & Juan Francisco Saldarriaga. 2022. 'Targeted harassment of academics by Hindutva: A Twitter analysis of the India-US connection'. May 3.

Ainge Roy, Eleanor. 2017. 'New Zealand river granted same legal rights as human being'. *Guardian*, Mar. 16.

Ameerudheen, T. A. 2019. 'Gender justice activist and a devout Hindu: Meet the women who made history by entering Sabarimala'. *Scroll*, Jan. 2.

Anand, Geeta. 2016. 'Forging a path for women, deep into India's sacred shrines'. *New York Times*, Apr. 29.

Anand, Utkarsh. 2020. 'SC refuses to set aside election of Kerala MP over remarks against Women's entry into Sabarimala'. *News18*, May 30.

Anand, Utkarsh. 2020. 'Faith vs right to pray: Why CJI Bobde constituted a 9-judge bench to hear Sabarimala review pleas from today'. *News18*, Jan. 13.

Ashraf, Ajaz. 2019. 'On Sabarimala, nationalism and the rule of law, the Congress is being more hypocritical than the BJP'. *Scroll*, Jan. 10.

Ashraf, Syed Firdaus. 2019. 'REVEALED: How two women entered Sabarimala temple'. *Rediff*, Jan. 3.

Babu, Ramesh. 2018. 'Won't allow RSS to turn Sabarimala into another Ayodhya, says Kerala CM Pinarayi Vijayan'. *Hindustan Times*, Nov. 20.

Bagriya, Ashok. 2019. 'A year after landmark press conference, little has changed in Supreme Court's running'. *Hindustan Times*, Jan. 12.

Bhardwaj, Prachi. 2020. 'Sabarimala | Can reference be made in a review petition? 9-judge bench to decide along with other issues'. *SCC Online Blog*, Feb. 5.

Bhaskar, B. R. P. 2018. 'The Sabarimala judgement: When reason triumphed over prejudice'. *News Minute*, Sep. 30.

Bhattacharya, Pramit. 2014. 'Spittoons, clotheslines, and the absurdity of Indian labour laws'. *Livemint*, Jun. 27.

Bose, Saikat Kumar. 2021. '4 women judges in Supreme Court after historic oath Today'. *NDTV*, Sep. 1.

Chanda-Vaz, Urmi. 2018. 'Shashi Tharoor's 'Why I Am a Hindu' is a timely reminder of why Hinduism must retain its pluralism'. *Scroll*, Feb. 18.

Chatterji, Saubhadhra. 2017. 'Kerala cow slaughter: Congress distances itself, Rahul Gandhi says it's 'barbaric, thoughtless''. *Hindustan Times*, May 29.

Chhibber, Maneesh. 2020. 'SC collegium willing, this Karnataka judge could become first woman Chief Justice of India'. *Print*, May 29.

Daniyal, Shoaib. 2018. 'I want to resist the hijacking of Hinduism by Hindutva: The Shashi Tharoor interview'. *Scroll*, Feb. 11.

Das Acevedo, Deepa. 2019. 'The battle for Sabarimala'. *Foreign Affairs*, Apr. 4.

Dasgupta, Piyasree. 2019. 'Sabarimala: Only one of the 5 women petitioners has stood her ground'. *Huffington Post*, Jan. 3.

Deshpande, Rohan. 2020. 'Prashant Bhushan contempt verdict by Supreme Court betrays curious double standards'. *Scroll*, Aug. 19.

Devasia, T. K. 2019. "Miss my children': Kanaka Durga, woman who entered Sabarimala, says she is not afraid of fighting for just cause'. *FirstPost*, Feb. 9.

Dixon, S. 2023. 'Twitter accounts with the most followers worldwide 2023'. *Statista.com*, Jan. 25.

Doctor, Vikram. 2018. 'Hoping for divine justice: When gods become litigants'. *Economic Times*, Aug. 11.

Dutt, Shriaya. 2019. "Main bhi Chowkidar' was way ahead of 'Chowkidar Chor Hai' campaign online'. *Tribune*, May 29.

Easwar, Rahul. 2018. 'We respect SC verdict but most of us feel homosexual behaviour is deviation'. *Print*, Sep. 6.

Easwar, Rahul. 2016. 'Why Sabarimala has restrictions on women, Rahul Easwar explains'. *Covai Post*, Jan. 15.

Echavez, Charissa. 2015. 'Indian women protest against menstruation taboo statement, spread #HappyToBleed message in social media'. *Science Times*, Nov. 23.

Ganz, Kian. 2017. 'How Supreme Court chooses the Chief Justice of India'. *LiveMint*, May 17.

Garner, Dwight. 2020. 'Isabel Wilkerson's 'Caste' is an 'Instant American Classic' about our abiding sin'. *New York Times*, Jul. 31.

Gettleman, Jeffrey, Hari Kumar & Kai Schultz. 2018. 'Hundreds of cases a day and a flair for drama: India's crusading Supreme Court'. *New York Times*, Sep. 27.

Ghadyaipatil, Abhiram. 2016. 'Trupti Desai: The woman who took on a 400-year-old tradition and won'. *LiveMint*, Apr. 12.

Gopinathan, Sharanya. 2018. 'Harassed, abused, forced into hiding: A woman's ordeal for attempting Sabarimala trek'. *News Minute*, Oct. 23.

Haneef, Mahir. 2022. 'Kerala high court bids farewell to two judges'. *Times of India*, Apr. 8.

Haneef, Mahir. 2018. 'Sabarimala: Rahul Easwar opposes BJP's plea for barring non-Hindus'. *Times of India*, Nov. 30.

Haneef, Mahir. 2016. 'Justice K. S. Paripoornan passes away'. *Times of India*, Feb. 3.

Ilaiah Shepherd, Kancha. 2018. 'To be or not to be'. *Indian Express*, Mar. 24.

Ittyipe, Minu & Anand Kochukudy. 2018. 'Meet Rahul Easwar, the angry face of the Sabarimala temple protests'. *Arré*, Oct. 24.

Jain, Ritika. 2017. 'Even gods have rights, argues petition on Sabarimala issue'. *DNA India*, Feb. 21.
John, Haritha. 2021. 'Kerala BJP chief K Surendran loses Konni and Manjeshwar, Sabarimala plank fails'. *News Minute*, May 2.
Kakkar, Shruti. 2022. 'Vedanta-NALCO Dispute: Attorney General seeks time to respond to Supreme Court's suggestions for settlement'. *LiveLaw.in*, Apr. 12.
Kanth, Ajay. 2018. 'Sabarimala: Controlling women devotees at 18 holy steps tough task, admit police'. *New Indian Express*, Oct. 12.
Kashyap, Gauri. 2022. 'Next 9 Chief Justices of India'. *Supreme Court Observer*, May 18.
Kochukudy, Anand. 2019. 'How Shashi Tharoor beat the Modi wave and Sabarimala anger for a third straight victory'. *Quartz India*, May 27.
Koshy, Sneha Mary. 2019. 'Temple purification not due to entry of women, claims Sabarimala priest'. *NDTV*, Feb. 5.
Koshy, Sneha Mary. 2018. "Accept Sabarimala order, no woman will be barred': Kerala Chief Minister'. *NDTV*, Oct. 3.
Kumar, Ashwani. 2018. 'Book review: Shashi Tharoor's 'Why I am a Hindu' is an emphatic denunciation of Hindutva'. *Financial Express*, Mar. 11.
Kumari, Prerna. 2018. 'A Sabarimala petitioner explains how she misunderstood the issue'. *Organiser*, Oct. 16.
Lalwani, Vijayta. 2019. "Anti-judicial': Activists, lawyers protesting against SC and CJI Ranjan Gogoi detained by police'. *Scroll*, May 7.
Madhukar, Jayanthi. 2013. 'Creation of 'God's own country''. *Bangalore Mirror*, Aug. 7.
Mahapatra, Dhananjay. 2019. 'Author of Ayodhya Verdict not named, but it bears Chandrachud's imprint'. *Times of India*, Nov. 10. Author of Ayodhya Verdict Not Named, But It Bears Chandrachud's Imprint.
Malhan, Amritesh. 2020. '10 things to know about India's new gold playbook: What's in it for you and the govt?' *Economic Times*, Aug. 3.
Mandhani, Apoorva. 2020. 'Before Sabarimala, there were only 15 nine-judge bench rulings. Here are 5 landmark cases'. *Print*, Jan. 16.
Mandhani, Apoorva. 2019. 'Gogoi keeps up CJI tradition of retiring with a bang—has 4 big verdicts in last 2 weeks'. *Print*, Nov. 2.
Manoj, P. 2020. 'Sethusamudram ship channel project set to be beached'. *The Hindu Business Line*, Dec. 29.
Mary, John. 2006. 'India actress 'defiles' shrine'. *BBC News*, Jul. 3.
Mathew, Liz. 2019. 'Sabarimala row: Sonia Gandhi stops black band protest by Congress MPs'. *Indian Express*, Jan. 4.
Meethal, Amiya. 2019. 'Bindu Ammini, husband were with CPI(ML) earlier'. *Deccan Chronicle*, Jan. 3.
More, Manoj Dattatrye. 2018. 'Trupti Desai profile: From local activism in Pune to national stature with Shani Shingnapur entry'. *Indian Express*, Nov. 17.
More, Manoj. 2016. 'Bhumata Brigade: Housewives, driving instructor, student: The women behind temple protest'. *Indian Express*, Jan. 29.
Murthy, Sushmita. 2016. 'An equalising templeton'. *Deccan Chronicle*, Apr. 17.
Mustafa, Faizan. 2020. 'SC holds Prashant Bhushan guilty of contempt: What the verdict means'. *Indian Express*, Aug. 16.

Mustafa, Faizan. 2020. 'Strange and Arbitrary bail orders: Are Indian judges going too far?.' *Wire*, Apr. 28.

Nair, Preetha. 2019. 'My private member bill exposed BJP's 'double standards' on Sabarimala: NK Premachandran'. *Outlook*, Jun. 27.

Narayan, Vishal. 2015. '#Happytobleed: 20 year old challenges temple priest'. *Citizen*, Nov. 24.

Nijeesh, T. P. 2016. 'Amma knew about astrology: Parappanangadi Unnikrishna Panikkar'. *Times of India*, Dec. 7.

Nivedhitha K. 2019. 'Sabarimala review: The curious case of review petitions' adjudication'. *The Leaflet*, Nov. 21.

Patel, Anand. 2019. 'Nearly 50 per cent MPs in new Lok Sabha have criminal records'. *India Today*, May 25.

Philip, Shaju. 2021. 'Kerala government decides to withdraw Sabarimala, anti-CAA protest cases'. *Indian Express*, Feb. 25.

Pillai, Amrita & Reshma Sekhar. 2018. 'The art of writing a judgement'. *Hindu*, Jul. 24.

Raghunath, Arjun. 2020. 'Sabarimala temple's daily revenue drops 97% to Rs 10 lakh; temple in acute financial crisis'. *Deccan Herald*, Nov. 22.

Raghunath, Arjun. 2020. 'Covid-19 clouds demand for Sabarimala 'melsanthi' post'. *Deccan Herald*, Aug. 11.

Rajagopal, Krishnadas. 2021. 'CJI Bobde's tenure draws to a close'. *Hindu*, Apr. 23.

Rajagopal, Krishnadas. 2016. 'New Bench to hear Sabarimala entry case'. *Hindu*, Jul. 8.

Raj, Suhasini & Kai Schultz. 2018. 'Religion and women's rights clash, violently, at a shrine in India'. *New York Times*, Oct. 18.

Rajiv, G., et al. 2012. 'Managing Gods' wealth: Kerala's four Devaswoms together earn Rs 1000 crore annually'. *Times of India*, Sep. 4.

Saluja, Pallavi. 2020. 'The next judges of the Supreme Court: Which High Court Chief Justices are most likely to be elevated? Will we see a woman CJI this decade?' *Bar and Bench*, Jul. 17.

Sanjana. 2016. '#HappytoBleed'. *My Independent Wings*, Apr. 10.

Sankritik, Abhishek. 2020. 'Sabarimala review: Kantaru Rajeevaru v. Indian Young Lawyers' Association: Day 3 Arguments: 6 February 2020'. *Supreme Court Observer*, Feb. 3.

Sankritik, Abhishek. 2020. 'Sabarimala review: Kantaru Rajeevaru v. Indian Young Lawyers' Association: Day 1 Arguments: 13 January 2020'. *Supreme Court Observer*, Jan. 13.

Schultz, Kai. 2019. 'Her visit to a men-only temple went smoothly. Then the Riots started'. *New York Times*, Jan. 18.

Sengupta, Arghya. 2019. 'Much is legally incorrect about the Sabarimala judgment'. *The Telegraph Online*, Nov. 20.

Shetty, Poorna. 2009. 'Pink chaddis v the moral police'. *The Guardian*, Feb. 12.

Solomon, Saskia. 2019. 'The false scientific claims made during Modi's first term'. *The Caravan*, Jun. 26.

Sundaram, Dheepa. 2018. 'Globalizing Darśan: Online Puja'. *Globalizing Dharma*, Oct. 3.

Swamy, Rohini. 2020. 'Faced with financial crunch, Sabarimala & 1,200 Kerala temples plan to monetise gold'. *The Print*, Aug. 28.

Tharoor, Shashi. 2018. 'Why Sabarimala issue leaves instinctive liberals like me torn: Shashi Tharoor'. *The Print*, Nov. 10.

Varier, Megha. 2016. 'Rahul Easwar dares Trupti Desai to enter Sabarimala, says 500 women will stop her'. *The News Minute*, Dec. 1.

Varma, Vishnu. 2019. 'Kerala bye-election results 2019 highlights: State's voters stick to LDF, UDF; BJP blanked out'. *Indian Express*, Oct. 25.

Varma, Vishnu. 2017. 'Kerala 'love-jihad case': Hadiya pleads in new video-'Please get me out, I will get killed soon''. *Indian Express*, Oct. 27.

Yadavar, Swagata. 2020. 'India's maternal mortality ratio dips to 1: Assam has highest and Kerala lowest'. *The Print*, Jul. 16.

Yamunan, Sruthisagar. 2018. 'One of India's most controversial judges has retired'. *Quartz India*, Oct. 2.

Yamunan, Sruthisagar & Ipsita Chakravarty. 2019. 'Interview: 'I've lost everything. Financially, mentally, everything,' says ex-SC staffer in CJI case'. *Scroll*, May 9.

Scholarly Works

Adcock, C. S. 2016. 'Violence, Passion, and the Law: A Brief History of Section 295A and Its Antecedents'. *Journal of the American Academy of Religion* 84, no. 2: 337–351.

Aiyer, Ulloor S. Parameswara. 1998. *Progress of Travancore under H.H. Sree Moolam Tirunal*. Thiruvananthapuram: Government of Kerala.

Agnes, Flavia. 2016. 'Personal Laws'. In *The Oxford Handbook of the Indian Constitution*, ed. Sujit Choudhry, Madhav Khosla, and Pratap Bhanu Mehta, 903–920. Oxford: Oxford University Press.

Anand, A. S. 2003. 'Judicial Review – Judicial Activism – Need for Caution'. In *Law & Justice: An Anthology*, ed. Soli J. Sorabjee, 377–387.

Anitha S., et al. 2008. 'Final Report: Gendering Governance or Governing Women? Politics, Patriarchy, and Democratic Decentralisation in Kerala State, India'. Thiruvananthapuram: Centre for Development Studies.

Appadurai, Arjun. 2008 [1981]. *Worship and Conflict under Colonial Rule: A South Indian Case*. Cambridge: Cambridge University Press.

Appadurai, Arjun. 1977. 'Kings, Sects and Temples in South India, 1350–1700 A.D'. *Indian Economic Social History Review* 14, no. 1: 47–73.

Appadurai, Arjun & Carol Appadurai Breckenridge. 1976. 'The South Indian Temple: Authority, Honour and Redistribution'. *Contributions to Indian Sociology* 10, no. 2: 187–211.

Arafath, P. K. Yasser. 2021. 'Southern Hindutva: Rhetoric, Parivar Kinship and Performative Politics in Kerala, 1925–2015'. *Economic and Political Weekly* 56, no. 2: 51–60.

Arunima, G. 2003. *There Comes Papa: Colonialism and the Transformation of Matriliny in Kerala, Malabar, c. 1850–1940*. Hyderabad: Orient BlackSwan.

Austin, Granville. 1999 [1966]. *The Indian Constitution: Cornerstone of a Nation*. New Delhi: Oxford India Paperbacks.

Bacchetta, Paola. 1993. 'All Our Goddesses are Armed: Religion, Resistance, and Revenge in the Life of a Militant Hindu Nationalist Woman'. *Bulletin of Concerned Asian Scholars* 25, no. 4: 38–52.

Bachofen, Johann Jakob. 2006 [1861]. *An English Translation of Bachofen's Mutterrecht (mother Right) (1861): v. 3: A Study of the Religious and Juridical Aspects of Gynecocracy in the Ancient World "Orchomenus and the Minyan's" and "India and Central Asia,"* trans. David Partenheimer. New York: Edwin Mellen Press.

Bajpai, Rochona. 2011. *Debating Difference: Group Rights and Liberal Democracy in India.* New Delhi: Oxford University Press.

Balakrishnan, K. G. 2008. 'Growth of Public Interest Litigation in India'. Fifteenth Annual Lecture, Singapore Academy of Law, Oct. 8.

Banerjee, Himadri. 2014. 'Sikhs Living Beyond Punjab in India'. In *The Oxford Handbook of Sikh Studies*, ed. Pashaura Singh and Louis E. Fenech, 534–544. Oxford: Oxford University Press.

Barton, R. F. 1949. *The Kalingas: Their Institutions and Custom Law.* Chicago: The University of Chicago Press.

Basu, Amrita. 1993. 'Feminism Inverted: The Real Women and Gendered Imagery of Hindu Nationalism'. *Bulletin of Concerned Asian Scholars* 25, no. 4: 25–37.

Basu, Tapan et al. 1993. *Khaki Shorts and Saffron Flags: A Critique of the Hindu Right.* Hyderabad: Orient Longman.

Baxi, Upendra. 2000. 'The Avatars of Indian Judicial *Activism*: Explorations in the Geographies of [In]justice'. In *Fifty Years of the Supreme Court of India: Its Grasp and Reach*, ed. S. K. Verma, 156–209. Delhi: Oxford University Press.

Baxi, Upendra. 1985. 'Taking Suffering Seriously: Social Action Litigation in the Supreme Court of India'. *Third World Legal Studies* 4: 107–132.

Bayly, Susan. 1984. 'Hindu Kingship and the Origin of Community: Religion, State and Society in Kerala, 1750–1850'. *Modern Asian Studies* 18, no. 2: 177–213.

Beck, Guy L. 1995. *Sonic Theology: Hinduism and Sacred Sound.* Delhi: Motilal Banarsidass.

Bedi, Tarini. 2016. *The Dashing Ladies of Shiv Sena: Political Matronage in Urbanizing India.* Albany: State University of New York Press.

Bernstein, Anya. 2017. 'Before Interpretation'. *University of Chicago Law Review* 84, no. 2: 567–653.

Bhagwati, P. N. 2005. Religion and Secularism Under the Indian Constitution. In *Religion and Law in Independent India*, Second Edition. ed. Robert D. Baird, 35–50. New Delhi: Manohar.

Bhalla, Deepti Omchery. 2006. *Vanishing Temple Arts.* Gurgaon: Shubhi Publications.

Bhatia, Gautam. 2019. *The Transformative Constitution: A Radical Biography in Nine Acts.* Noida: Harper Collins.

Bhatia, Gautam. 2016. 'Freedom from Community: Individual Rights, Group Life, State Authority and Religious Freedom under the Indian Constitution'. *Global Constitutionalism* 5, no. 3: 351–382.

Bhattacharya, Shreejoyee. 2016. 'Anticipatory Bail'. Working paper. https://ssrn.com/abstract=2902141

Bhuwania, Anuj. 2017. *Courting the People: Public Interest Litigation in Post-Emergency India.* Cambridge: Cambridge University Press.

Blackstone, William. 1979. *Commentaries on the Laws of England*, Vol. 1. Chicago & London: The University of Chicago Press.

Birla, Ritu. 2009. *Stages of Capital: Law, Culture, and Market Governance in Late Colonial India.* Durham: Duke University Press.

Bohannan, Paul. 1997 [1969]. 'Ethnography and Comparison in Legal Anthropology'. In *Law in Culture and Society*, ed. Laura Nader, 401–419. Berkeley: University of California Press.

Bohannan, Paul. 1989 [1957]. *Justice and Judgment among the Tiv*. Prospect Heights: Waveland Press.

Breckenridge, Carol A. 1977. *The Sri Minaksi Sundaresvarar Temple: Worship and Endowments in South India, 1833–1925*. Thesis, University of Wisconsin-Madison.

Cabatingan, Lee. 2018. 'Fashioning the Legal Subject: Popular Justice and Courtroom Attire in the Caribbean'. *PoLAR: Political and Legal Anthropology Review* 41, no. 1: 69–84.

Caldwell, Sarah. 1999. *Oh Terrifying Mother: Sexuality, Violence, and Worship of the Goddess Kāli*. New Delhi & New York: Oxford University Press.

Chacko, Elizabeth. 2003. 'Marriage, Development, and the Status of Women in Kerala, India'. *Gender and Development* 11, no. 2: 52–59.

Chandrakant, Kamala. 2008 [1978]. *Dasha Avatar, No. 10002*. Mumbai: Amar Chitra Katha.

Chatterjee, Partha, 1989. 'The Nationalist Resolution of the Women's Question'. In *Recasting Women: Essays in Colonial History*, ed. Kumkum Sangari and Sudesh Vaid, 233–253. New Delhi: Kali for Women.

Chiriyankandath, James. 1993. "Communities at the Polls': Electoral Politics and the Mobilization of Communal Groups in Travancore'. *Modern Asian Studies* 27, no. 3: 643–665.

Clothey, Fred W. 1978. Theogony and Power in South India: Some Clues from the Aiyappan Cult. In *Religion and the Legitimation of Power in South India*, ed. Bardwell L. Smith, 1–13. Leiden: Brill.

Coleman, E. Gabriella. 2013. *Coding Freedom: The Ethics and Aesthetics of Hacking*. Princeton: Princeton University Press.

Coleman, Tracy. 2018. 'Avatāra'. Oxford Bibliographies Online: Hinduism. DOI: 10.1093/OBO/9780195399318-0009

Comaroff, John L. & Simon Roberts. 1981. *Rules and Processes: The Cultural Logic of Dispute in an African Context*. Chicago: The University of Chicago Press.

Conley, John M. & William M. O'Barr. 2005 [1988]. *Just Words: Law, Language and Power*. Second Edition. Chicago: The University of Chicago Press.

Conley, John M. & William M. O'Barr. 1993. 'Legal Anthropology Comes Home: A Brief History of the Ethnographic Study of Law'. *Loyola Los Angeles Law Review* 27, no. 1: 41–64.

Daniel, E. Valentine. 1984. *Fluid Signs: Being a Person the Tamil Way*. Berkeley: University of California Press.

Das Acevedo, Deepa. 2023. What's Law Got to Do with It? Anthropological Engagement with Legal Scholarship *Law & Social Inquiry* 48, no. 1: 1–13.

Das Acevedo, Deepa. 2022. 'Sweet Old-Fashioned Notions: Legal Engagement with Anthropological Scholarship'. *Alabama Law Review* 73, no. 4: 719–732.

Das Acevedo, Deepa. Work in progress. 'Transformative Temple Entry Jurisprudence?'

Das Acevedo, Deepa. 2021b. '(Im)mutable Race?' *Northwestern University Law Review Online* 116: 88–119.

Das Acevedo, Deepa. 2021a. 'From Mythic Saviors to #MeToo at the Indian Supreme Court'. *Asian Journal of Law and Society* 8, no. 2: 226–254.

Das Acevedo, Deepa. 2020. 'Just Hindus'. *Law & Social Inquiry* 45, no. 4: 965–994.

Das Acevedo, Deepa. 2018. 'Gods' Homes, Men's Courts, Women's Rights'. *I•CON: International Journal of Constitutional Law* 16, no. 2: 552–573.

Das Acevedo, Deepa. 2016c. 'Divine Sovereignty, Indian Property Law, and the Dispute over the Padmanabhaswamy Temple'. *Modern Asian Studies* 50, no. 3: 841–865.

Das Acevedo, Deepa. 2016b. 'Celibate Gods and "Essential Practices" Jurisprudence at Sabarimala, 1991–2011'. In *Filing Religion: State, Hinduism, and Courts of Law*, ed. Daniela Berti, Gilles Tarabout, and Raphaël Voix, 101–123. New Delhi: Oxford University Press.

Das Acevedo, Deepa. 2016a. 'Temples, Courts, and Dynamic Equilibrium in the Indian Constitution'. *American Journal of Comparative Law* 64, no. 3: 555–582.

Das Acevedo, Deepa. 2013b. 'Secularism in the Indian Context'. *Law & Social Inquiry* 38, no. 1: 138–167.

Das Acevedo, Deepa. 2013a. Religion, Law, and the Making of a Liberal Indian State. PhD Dissertation submitted to the Department of Anthropology, The University of Chicago.

Dasgupta, Anirban. 2017. 'Land Reform in Kerala and West Bengal: Two Stories of Left Reformism and Development'. In *The Land Question in India: State, Dispossession, and Capitalist Transition*, ed. Anthony P. D'Costa and Achin Chakraborty, 242–264. Oxford: Oxford University Press.

Davis Jr., Donald R. 2007. 'Law and 'Law Books' in the Hindu Tradition'. *German Law Journal* 9, no. 3: 309–326.

Davis, Richard H. 2010. 'Temples, Deities, and the Law'. In *Hinduism and Law: An Introduction*, ed. Timothy Lubin, Donald R. Davis Jr., and Jayanth K. Krishnan, 195–206. Cambridge: Cambridge University Press.

Davis, Richard H. 1997. *Lives of Indian Images*. Princeton: Princeton University Press.

De, Rohit. 2018. *A People's Constitution: The Everyday Life of Law in the Indian Republic*. Princeton & Oxford: Princeton University Press.

Debroy, Bibek. 2001. 'Why We Need Law Reform'. *Seminar* 497. https://www.india-seminar.com/2001/497/497%20bibek%20debroy.htm

Dempsey, Corinne G. 1998. 'Rivalry, Reliance, and Resemblance: Siblings as Metaphor for Hindu-Christian Relations in Kerala State'. *Asian Folklore Studies* 57, no. 1: 51–70.

Devika, J. 2019b. 'Against Aachaaram: Lalitambika Antharjanam'. *Kafila*, Aug. 29.

Devika, J. 2019a. 'Against Aachaaram: A Dossier from Malayalam–Announcement'. *Kafila*, Jul. 18.

Devika, J. 2010. 'The Capabilities Approach in the Vernacular: The History in Kerala'. *Economic and Political Weekly* 45, no. 26/27: 269–277.

Devika, J. 2006. 'Negotiating Women's Social Space: Public Debates on Gender in Early Modern Kerala, India'. *Inter-Asia Cultural Studies* 7, no. 1: 43–61.

Dhavan, Rajeev. 2001. 'The Road to Xanadu: India's Quest for Secularism'. In *Religion and Personal Law in Secular India*, ed. Gerald Larson, 301–329. Bloomington: Indiana University Press.

Dhavan, Rajeev & Fali S. Nariman. 2000. 'The Supreme Court and Group Life: Religious Freedom, Minority Groups and Disadvantaged Communities'. In *Supreme But Not Infallible—Essays in Honour of the Supreme Court of India*, ed. B. N. Kirpal, Ashok H. Desai, Gopal Subramaniam, Raju Ramachandran, and Rajeev Dhavan, 159-192. New Delhi: Oxford University Press.

Di Varthema, Ludovico. 1863. *The Travels of Ludovico di Varthema in Egypt, Syria, Arabia Deserta and Arabia Felix, in Persia, India, and Ethiopia, A.D. 1503 to 1508*. London: Hakluyt Society.

Dirks, Nicholas B. 1996. *The Hollow Crown: Ethnohistory of an Indian Kingdom*. Second Edition. Ann Arbor: The University of Michigan Press.

Doniger, Wendy. 2014. *On Hinduism*. Oxford: Oxford University Press.

Donovan, James M. 2008. *Legal Anthropology: An Introduction*. Plymouth: AltaMira Press.

Elkins, Zachary, Tom Ginsburg & James Melton. 2009. *The Endurance of National Constitutions*. Cambridge: Cambridge University Press.

Engels, Friedrich. 1902 [1844]. *The Origin of the Family, Private Property and the State*, trans. Ernest Untermann. Chicago: C. H. Kerr.

Erlanger, Howard et al. 2005. 'Is It Time for a New Legal Realism?' *Wisconsin Law Review* 2005, no. 2: 335-363.

Fallers, Lloyd A. 1969. *Law without Precedent: Legal Ideas in Action in Courts of Colonial Busoga*. Chicago: The University of Chicago Press.

Fischel, William A. 2001. 'Why Are There NIMBYs?' *Land Economics* 77, no. 1: 144-152.

Fleming, Christopher T. Forthcoming. *Equity and Trusts in Sanskrit Jurisprudence*. Oxford: British Academy Monographs.

Franke, Richard W. 2008. 'Local Planning: The Kerala Experiment'. In *Real Utopia: Participatory Society for the 21st Century*, ed. Chris Spannos, 130-135. Oakland: AK Press.

Franke, Richard W. & Barbara H. Chasin. 1997. 'Power to the Malayalee People'. *Economic and Political Weekly* 32, no. 48: 3061-3065, 3067-3068.

Frykenberg, Robert Eric. 2008. *Christianity in India: From Beginnings to the Present*. Oxford: Oxford University Press.

Frykenberg, Robert Eric. 2000. 'The Construction of Hinduism as a 'Public' Religion: Looking Again at the Religious Roots of Company Raj in South India'. In *Religion and Public Culture: Encounters and Identities in Modern South India*, ed. Keith E. Yandell and John J. Paul, 3-26. Richmond & Surrey: Curzon.

Fuller, C. J. 2004[1992]. *The Camphor Flame: Popular Hinduism and Society in India*. Princeton: Princeton University Press.

Fuller, C. J. 1988. 'Hinduism and Scriptural Authority in Modern Indian Law'. *Comparative Studies in Society and History* 30, no. 2: 225-248.

Fuller, C. J. 1984. *Servants of the Goddess: The Priests of a South Indian Temple*. Cambridge: Cambridge University Press.

Fuller, C. J. 1975. 'The Internal Structure of the Nayar Caste'. *Journal of Anthropological Research* 31, no. 4: 283-312.

Galanter, Marc. 2014. 'Snakes and Ladders: Suo Motu Intervention and the Indian Judiciary'. *Florida International University Law Review* 10, no. 1: 69-83.

Galanter, Marc. 1964. 'Temple-Entry and the Untouchability (Offences) Act, 1955'. *Journal of the Indian Law Institute* 6, nos. 2 & 3: 185-195.

Gauri, Varun. 2009. 'Public Interest Litigation in India: Overreaching or Underachieving?' World Bank Dev. Research, Policy Research Working Paper No. 5109.

Geertz, Clifford. 2003 [1983]. *Local Knowledge: Further Essays in Interpretive Anthropology*. New York: Basic Books.

Geertz, Clifford. 1975. 'On the Nature of Anthropological Understanding'. *American Scientist* 63, no. 1: 47-53.

George, Jasper Vikas. 2005. 'Social Change and Public Interest Litigation in India'. Mar. 8. http://www.ssvk.org/social_change_public_interest_litigation_in_india.pdf

Gluckman, Max. 1997 [1969]. 'Concepts in the Comparative Study of Tribal Law'. In *Law in Culture and Society*, ed. Laura Nader, 349-374. Berkeley: University of California Press.

Gluckman, Max. 1967 [1955]. *The Judicial Process among the Barotse of Northern Rhodesia*. Manchester: Manchester University Press.

Good, Anthony. 2004. *Worship and the Ceremonial Economy of a Royal South Indian Temple*. Lewiston: Edwin Mellen Press.

Goodale, Mark. 2017. *Anthropology and Law: A Critical Introduction*. Princeton: Princeton University Press.

Greenhouse, Carol J. 1986. *Praying for Justice: Faith, Order, and Community in an American Town*. Ithaca: Cornell University Press.

Gulliver, P. H. 1963. *Social Control in an African Society: A Study of the Arusha, Agricultural Masai of Northern Tanganyika*. Boston: Boston University Press.

Halliburton, Murphy. 1998. 'Suicide: A Paradox of Development in Kerala'. *Economic and Political Weekly* 33, no. 36/37: 2341-2345.

Hansen, Thomas Blom. 1994. 'Controlled Emancipation: Women and Hindu Nationalism'. *European Journal of Development Research* 6, no. 2: 82-94.

Hardgrave, Robert L. Jr. 1977. 'The Mappilla Rebellion, 1921: Peasant Revolt in Malabar'. *Modern Asian Studies* 11, no. 1: 57-99.

Heng, Geraldine. 2018. *The Invention of Race in the European Middle Ages*. Cambridge: Cambridge University Press.

Holt, John Clifford. 2004. *The Buddhist Viṣṇu: Religious Transformation, Politics, and Culture*. New York: Columbia University Press

Induchudan, V. T. 1971. *The Golden Tower: A Historical Study of the Tirukkulasekharapuram and Other Temples*. Trichur: Cochin Devaswom Board.

Induchudan, V. T. 1969. *The Secret Chamber: A Historical, Anthropological, and Philosophical Study of the Kodungallur Temple*. Thrissur: Cochin Devaswom Board.

Jackson, William J. 1994. 'Name-Devotion in Indian Religions and Kaveri Delta Namasiddhanta'. *Journal for the Study of Religion* 7, no. 2: 33-55.

Jacobsohn, Gary Jeffrey. 2010. *Constitutional Identity*. Cambridge & London: Harvard University Press.

Jacobsohn, Gary Jeffrey. 2009. 'Chapter Seven: The Sounds of Silence: Militant and Acquiescent Constitutionalism'. In *The Supreme Court and the Idea of Constitutionalism*, ed. Steven Kautz, Arthur Melzer, Jerry Weinberger, and M. Richard Zinman, 131-161. Philadelphia: University of Pennsylvania Press.

Jayashankar, S. 1999. *Temples of Kerala*. Delhi: Controller of Publications.

Jeffrey, Robin. 2004-2005. 'Legacies of Matriliny: The Place of Women and the 'Kerala Model''. *Pacific Affairs* 77, no. 4: 647-664.
Jeffrey, Robin. 1992. *Politics, Women and Well-Being: How Kerala Became a 'Model'*. Basingstoke & New York: Palgrave MacMillan.
Jeffrey, Robin. 1976. 'Temple-Entry Movement in Travancore 1860-1940'. *Social Scientist* 4, no. 8: 3-27.
Jenett, Dianne. 2005. 'A Million 'Shaktis' Rising: Pongala, a Women's Festival in Kerala, India'. *Journal of Feminist Studies in Religion* 21, no. 1: 35-55.
Joseph, J. K. et al. 2020. 'Pilgrim Satisfaction in a Mass Religious Gathering: Study from Sabarimala Destination, Kerala State of India'. *Journal of Religion and Health* 59, no. 4: 1713-1727.
Kahn, Jeffrey S. 2022. 'Anthropology, Law, and the Problem of Incommensurability'. *Alabama Law Review* 73, no. 4: 783-801.
Kahn, Jeffrey S. 2019. *Islands of Sovereignty: Haitian Migration and the Borders of Empire*. Chicago: The University of Chicago Press.
Kane, P. V. 1941. *History of Dharmaśāstra (Ancient and Mediæval Religious and Civil Law)*, Vol. II, Part II. Poona: Bhandarkar Oriental Research Institute.
Katz, Nathan. 2000. *Who are the Jews of India?* Berkeley & Los Angeles: University of California Press.
Kaviraj, Sudipta. 2000. 'Modernity and Politics in India'. *Daedalus* 129, no. 1: 137-162.
Kent, Eliza. 2004. *Converting Women: Gender and Protestant Christianity in Colonial South India*. New York: Oxford University Press.
Khan, Dominique-Sila. 2009. *Sacred Kerala: A Spiritual Pilgrimage*. New Delhi: Penguin Books India.
Khilnani, Sunil. 1997. *The Idea of India*. New York: Farrar, Straus and Giroux.
Kooiman, Dick. 2005. 'Invention of Tradition in Travancore: A Maharaja's Quest for Political Security'. *Journal of the Royal Asiatic Society* 15, no. 2: 151-164.
Kooiman, Dick. 1992. 'State Formation in Travancore: Problems of Revenue, Trade, and Armament'. In *Ritual, State and History in South Asia: Essays in Honour of J. C. Heesterman*, ed. A. W. Van Den Hoek, D. H. A. Kolff, and M. S. Oort, 587-609. Leiden, New York, Köln: Brill.
Kumar, Neha. 2019. "Is Twitter for Celebrities Only?': A Qualitative Study of Twitter Use in India'. In *#identity: Hashtagging Race, Gender, Sexuality, and Nation*, ed. Abigail De Kosnik and Keith P. Feldman, 237-248. Ann Arbor: University of Michigan Press.
Kumari, Nirmala K. 1998. *History of the Hindu Religious Endowments in Andhra Pradesh*. New Delhi: Northern Book Centre.
Kurien, Prema. 2008. 'A Socio-Cultural Perspective on Migration and Economic Development: Middle Eastern Migration from Kerala, India'. In *Migration and Development Within and Across Borders: Research and Policy Perspectives on Internal and International Migration*, ed. Josh DeWind and Jennifer Holdaway, 189-218. Geneva & New York: International Organization for Migration and Social Science Research Council.
Kurup, K. K. N. 1973. *The Cult of Teyyam and Hero Worship in Kerala*. Calcutta: Indian Publications.
Laine, James W. 2012. 'Resisting My Attackers; Resisting My Defenders: Representing the Shivaji Narratives'. In *Engaging South Asian Religions: Boundaries,*

Appropriations, and Resistances, ed. Mathew N. Schmalz and Peter Gottschalk, 153–172. Albany: State University of New York Press.

Lamb, Ramdas. 2002. *The Ramnamis, Ramnam, and Untouchable Religion in Central India*. Albany: State University of New York Press.

Leach, Edmund R. 2020 [1954]. *Political Systems of Highland Burma: A Study of Kachin Social Structure*. Oxford & New York: Routledge.

Lemons, Katherine. 2019. *Divorcing Traditions: Islamic Marriage Law and the Making of Indian Secularism*. Ithaca: Cornell University Press.

Llewellyn, Karl N. & E. Adamson Hoebel. 1941. *The Cheyenne Way: Conflict and Case Law in Primitive Jurisprudence*. Norman & London: University of Oklahoma Press.

Lowy, Michael J. 1973b. 'Rebuttal to Pospisil'. *American Anthropologist* 75, no. 4: 1173–1174.

Lowy, Michael J. 1973a. 'Review: Anthropology of Law: A Comparative Theory'. *American Anthropologist* 75, no. 4: 953–957.

Lubet, Steven. 2018. *Interrogating Ethnography: Why Evidence Matters*. New York: Oxford University Press.

Malinowski, Bronislaw. 1985 [1926]. *Crime and Custom in Savage Society*. Totowa: Littlefield, Adams & Company.

Mallampalli, Chandra. 2010. 'Escaping the Grip of Personal Law in Colonial India: Proving Custom, Negotiating Hindu-ness'. *Law and History Review* 28, no. 4: 1043–1065.

Mani, Lata. 1998. *Contentious Traditions: The Debate on Sati in Colonial India*. Berkeley: University of California Press.

Mannathukkaren, Nissim. 2010. 'The 'Poverty' of Political Society: Partha Chatterjee and the People's Plan Campaign in Kerala, India'. *Third World Quarterly* 31, no. 2: 295–314.

Mathur, P. R. G. 2019. *Sacred Complex of the Sabarimala Ayyappa Temple*. New Delhi: B.R. Publishing.

Mathur, P. R. G. 2009. *Sacred Complex of the Guruvayur Temple*. New Delhi: Indira Gandhi National Centre for the Arts.

Mazumdar, Sucheta. 1995. 'Women on the March: Right-Wing Mobilization in Contemporary India'. *Feminist Review* 49, no. 1: 1–28.

Mazzarella, William. 2003. *Shoveling Smoke: Advertising and Globalization in Contemporary India*. Durham & London: Duke University Press.

Mehta, Pratap Bhanu. 2010. 'What is Constitutional Morality?' *Seminar* 615.

Menon, Nandagopal R. 2010. 'Imagined Kerala'. *Economic and Political Weekly* 45, no. 34: 22–23 & 25.

Menon, Nikhila. 2020. *Mobility as Capability: Women in the Indian Informal Economy*. Cambridge & New York: Cambridge University Press.

Menon, P. Shungoony. 1983 [1878]. *A History of Travancore from the Earliest Times*. Trivandrum: Kerala Gazetteers.

Menon, Parvathi. 2020. 'Sabarimala and Women's Identity in Kerala'. *Social Scientist* 48, no. 3/6: 3–24.

Menon, Priya. 2020. 'Kerala's Own Petrofiction: Literary Interventions in Gulf Migration Studies'. *Ala: A Kerala Studies Blog*, no. 23, July 31.

Menski, Werner F. 2001. *Modern Indian Family Law*. Richmond: Curzon Press.

Merry, Sally Engle. 2016. *The Seductions of Quantification: Measuring Human Rights, Gender Violence, and Sex Trafficking*. Chicago: The University of Chicago Press.
Merry, Sally Engle. 1990. *Getting Justice and Getting Even: Legal Consciousness among Working-Class Americans*. Chicago: The University of Chicago Press.
Mertz, Elizabeth. 2007. *The Language of Law School: Learning to "Think Like a Lawyer."* Oxford: Oxford University Press.
Miller, Barbara Stoller, ed. & trans. 1997. *Gītagovinda of Jayadeva: Love Song of the Dark Lord*. Delhi: Motilal Banarsidass.
Mishra, Nilakantha. 2006. 'Temple Administration—Past and Present'. *Orissa Review (now Odisha Review)*, July: 28–35.
Mohan, Sriram. 2015. 'Locating the 'Internet Hindu' Political Speech and Performance in Indian Cyberspace'. *Television & New Media* 16, no. 4: 339–345.
Moodie, Deonnie. 2019. *The Making of a Modern Temple and a Hindu City: Kālīghāṭ and Kolkata*. New York: Oxford University Press.
Moore, Sally Falk. 1983 [1978]. *Law as Process: An Anthropological Approach*. London: Routledge & Kegan Paul.
Moorthy, K. K. 1991. *The Kovils of Kerala: An 18 Petal Fragrant Rose*. Tirupati: Message Publications.
Morgan, Lewis H. 1877. *Ancient Society: Researches in the Lines of Human Progress from Savagery through Barbarism to Civilization*. New York: Henry Holt.
Moynihan, Daniel Patrick & Suzanne Weaver. 1978. *A Dangerous Place*. Boston: Atlantic-Little, Brown.
Mudaliar, Chandra. 1976. *State and Religious Endowments in Madras*. Madras: University of Madras Press.
Mukhopadhyay, Swapna, ed. 2007. *The Enigma of the Kerala Woman: A Failed Promise of Literacy*. New Delhi: Social Science Press.
Nadel, S. F. 1956. 'Reason and Unreason in African Law'. *Africa* 26, no. 2: 160–173.
Nader, Laura. 1990. *Harmony Ideology: Justice and Control in a Zapotec Mountain Village*. Stanford: Stanford University Press.
Nader, Laura. 1997 [1969]. *Law in Culture and Society*. Berkeley: University of California Press.
Nader, Laura. 1972. 'Up the Anthropologist—Perspectives Gained From Studying Up'. In *Reinventing Anthropology*, ed. Dell Hymes, 284–311. New York: Pantheon Books.
Nader, Laura. 1965. 'The Anthropological Study of Law'. *American Anthropologist* 67, no. 6: 3–32.
Nair, R. Raman & L. Sulochana Devi. 2010. *Chattampi Swami: An Intellectual Biography*. Trivandrum: Centre for South Indian Studies.
Nanda, Meera. 2011. *The God Market: How Globalization is Making India More Hindu*. New York: Monthly Review Press.
Neo, Jaclyn. 2018. 'Definitional Imbroglios: A Critique of the Definition of Religion and Essential Practice Tests in Religious Freedom Adjudication'. *I•CON: International Journal of Constitutional Law* 16, no. 2: 574–595.
Osella, Filippo & Caroline Osella. 2003. "'Ayyappan Saranam': Masculinity and the Sabarimala Pilgrimage in Kerala'. *Journal of the Royal Anthropological Institute* 9: 729–753.
Osella, Filippo & Caroline Osella. 2000. *Social Mobility in Kerala: Modernity and Identity in Conflict*. London & Sterling: Pluto Press.

Ouwerkerk, Louise. 1994. *No Elephants for the Maharaja: Social and Political Change in the Princely State of Travancore (1921-1947)*, ed. Dick Kooiman. New Delhi: Manohar.

Padmanabhan, S. 1977. *South Indian Temples: An Illustrated Book on the Origin, Development and Importance of South Indian Temples*. Nagercoil: Kumaran Pathippagam.

Pal, Joyojeet, et al. 2017. 'Innuendo as Outreach: @narendramodi and the Use of Political Irony on Twitter'. *International Journal of Communication* 11: 4197-4218.

Parashar, Archana. 1992. *Women and Family Law Reform in India: Uniform Civil Code and Gender Equality*. New Delhi: Sage Publications.

Parthasarathy, Suhrith. 2020. 'An Equal Right to Freedom of Religion: A Reading of the Supreme Court's Judgment in Sabarimala'. *Oxford Human Rights Hub Journal* 3, no. 2: 123-150.

Percot, Marie & S. Irudaya Rajan. 2007. 'Female Emigration from India: Case Study of Nurses'. *Economic and Political Weekly* 42, no. 4: 318-325.

Pillai, Manu S. 2015. *The Ivory Throne: Chronicles of the House of Travancore*. New Delhi: HarperCollins.

Pillai, V. R. Parameswaran. 1986. *Temple Culture of South India*. New Delhi: Inter-India Publications.

Pospisil, Leopold. 1973. 'Anthropology of Law: A Rejoinder to Lowy'. *American Anthropologist* 75, no. 4: 1170-1173.

Pospisil, Leopold. 1971. *The Anthropology of Law: A Comparative Theory*. New York: Harper & Row.

Pospisil, Leopold. 1958. *Kapauku Papuans and Their Law*. New Haven: Yale University Publications in Anthropology No. 54.

Presler, Franklin A. 1987. *Religion under Bureaucracy: Policy and Administration for Hindu Temples in South India*. Cambridge: Cambridge University Press.

Price, Pamela G. 2008 [1996]. *Kingship and Political Practice in Colonial India*. Cambridge: Cambridge University Press.

Quack, Johannes. 2011. *Disenchanting India: Organized Rationalism and Criticism of Religion in India*. Oxford: Oxford University Press.

Radhakrishnan, P. 1981. 'Land Reforms in Theory and Practice: The Kerala Experience'. *Economic and Political Weekly* 16, no. 52: A129-A131, A133, A135-A137.

Raimon, S., ed. 2006. *Selected Documents on Vaikom Satyagraha*. Thiruvananthapuram: Government of Kerala.

Raimon, S., ed. 2005. *Thiranjedutha Rajakeeya Vilambarangal (Selected Proclamations of the Sovereign)*, trans. Mallika Das. Thiruvananthapuram: Government of Kerala.

Rao, Anupama. 2009. *The Caste Question: Dalits and the Politics of Modern India*. Berkeley, Los Angeles & London: University of California Press.

Riley, Dylan J. & Manali Desai. 2007. 'The Passive Revolutionary Route to the Modern World: Italy and India in Comparative Perspective'. *Comparative Studies in Society and History* 49, no. 4: 815-847.

Riles, Annelise. 2005. 'A New Agenda for the Cultural Study of Law: Taking on the Technicalities'. *Buffalo Law Review* 53, no. 3: 973-1033.

Robinson, Nick. 2013b. 'Structure Matters: The Impact of Court Structure on the Indian and U.S. Supreme Courts'. *American Journal of Comparative Law* 61, no. 1: 173–208.

Robinson, Nick. 2013a. 'A Quantitative Analysis of the Indian Supreme Court's Workload'. *Journal of Empirical Legal Studies* 10, no. 3: 570–601.

Robinson, Nick. 2009b. 'Too Many Cases'. *Frontline* 26, no. 1.

Robinson, Nick. 2009a. 'Expanding Judiciaries: India and the Rise of the Good Governance Court'. *Washington University Global Studies Law Review* 8, no. 1: 1–70.

Robinson, Nick et al. 2011. 'Interpreting the Constitution: Supreme Court Constitution Benches since Independence'. *Economic and Political Weekly* 46, no. 9: 27–31.

Rodrigues, Usha M. & Mochael Niemann. 2019. 'Political Communication Modi Style: A Case Study of the Demonetization Campaign on Twitter'. *International Journal of Media & Cultural Politics* 15, no. 3: 361–379.

Roopesh, O. B. 2017. 'When 'Anybody Can Be Brahmin': Appointment of Dalit Priests to Kerala Temples'. *Economic and Political Weekly* 52, no. 46: 12–15.

Rosen, Lawrence. 1998 [1989]. *The Anthropology of Justice: Law as Culture in Islamic Society*. Cambridge: Cambridge University Press.

Saradamoni, K. 1994. 'Women, Kerala and Some Development Issues'. *Economic and Political Weekly* 29, no. 9: 501–509.

Sarkar, H. 1978. *An Architectural Survey of Temples of Kerala*. New Delhi: Archaeological Survey of India.

Sarkar, Tanika. 1991. 'The Women of the Hindutva brigade'. *Bulletin of Concerned Asian Scholars* 25, no. 4: 16–24.

Sarkar, Tanika. 1993. 'The Women of the Hindutva brigade'. *Bulletin of Concerned Asian Scholars* 25, no. 4: 16–24.

Sarkar, Tanika & Urvashi Butalia, eds. 1995. *Women and Right Wing Movements: Indian Experiences*. London & New Jersey: Zed Books.

Sasikumar, Harikrishnan. 2020. Social Spaces and the Public Sphere: A Spatial-history of Modernity in Kerala, India. PhD Dissertation submitted to the School of Law and Government, Dublin City University.

Schapera, Isaac. 1938. *A Handbook of Tswana Law and Custom*. London: Oxford University Press for the International African Institute.

Scheppele, Kim Lane. 2004. 'Constitutional Ethnography: An Introduction'. *Law and Society Review* 38, no. 3: 389–406.

Sekar, Radhika. 1992. *The Śabarimalai Pilgrimage and Ayyappan Cultus*. Delhi: Motilal Banarsidass Publishers.

Sekhri, Abinhav. 2019. 'Anticipatory Bail and Jurisdiction'. *The Criminal Law Blog*, July 31.

Sen, Atreyee. 2007. *Shiv Sena Women: Violence and Communalism in a Bombay Slum*. Bloomington: Indiana University Press.

Sen, Ronojoy. 2010. *Articles of Faith: Religion, Secularism, and the Indian Supreme Court*. New Delhi: Oxford University Press.

Sengupta, Arghya. 2019. *Independence and Accountability of the Indian Higher Judiciary*. New Delhi: Cambridge University Press.

Sethi, Manisha. 2002. 'Avenging Angels and Nurturing Mothers: Women in Hindu Nationalism'. *Economic and Political Weekly* 37, no. 16: 1545–1552.
Sewell Jr., William H. 1997. 'Geertz, Cultural Systems, and History: From Synchrony to Transformation'. *Representations* 59 (Summer): 35–55.
Simmons, Caleb. 2020. *Devotional Sovereignty: Kingship and Religion in India*. New Delhi: Oxford University Press.
Singh, Bhagat. 2020 [1930]. 'Why I am an Atheist'. *Marxists Internet Archive*.
Sreedhar Mini, Darshana. 2016. 'Attukal 'Pongala': The 'Everydayness' in a Religious Space'. *Journal of Ritual Studies* 30, no. 1: 63–73.
Sreenivasan, K. 2003. 'Kerala's Integrated Culture: Its Present-day Distortions'. In *Issues in Kerala Historiography*, ed. K. K. Kusuman, 183–191. Thiruvananthapuram: University of Kerala.
Srinivasan, K. R. 1971. *Temples of South India*. New Delhi: National Book Trust.
Stein, Burton. 1977. 'Temples in Tamil Country, 1300–1750 A.D'. *Indian Economic Social History Review* 14, no. 1: 11–45.
Stein, Burton. 1960. 'The Economic Function of a Medieval South Indian Temple'. *The Journal of Asian Studies* 19, no. 2: 163–176.
Stein, Burton. 1958. The Tirupati Temple: An Economic Study of a Medieval South Indian Temple. Doctoral dissertation, University of Chicago.
Subrahmanian, Maya. 2019. 'Autonomous Women's Movement in Kerala: Historiography'. *Journal of International Women's Studies* 20, no. 2: 1–10.
Sullivan, Winnifred Fallers. 2005. *The Impossibility of Religious Freedom*. Princeton: Princeton University Press.
Talbot, Ian & Gurharpal Singh. 2009. *The Partition of India*. Cambridge: Cambridge University Press.
Talesh, Shauhin, Elizabeth Mertz & Heinz Klug. 2021. *Research Handbook on Modern Legal Realism*. Cheltenham: Edward Elgar Publishing.
Tarabout, Gilles. 2015. 'Religious Uncertainty, Astrology and the Courts in South India'. In *Of Doubt and Proof: Ritual and Legal Practices of Judgment*, ed. Daniela Berti and Anthony Good, Gilles Tarabout, 59–75. Farnham: Ashgate Publishing.
Tarabout, Gilles. 1986. *Sacrifier et donner à voir en pays Malabar*. Paris: École Française d'Extrême-Orient.
Tejani, Riaz. 2013. 'Little Black Boxes: Legal Anthropology and the Politics of Autonomy in Tort Law'. *University of New Hampshire Law Review* 11, no. 2: 129–170.
Thakur, Mandar Anant. 2008. 'People's Role and Contribution in Nasik Kalaram Temple Entry Satyagraha'. *Proceedings of the Indian History Congress* 69: 833–838.
Tharamangalam, Joseph. 1981. *Agrarian Class Conflict: The Political Mobilization of Agricultural Labourers in Kuttanad, South India*. Vancouver & London: University of British Columbia Press.
Thiruvengadam, Arun K. 2013. 'Swallowing a Bitter PIL? Reflections on Progressive Strategies for Public Interest Litigation in India'. In *Transformative Constitutionalism: Comparing the Apex Courts of Brazil, India, and South Africa*, ed. Oscar Vilhena, Upendra Baxi, and Frans Viljoen, 519–531. Pretoria: Pretoria University Law Press.

Thomas, Sonja. 2022. 'The Ingredients of Casteism: Holy Week and Syrian Christian Food Practices in Kerala, India'. *South Asia: Journal of South Asian Studies* 45, no. 3: 401–416.
Trivedi, Prashant K. et al. 2016. 'Does Untouchability Exist Among Muslims? Evidence from Uttar Pradesh'. *Economic and Political Weekly* 51, no. 15: 32–36.
Udupa, Sahana. 2018. 'Enterprise Hindutva and Social Media in Urban India'. *Contemporary South Asia* 26, no. 4: 453–467.
Udupa, Sahana. 2015. 'INTERNET HINDUS: Right-Wingers as New India's Ideological Warriors'. In *Handbook of Religion and the Asian City: Aspiration and Urbanization in the Twenty-First Century*, ed. Peter van der Veer, 432–449. Berkeley: University of California Press.
Vaidyanathan, K. R. 1982. *Temples and Legends of Kerala*. Bombay: Bharatiya Vidya Bhavan.
Vakil, Raeesa. 2022. 'Representation and Legitimacy in the Supreme Court: Adjudicating Law and Religion in India'. *Studies in Indian Politics*, DOI: 10.1177/23210230221083064.
Vandenhole, Wouter. 2002. 'Human Rights Law, Development, and Social Action Litigation in India'. *Asia Pacific Journal on Human Rights & the Law* 3, no. 2: 136–210.
Vijayan, Aleyamma. 2004. 'Decentralization Process and Women: the Case of Kerala, India'. In *Gender, Citizenship and Governance: A Global Sourcebook*, ed. Minke Valk, Sarah Cummings, and Henk van Dam, 29–40. Oxford: Oxfam GB.
Viswanath, Rupa. 2016. 'Economies of Offense: Hatred, Speech, and Violence in India'. *Journal of the American Academy of Religion* 84, no. 2: 352–363.
Wahi, Namita. 2016. 'Property'. In *The Oxford Handbook of the Indian Constitution*, ed. Sujit Choudhry, Madhav Khosla, and Pratap Bhanu Mehta, 943–966. Oxford: Oxford University Press.
Warrier, M. I., E. P. Narayana Bhattathiry & K. Radhakrishna Warrier. 2009. *Malayalam-English Dictionary*. Kottayam: DC Press.
Wilson, Elisabeth. 2016. 'Outward Bound with Ayyappan: Work, Masculinity, and Self-Respect in a South Indian Pilgrimage Festival'. *Religion and Gender* 6, no. 1: 118–136.
Younger, Paul. 2002. *Playing Host to Deity: Festival Religion in the South Indian Tradition*. New York: Oxford University Press.

Case Law

Acharya Jagadishwarananda Avadhuta v. Commissioner of Police, Calcutta, AIR 1984 SC 51 ("Ananda Marga I")
A. S. Narayana Deekshitulu v. State of Andhra Pradesh, AIR 1995 SC 1805
A. S. Yanglung v. State of Manipur, 2020 SCC OnLine Mani 13 (Jan. 27, 2020)
Bijoe Emmanuel v. State of Kerala, 1987 AIR 748
Binu v. State of Kerala, 2019 SCC OnLine Ker 429 (Jan. 31, 2019)
B. K. Hemanth Kumar v. Sri M. Narayanappa, Original Suit Nos. 3928/1994 and 4426/1995 (Bangalore District Court, Feb. 3, 2018)
Bumper Development Corp. v. Commissioner of Police, [1991] 1 W.L.R. 1362, [1991] 4 All E. R. 638 (C. A.)
Carlisle v. United States 517 U.S. 416 (1996)

Chaturgun Turha and Ors. vs Jamadar Mian on 22 December, AIR 1961 Pat 374
Commissioner, Hindu Religious Endowments v. Sri Lakshmindra Thirtha Swamiar of Sri Shirur Mutt, AIR 1954 SC 282 ("Shirur Mutt")
Commissioner, Police v. Acharya Jagadishwaranandha Avadhuta, (2004) 12 SCC 770 ("Ananda Marga II")
Durgah Committee, Ajmer v. Syed Hussain Ali, AIR 1961 SC 1402
Gurbaksh Singh Sibbia v. State of Punjab, (1980) 2 SCC 565
Indian Young Lawyers Association v. State of Kerala, 2018 SCC OnLine SC 1690
Indra Sawhney v. Union of India, AIR 1993 SC 477
Jayamala vs State of Kerala, O.P. (Criminal) No. 1332 of 2011(Q) (April 12, 2011)
Joseph Shine v. Union of India, (2019) 3 SCC 39
Kantaru Rajeevaru v. IYLA, Review Petition (Civil) 2020 Supreme Court Cases 1 (Nov. 14, 2019) ("Kantaru Rajeevaru")
Kantaru Rajeevaru v. IYLA, Review Petition (Civil) No. 3358 of 2018, in Writ Petition (Civil) No. 373 of 2006 (Feb. 10, 2020) ("Kantaru February order")
Kantaru Rajeevaru v. IYLA, Review Petition (Civil) No. 3358 of 2018, in Writ Petition (Civil) No. 373 of 2006 (May 11, 2020) ("Kantaru May order")
Kesavananda Bharati Sripadagalvaru v. State of Kerala, (1973) 4 SCC 225
K. Sivadasan v. State of Kerala, 2019 SCC OnLine Ker 572 (Feb. 13, 2019)
K. S. Puttaswamy v. Union of India, (2017) 10 SCC 1
Manoj Narula v. Union of India, (2014) 9 SCC 1
Marthanda Varma v. State of Kerala, (2021) 1 Supreme Court Cases 225
M. Siddiq v. Mahant Suresh Das, (2020) 1 Supreme Court Cases 1
Mohd. Hanif Qureshi & Others v. State of Bihar, 1958 AIR 731
Noorjehan Safia Niaz & Ors v. State of Maharashtra, 2016 SCC OnLine Bom 5394
Pramatha Nath Mullick v. Pradyumna Kumar Mullick, (1925) 27 BOMLR 1064
Ravi v. State of Kerala, 2019 SCC OnLine Ker 428 (Jan. 31, 2019)
Romila Thapar v. Union of India, (2018) 10 SCC 753
S. Mahendran v. The Secretary, Travancore Devaswom Board, AIR 1993 Ker 42
S. P. Gupta v. Union of India, 1981 Supp (1) SCC 87
Secretary, Ministry of Defense v. Babita Puniya, Civil Appeal Nos. 9367–9369 of 2011 (Feb. 17, 2020)
Seshammal v. State of Tamil Nadu, (1972) 2 SCC 11
Shastri Yagnapurushdasji v. Muldas Bhudardas Vaishya, AIR 1966 SC 1119 ("Satsang case")
Shri Govindlalji v. State of Rajasthan, AIR 1963 SC 1638
Sivan v. State of Kerala, 2019 SCC OnLine Ker 1006 (Mar. 26, 2019).
Sree Prasad v. State of Kerala, 2019 SCC OnLine Ker 512 (Feb. 11, 2019)
Sreekumar v. State of Kerala, 2019 SCC OnLine Ker 1305 (Apr. 3, 2019)
Sri Venkataramana Devaru v. State of Mysore, AIR 1958 SC 255 (1957)
Rajasthan. v. Union of India (1977) 3 S.C.C. 634
Subramanian Swamy v. Union of India, Writ Petition (Criminal) No. 184 of 2014.
Supreme Court Advocates-on-Record Association v. Union of India, (2016) 5 SCC 1
Sushila Aggarwal v. NCT of Delhi, (2020) 5 SCC 1
S. P. Mittal v. Union of India, (1983) 1 SCR 729
S. R. Bommai v. Union of India (1994) 3 SCC 1
Trest v. Cain 522 U.S. 87 (1997)

Trest v. Whitley, 94 F. 3d 1005 (1996)
Union of India v. Annie Nagaraja, Civil Appeal Nos. 2182–87 of 2020, S.L.P. (C) Nos. 30791–96 of 2015 (Mar. 17, 2020)
Vipin v. State of Kerala, 2019 SCC OnLine Ker 326 (Jan. 22, 2019)

Litigation Materials

Brief for the *Amicus Curiae*, Raju Ramachandran, Indian Young Lawyers Association v. State of Kerala, W.P. (Civil) No. 373 of 2006
Brief for Intervenor-Applicant No. 10, Nikita Azad (Arora), Indian Young Lawyers Association v. State of Kerala, W.P. (Civil) No. 373 of 2006
Brief for Intervenor-Applicant No. 30, People for Dharma, Indian Young Lawyers Association v. State of Kerala, W.P. (Civil) No. 373 of 2006
Brief for Respondent No. 6, Nair Service Society, Indian Young Lawyers Association v. State of Kerala, W.P. (Civil) No. 373 of 2006
Brief for Respondent No. 19, Raja of Pandalam, Indian Young Lawyers Association v. State of Kerala, W.P. (Civil) No. 373 of 2006

Statutes or Bills

Bombay Hindu Temple Worship (Removal of Disabilities) Act (1938)
Constitution (Eighty-sixth Amendment) Act (2002)
Criminal Procedure Code (1973)
Factories Act, 1948 (Act 63 of 1948)
Kerala Hindu Places of Public Worship (Authorisation of Entry) Act, 1965 (Act 7 of 1965)
Kerala Hindu Places of Public Worship (Authorization of Entry) Rules (1965)
Kerala Joint Hindu Family System (Abolition) Act, 1975 (Act 30 of 1976)
Madras Endowments and Escheats Regulation of 1817 (Regulation 7 of 1817)
Madras Temple Entry Authorization and Indemnity Act (1939)
Maharashtra Hindu Place of Worship (Entry Authorisation) Act (1956)
National Judicial Appointments Commission Act (2014)
Protection of Civil Rights Act, 1955 (Act 22 of 1955)
Sabarimala Sree Dharma Sastha Temple (Special Provision) Bill (2019)
Tamil Nadu Hindu Religious and Charitable Endowments (Amendment) Act (2013)
Travancore-Cochin Hindu Religious Institutions Act (1950)
Madras Hindu Religious & Charitable Endowment Act (1951)
Madras Hindu Religious & Charitable Endowment (Amendment) Act, 2008 (Act 31 of 2008)
Madras Hindu Religious & Charitable Endowment (Amendment) Act, 2017 (Act 9 of 2017)

Primary Sources

Aiyer, Sir C. P. Ramaswami. 1943. Copy of Correction Memo from Sir Frank H. Brown, editor of the *Asiatic Review*. File 3316/44, Bundle 174, Serial No. 12 (1944–49). Thiruvananthapuram: Kerala State Archives.
Azad, Nikita. 2015b. '#HappyToBleed: An Initiative against Sexism'. *Countercurrents*. Nov. 23.
Azad, Nikita. 2015a. "A Young Bleeding Woman' Pens An Open Letter To The 'Keepers' of Sabarimala Temple'. *Youth ki Awaaz*. Nov. 20.

Bayi, Parvathi. 1815. Proclamation 13 (December 29). In Raimon, ed. (2005, 19–20). Trans. Mallika Das.
Bayi, Parvathi. 1823. Proclamation 98 (March 23). In Raimon, ed. (2005, 165–166). Trans. Mallika Das.
Complainant. 2019. 'Press Release by former Supreme Court employee and complainant in sexual harassment against CJI'. April 30.
Easwar, Rahul. 2020. *@RahulEaswar*, July 14. On file with author.
Extracts from the Debates of the Legislative Assembly of the Province of Madras Regarding the Malabar Temple Entry Bill, 1938. *Fort St. George Gazette*, August 30, File 64–65, Bundle 1129 (1904–56). Thiruvananthapuram: Kerala State Archives.
Government of India. nd. 'Lord Padmanabha and His Dasas'. Indian Culture: Discover, Learn, Immerse, Connect.
Government of India. 2020a. *Sample Registration System Statistical Report Detailed Tables*.
Government of India. 2020b. *Sample Registration System (SRS) Based Abridged Life Tables 2014–18*.
Government of India. 2020c. *National Sample Survey (75th Round, 2017–2018): Household Consumption on Education in India*.
Government of India. 2020d. *Annual Report: Periodic Labour Force Survey (PLFS) (July 2018–June 2019)*.
Government of India. 2020e. *Accidental Deaths and Suicides in India 2019*.
Government of India. 2011. *Census 2011: C-1 Population by Religious Community*.
Government of Kerala. 2017. *Annual Vital Statistics Report–2016*.
Idicheria, P. 1942. Proposal to the Chief Secretary to Government (Sep. 24). File 107, Bundle 627 (1936–43). Thiruvananthapuram: Kerala State Archives.
India Cellular and Electronics Association. 2020. *Contribution of Smartphones to Digital Governance in India*. July.
Law Commission of India. 2017. Report No. 268: Amendments to Criminal Procedure Code, 1973–Provisions Relating to Bail.
Law Commission of India. 1969. 41st Report on the Code of Criminal Procedure, 1898. Vol. I.
Mehra, Kushal. 2017. 'My Interview with Anjali George'. *Cārvāka*, May 19.
Menon, K. Kuttikrishna. 1964. *Report of the High Level Committee for Unification of Laws relating to Hindu Religious Institutions and Endowments*. Trivandrum: Government of Kerala.
Paripoornan, K. S., B. M. Thulasidas & D. R. Kaarthikeyan. *Report of the High Power Commission to Enquire into the Affairs of the Travancore Devaswom Board* (Dec. 19, 2007) ("Paripoornan Commission Report").
Saheli Women's Resource Center et al. 2019. 'Supreme Injustice'. May 7.
Sunder Rajan, Kaushik, 2015. Syllabus: ANTH 42000: Anthropological Fieldwork Methods 1.
Thirunal, Chithira. 1936. Proclamation 306 (November 12). In Raimon, ed. (2005, 589–596). Trans. Mallika Das.
Thirunal, Moolam. 1922. Proclamation 299 (April 12). In Raimon, ed. (2005, 571–575). Trans. Mallika Das.
Tirunal, Uthradom. 2010. *Travancore: The Footprints of Destiny: My Life and Times under the Grace of Lord Padmanabha*. Delhi: Konark Publishers.

Transparency International. 2018. *Corruption Perceptions Index.*
Wadhawan, Neha. 2018. *India Labour Migration Update 2018.* Geneva: International Labour Organization.
World Bank. 2018a. *Literacy Rate, Adult Female (% of Females Ages 15 and Above).*
World Bank. 2018b. Birth Rate, Crude (Per 1,000 People) – United Kingdom.
World Bank. 2018c. Birth Rate, Crude (Per 1,000 People) – United States.
World Bank. 2018d. Fertility Rate, Total (Births Per Woman) – United Kingdom.
World Bank. 2018e. Fertility Rate, Total (Births Per Woman) – United States.

Index

For the benefit of digital users, indexed terms that span two pages (e.g., 52–53) may, on occasion, appear on only one of those pages.

#HappyToBleed, 136–37
#ReadyToWait, 43, 138

aachaaram, 42–43
Ambedkar, B.R., 58, 82–83, 144–46
amicus, 98, 117–19, 123, 144
Ammini, Bindu, 45–47, 51–52, 143
Ananda Marga, 181
Ananda Marga, 119–20, 181
Anizham Thirunal, 26–28, 30–32
anthropology, 9, 10–11, 15, 20, 23, 67, 86–87, 99–101, 102–3, 111, 132–33, 158, 165
anticipatory bail, 48–49
Appan, 101–2
Article 17, 34–35, 47, 80–81, 82–83, 85, 87, 138
Article 25, 35–36, 73, 77–78, 83–84, 111, 127, 129–30, 176
   Article 25(2), 33–34, 35
   Article 25(2)(a), 34, 36, 73–74
Article 26, 35–36, 73, 74, 77–78, 127, 150–51, 176–77
avarna, 19–20, 23, 44, 46, 47, 144–46, 147
Ayyan, 101–2
Azad, Nikita, 72, 131, 132–35, 136–38, 140

Bal, Vidya, 139, 140–41
Bharatiya Janata Party (BJP), 19, 51–52, 53–55, 63–64, 137
Bhumata Brigade, 138, 142
Blackstone, Sir William, 113
Bobde, S.A., 152, 153, 157–58
British (colonial power), 18–19, 26–29, 31, 124–25, 145–46
Buddhism, 101–2

Chandrachud, D.Y., 60–61, 68, 73, 79–83, 84, 88–90, 154–55
Chandrika, S., 117–19, 122, 129
Chennai, 4, 7, 10, 138
Chithira Thirunal, 29–30
Christianity, 4–5, 18, 19–20, 23, 51, 76, 133–34
CJI Scandal, 61–62, 63
Cochin, 10, 27, 33, 114–16
colonial, 5, 20, 31, 32, 33, 50, 124–25
Common Law, 15, 56–57, 59–60, 124
communism, 17–18, 21, 26, 38, 51
Congress, 19, 50–55, 145
constitutional ethnography, 165
constitutional morality, 58
CPI(M), 47–48, 50, 51, 53–55, 143
cultivated attentiveness, 170–71

deity, 30–31, 75–76, 80–82, 85–86, 95, 99–102, 104, 138–39, 158–59
democracy/democratic, 2–3, 17, 25, 26, 32, 35–36, 38, 54, 68, 87, 126–28, 140, 141, 152
Desai, Trupti, 14, 44, 131, 132–33, 134, 138–44, 146, 148
devaprasnam, 93–95, 97, 98, 107, 109–10
Devaswom, 5–6, 29, 117
dharmashastra, 124
dynamic equilibrium, 3, 37–38, 90–91, 159

Easwar, Rahul, 97, 103–8
elections, 2, 12, 14–15, 54–55
ethnography, 5, 9–11, 15, 86

feminism/feminist, 20–21, 42, 67, 139–42
fertile, 2, 75–76, 88, 104, 123

Gandhi, M.K., 144–45, 146
Gandhi, Rahul, 51, 54, 137
Gandhi, Sonia, 51–52
Gogoi, Ranjan, 61–63, 149–52, 154
Gopalakrishnan, Prayar, 135–36, 148
Guruvayur, 114–15, 144–45, 146

Haji Ali, 8–9, 139, 142
Hindu nationalism, 12, 17, 19, 35, 42, 46–47, 49–50, 53, 86, 90, 91, 135, 137, 141–42, 160

Indian Penal Code, 1–2, 58, 107–8, 145–46
  IPC § 295, 107–8
  IPC § 295(A), 108
IYLA (litigation), 32–33, 36–37, 38–39, 42–44, 47, 49–50, 51, 54–62, 63–65, 67–91, 97, 103–4, 111–12, 119, 121–22, 127, 128–29, 132–33, 134, 138, 147–48, 149–50, 154–55
IYLA, 83–84

Jaising, Indira, 138
Jayamala, 1–3, 13, 93–112, 159

Kanakadurga, 45–47, 51–52, 143
Kandararu Maheswararu, 7
Kandararu Mohanaru, 94–95
Kandararu Rajeevaru, 47, 143
Kantaru Rajeevaru, 63, 149–51, 152, 154–55, 157–58, 159
Kerala model, 17, 24
Kesavananda Bharati, 56, 67–68
Kochi, 10, 27, 44, 113, 143–44, 148

Lalit, U.U., 60–61, 157–58
locus standi, 70–71, 78
Lok Sabha, 50–52, 54–55

Madras, 10, 28, 31, 126–27
Madras Endowments and Escheats Regulation Act ("1817 Act"), 31
Malabar, 10, 18–19, 27, 31, 114–16

Malhotra, Indu, 49, 68, 78–79, 82–86, 104, 154–55
mandalam-makaravilakku, 99, 108–9, 156–57
Mangot, Krishnakumar, 5–7, 116–17
matriliny/matrilineal, 20–21, 24–25, 26–27, 38, 97
melsanthi, 94–95, 156–57
Menon, 123
menstruation, 17, 75–78, 134, 136–37, 138
Misra, Dipak, 63–65, 67–68, 69–70, 73, 98, 129, 147
Modia, Narendra, 47–48, 55, 62, 135, 137, 156
Moolam Thirunal, 29
Muslim/s, 18–20, 44, 51, 58, 76, 84, 103, 133–34, 139–40, 141–42, 150

Nair, 17–18, 20–21, 23, 72, 96, 107, 133–34
namajapam, 41–43, 61, 149
Nambudiri, 22–23, 42–43, 95, 96–97
Nariman, R.F., 68, 73, 76–79, 80, 82, 88–89, 149–50, 154–55
Nehru, Jawaharlal, 21, 50–52, 54
New York Times, 12
Niaz v. State of Maharashtra, 142
Niaz, Noorjehan Safia, 139–40, 141

orthodox/orthodoxy, 3, 145–46
orthoprax/orthopraxy, 22–24, 95, 96

Padmanabhaswamy, 2, 27–28, 96
Pandalam, 28, 50, 72, 93–94, 98, 102, 123
Paripoornan, K.S., 113–14, 116–19, 125–26, 129–30
patriarchy, 26, 136–37, 159
patrilineal(ity), 97
People for Dharma, 43, 81–82, 138
postcolonial, 21, 38, 123–24
precolonial, 30
public interest litigation (PIL), 48–49, 51–52, 57–58, 70–72, 75–79, 83–85, 117, 118–19, 131–32, 139, 150–51, 154
public morality, 58

puja, 137, 155–56
Purna and Pushkala, 85, 102

Ramachandran, Raju, 138
redistribution (of land), 21
religious freedom, 3, 22, 33–34, 36, 37–38, 73–77, 84, 89–90, 126–27, 150–51, 159–60
ritual, 1, 2, 9, 17, 23–24, 30, 41, 42–43, 47, 80–81, 94–95, 97, 99–100, 122, 123, 135, 138–39, 147

S. Mahendran, 13–14, 76, 78–79, 80, 110, 113–30, 149, 154–55
Sastha, 102, 125
satyagraha, 144–46, 147–48
secular/secularism, 32–39, 45, 56, 71, 73–74, 89, 90–91, 139–40
Sethi, Bhakti Pasrija, 49–50, 70, 83–84, 149
Shani Shingnapur, 138–39, 140, 142
Shirur Mutt, 73–74, 89, 126–27, 151–52, 153
Shiva, 30–31, 86, 100–2, 119–20, 125
Soman, Zakia, 139–40, 141
sovereign/sovereignty, 26, 27–28, 30–31, 32, 35, 37, 38, 59, 68, 86–91, 127–28, 148, 159
strike, 12, 25–26, 43–44, 46–47
Sudhakaran, G., 143
suo motu, 57–58

Tamil Nadu, 31–32, 54, 94
tantris, 77–78, 94–98, 103, 106–7, 126, 129–30, 155–56
Tharananallur, 95–96
Tharoor, Shashi, 52–54
Thazhamon, 95–98, 105–7, 142–43
The Hindu, 6–7
Times of India, 115–16
Travancore, 10, 26–32, 36–37, 38–39, 114–15, 120, 144–45
Travancore Devaswom Board (TDB), 47, 51, 70, 87, 96, 106, 114–15, 135, 155–56
Travancore Temple Entry Proclamation, 1936, 29–30
Travancore-Cochin Hindu Religious Institutions Act (1950), 32–33
Trivandrum, 7, 10, 27–28, 45, 95–96, 103, 104–5

untouchability, 29–30, 34–35, 47, 80–81, 82–83, 85, 87, 133–34, 138, 145, 159

vanitha mathil, 45–46
Vartak, Neelima, 139–41
Vedas, 124
Venkataramana Devaru, 147
Vijayan, Pinarayi, 45, 55
Vishnu, 86, 95–96, 101–2, 125